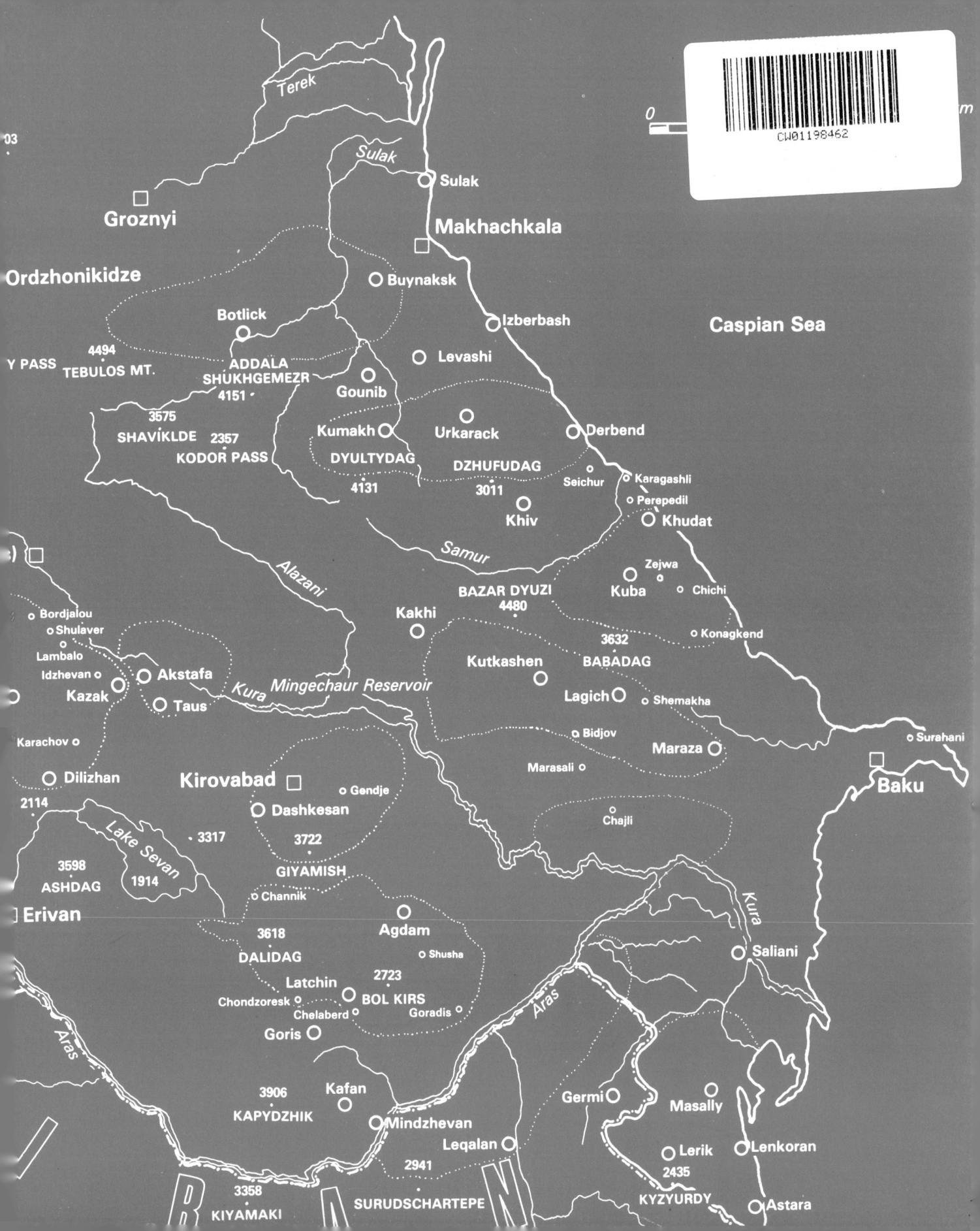

ORIENTAL RUGS

Volume 1 Caucasian

Ian Bennett

Antique Collectors' Club

© 1981 Oriental Textile Press Ltd.
World copyright reserved.

ISBN 0 902028 58 5

Reprinted 1993

All rights reserved. No part of this publication may be reproduced, stored in a retrieval system or transmitted in any form or by any means electronic, mechanical, photocopying, recording or otherwise, without the prior permission of the publishers in writing.

British Library CIP Data
Bennett, Ian
  Oriental Rugs
  Vol. 1: Caucasian
  1. Rugs, Oriental – Collectors and collecting
  I. Title
  746.7'5 NK2808

Printed in Aylesbury by BPCC Hazells Ltd. on Consort Satin from Donside Mills, Aberdeen

Published in England by Antique Collectors' Club Ltd,
Woodbridge, Suffolk, IP12 1DS

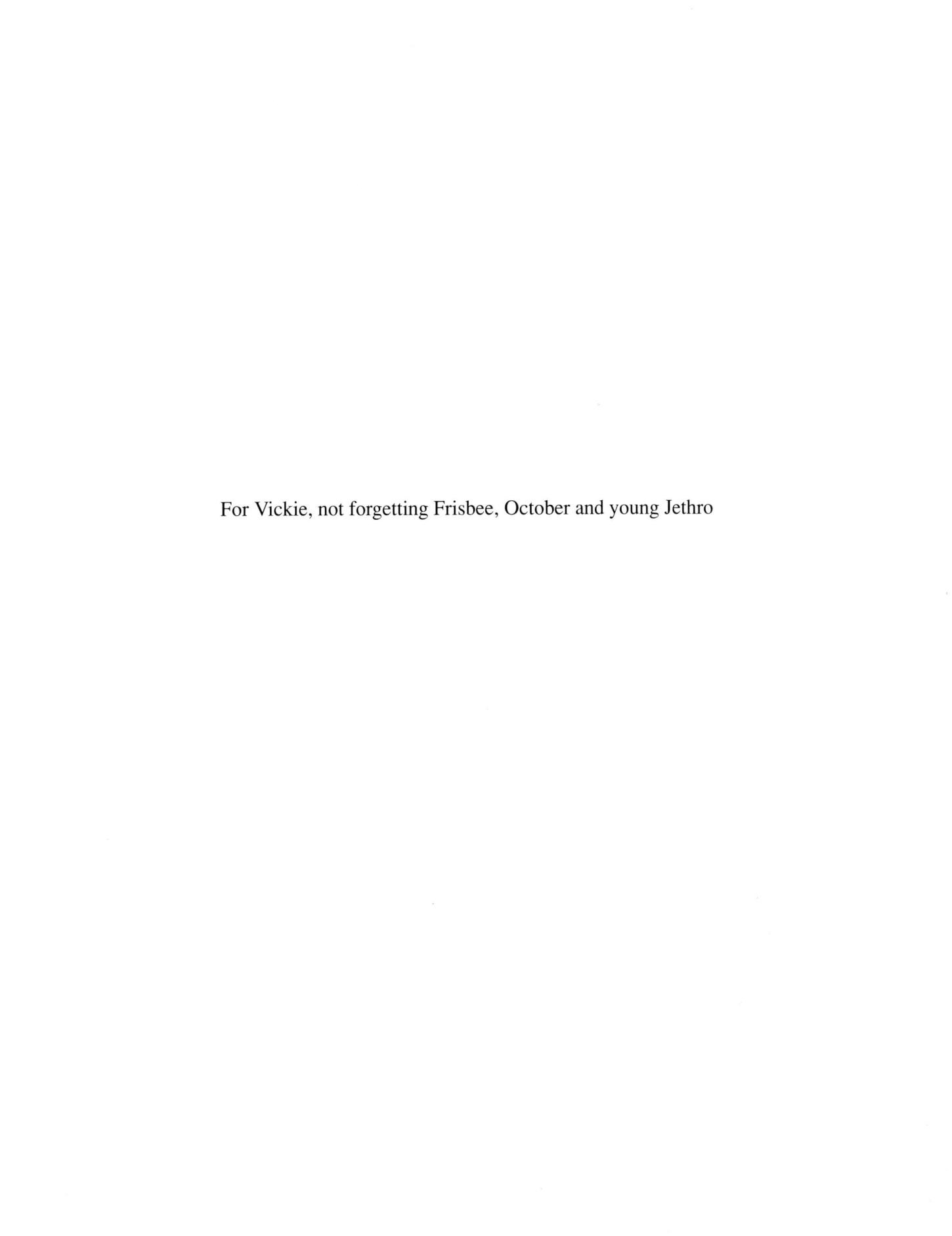

For Vickie, not forgetting Frisbee, October and young Jethro

ACKNOWLEDGEMENTS

In compiling a book such as this, an author is constantly asking questions, seeking advice and attempting to improve and refine his knowledge. The study of Oriental carpets is still in its infancy, although the lack of documentary evidence from before the 19th century, and the erosion of native cultures during the 19th and 20th centuries, has meant that there is little chance for us to advance much in the way of substantive knowledge. However, one hopes that there is still some way to go.

Naturally, a serious student of Oriental carpets will try to keep abreast of any new developments which find their way into print, but as much can be learned from the thousands of rugs which pass every year through the carpet trade in Europe and America, the vast majority of which then disappear once more into limbo, uncelebrated and, more disastrously, unpublished and unrecorded.

Happily, there is a growing trend among the younger dealers, the majority of whom seem to specialise in 19th and early 20th century tribal and village weavings, to keep records, either photographic or written or both, of interesting pieces which come their way. Thus scholars in the future will have far more material to work from than those in the past. Most such dealers are also only too willing to discuss their 'finds' and to pass on such information as they have and I have found the many discussions I have had over the past few months of invaluable help, not only in increasing my knowledge of Caucasian weavings but also in avoiding those dogmatic generalisations which one tends to make through too little actual first-hand knowledge of the objects themselves.

First, I would like to express my sincere thanks to the prestigious firm of Nagel and Co., without whose help on the photographic front this book would not have been possible. To the following dealers and scholars I would like to express my great gratitude for their time and enthusiasm: Peter Bausback; Raymond and Linda Benardout; David Black, Clive Loveless and Bruce Tozer of David Black Oriental Carpets Ltd.; Dennis R. Dodds; John Edelmann; Robert and Victor Franses; Julian Homer; Jenny Housego; Shirley Jarman; Jay Jones; Jean Lefèvre and Bert Blikslager of Lefèvre and Partners; Chris Legge; Alan Marcuson; Paul Nels; Yanni Petsopoulos; David Philpot; Robert and Lesley Pinner; Stephen Porter; Andrea Potter; Richard Purdon; Malcolm Puttick; Clive Rodgers and John Siudmak.

I should like to express a very special debt of thanks to Michael Franses, whose knowledge of all aspects of the Oriental carpet may be equalled somewhere in the world but is certainly not surpassed; he has always given freely of his time and knowledge to anyone who cares to ask and I have learned more from him than I would have thought possible.

Finally a grateful bow to my long-suffering publisher John Steel.

PUBLISHER'S FOREWORD

The illustrations in this book also feature in a German book on Caucasian rugs. In writing the English text the distinguished author did not have the opportunity to examine or handle the individual rugs. Therefore his comments must be interpreted on the basis of "what I would expect to find if I were to examine it".

Appreciating this limitation, the author and publisher agreed to adopt an entirely different approach based on the fact that the reader also has no chance to handle the actual rug and the information he will obtain will be gained solely from the illustration and what is said about it.

Accordingly the text discusses the illustrations on the most critical basis; they are seen not so much as individual pieces but in terms of the types. Thus dates indicated are the latest that are likely to be found, colours are discussed in terms of searching for chemical dyes and it is suggested to the reader which ones to check. The approach is, therefore, one of putting the reader on his guard, pointing out factors to consider and discussing possible alternative areas of origin. Collecting rugs is an art, not a science, and therefore the author makes suggestions for origins that may not be universally accepted. The reader is thus enabled to make his own comparisons and form his own views. What better way can there be of learning a subject?

In terms of antique furniture this approach is similar to illustrating a Sheraton bookcase dated perhaps 1790 and saying "This is a Sheraton bookcase but when was it made? The design is early but you must realise that it could just as well have been made in the Victorian classical revival. Therefore, it can be as late as c. 1890." The fact that it was genuine 1790 and had been sold in Christie's or Sotheby's for a vast price in no way invalidates these comments and indeed serves a valuable purpose in pointing out to the reader both what to look for and what to guard against. This will be familiar to those people who know the Antique Collectors' Club Price Guide series.

The adoption of this approach without explanation could also have caused embarrassment and misunderstanding, had the German and English versions been compared. Many of the rugs were auctioned in Germany by a highly knowledgeable and respected firm, and we wish to make it clear that there is here no implication or suggestion that the actual pieces were not as described by them.

CONTENTS

Introduction—History of Weaving in the Caucasus ...9
Kazak 18
    Star Kazak and Swastika Kazak 18
    Prayer Rugs...22
    Lori-Pambak...24
    Triple Medallion 28
    Sewan Kazaks...32
    Fachralo 40
    Fachralo Prayer Rugs...................................42
    Karachov...46
    Bordjalou..56
    Bordjalou Prayer Rugs.................................62
    Shikli Kazaks..66
    Shulaver Kazaks 70
    Lambalo Kazaks 72
    Tree or Garden Kazaks 76
    Hooked Polygons...78
    Compartmented 84
    Tile Pattern 88
Karabagh 90
    Chondzoresk 90
    Chelaberd...96
    Kasim-Usag..104
    Triple Medallion 108
    Prayer Rugs..112
    Boteh Rugs...114
    Hooked Diamond Medallion 116
    Small Shield Palmettes 118
    Herati Pattern...120
    Mina-Khani..122
    Carpets with 'European Designs' 124
    Lampa-Karabagh..126
    Zig-zag Medallions 127
    Goradis...128
Erivan..130
Gendje 132
    Floral Lattice..136
    Octagonal Medallions................................138
    'Tree of Life' Rugs 144
    Boteh Rugs...148
    Diagonal Stripes 150
Talish..152
    Met-hane 152
    Lattice Rugs...158
    Lenkoran 160
    Karadja...164

Moghan..166
    Medallion and Bar 169
    Hooked Diamonds 170
    Memlinc Gül...172
Chajli 174
Akstafa 176
    Prayer Rugs..182
Shirvan..184
    White Ground Prayer Rugs........................186
    Prayer Rugs..188
    Marasali 190
    Flower Shirvan 206
    Hexagon Columns 208
    Bidjov...214
    Saph Shirvan..216
Shirvan Baku 218
    Baku..218
    Surahani..218
    Khila 224
Kuba 238
    Afshan Pattern 240
    White Ground Kuba 248
    Karagashli 250
    Prayer Rugs..252
    Konagkend 256
    Chichi...268
    Perepedil 280
    Seichur...288
    Seichur with Western Flowers 292
    Bird Kuba...296
    Tree of Life Kuba 299
    Alpan-Kuba..300
    Zejwa 304
Daghestan..308
    Prayer Rugs..320
Lesghistan 326
Flat Weaves..336
    Slit-tapestry Rugs 336
    'Kuba' Kilim..339
    Brocaded Rugs...342
    Embroidered and Slit-tapestry Rugs...........346
    Soumaks...348
    'Dragon' Sileh 360
    'Verneh' Rugs 364
    Animal Covers 366
    Soumak Bags 369
Bibliography 374

INTRODUCTION
HISTORY OF WEAVING IN THE CAUCASUS

The rugs illustrated in this book are almost all from the 19th or early 20th centuries, for it is from this period that most rugs available to collectors are to be found Thus they represent the culmination of many centuries of craftsmanship, before politics and industry destroyed the native craft and replaced it with ghastly, *ersatz*, simulacrum. However, when looking at the main body of illustrations, it is important to realise that they represent only the *end* of a long tradition and not the tradition itself; the many different types of surviving 18th, 17th and possibly even 16th century Caucasian carpets testify to the brilliance of the tradition. Thus it is necessary for a history of early Caucasian weavings to appear here, albeit a brief one, so that the interested reader will be able to place the 19th and 20th century village rugs into their proper historical and aesthetic perspectives. There are appended also notes on dating and structure.

The history of early Caucasian weaving is especially confused. An indication of just how confused is given by the fact that the most famous group of 'classical' Caucasian carpets, the 'dragon' rugs, have been placed by various writers as wide apart historically as the 13th to the 18th centuries; although the current view is that the majority probably dates from the 17th century, there is by no means a consensus of opinion even now, and, unless new dating techniques are discovered which would shed unequivocal light on the matter, nor is there ever likely to be.

Unlike Turkish or Persian carpet production, there are almost no clues as to what Caucasian carpets might have looked like in the centuries before the earliest extant groups—i.e. the 'dragon' rugs, the earliest of which probably do not pre-date the end of the 16th century. Certainly the Armenians, whose role in weaving in the Transcaucasus is ubiquitous if as yet not fully explained, inhabited a vast area stretching from the Black Sea to the Caspian since at least the first century A.D. and had developed powerful kingdoms many centuries before that;[1] it would seem a reasonable supposition, therefore, that they had developed a weaving tradition hundreds of years older than the dragon rugs. However, in Armenian pictorial art, there are precious few indications of what their carpets might have looked like; the 11th century Gospel of Mugni in the Matenadaran Library, Erivan,[2] has a miniature of The Annunciation in which the Virgin rests her feet on what appears to be a mat with a plain gold field and a border containing a series of rectangles containing either four dots, a red square or a blue circle. This same style of weaving can be seen in several other early Armenian miniatures, including four of the Evangelists in a mid-13th century Gospel executed in Cilicia for Prince Sembat the Constable.[3] All of these latter pictures have much the same mats as the one previously described, having plain fields with borders containing geometric motifs; the only difference is that they each have a strip of Armenian script at the top end. That the composition of an Evangelist sitting in a chair with his feet resting on a mat became almost formularised in early Armenian pictorial art, can be seen from many other depictions including a series attributed to the most celebrated of early Armenian miniaturists, T'oros Roslin, in the Gospel of 1287;[4] in these miniatures, however, there are depicted carpets with more complex designs, with the split-palmette arabesque which is a feature of much early Armenian art, as it is of many other middle eastern cultures. Unfortunately, however, these carpets are not shown in sufficient detail for really objective comments to be made.

Early Armenian miniature painting is, therefore, of little help. Turning to that other great source of information, European painting, we find that such evidence as may be seen is ambivalent. Firstly, the majority of scholars take the view that the carpets with geometric designs which appear in Flemish and Italian paintings from the early 15th century are almost certainly Anatolian and not Caucasian; this view does not, of course, rule out the possibility that they may very well be the work of Armenian weavers. Certainly the carpets which appear in 15th century Flemish paintings with lozenge designs and hooked octagons (the so-called 'Memlinc' *gül*) resemble both Anatolian and, more strongly, Caucasian carpets of later dates and some, such as the diamond latch-hook carpet depicted in a 15th century Florentine painting of the Virgin and Child at Chantilly,[5] far more closely resemble Caucasian weavings. Many of the 'early Flemish' carpets, moreover, frequently have 'running vine' borders, not characteristic of early Anatolian carpets, but often encountered on the mats depicted in 12th and 13th century Armenian miniatures. Thus it may be that a good number of the weavings seen in 15th century European pictures, while Anatolian geographically, are the

---

1. For a history of Armenia and the Armenian people, the reader is referred to David Marshall Lang's *Armenia, Cradle of Civilization*, London 1970 and 1978.
2. Matenadaran Library MS no. 7736. Reproduced in Lydia A. Dournovo, *Armenian Miniatures*, London and Paris, 1961, p. 53.
3. Matenadaran Library MS no. 7644. The miniatures of St. Luke and St. Matthew are reproduced in Dournovo, op. cit., pp. 96, 97.
4. Matenadaran Library MS no. 197. Cf. Dournovo, op. cit., p. 113.
5. Attributed by Berenson to the mythical 'Amico di Sandro'; detail reproduced in Kurt Erdmann, *Oriental Carpets*, 2nd ed., Fishguard, 1976, fig. 23.

work of Armenians, who inhabited a large area of eastern Anatolia.

However, the shadowy presence of possibly Armenian rugs with geometric designs in the 15th century and earlier offers little developmental explanation for the emergence of the dragon rugs in the late 16th and early 17th centuries. As I explained above, the chronology of the dragon rugs itself poses considerable problems which have not, as yet, been satisfactorily resolved. Historically, there are two views of the development of the composition itself. The first view, developed by a generation of German scholars, suggested that dragon rugs, like western art, went through the usual phases of adolescence, maturity and decline; thus, those rugs with the most primitive, archaic, designs, such as the famous Graf rug in Berlin, largely destroyed in the Second World War, must be the oldest, being followed by the more sophisticated 'realistic' rugs which, in turn, were followed by the quite obviously late and degenerate types.

Neat and tidy as this view may appear, it imposes an aesthetic structure derived from a close study of western art upon an eastern cultural activity, which cannot be presumed to have developed in the same way. The approach of the second group of perhaps more radically minded experts, at the forefront of whom is the American Charles Grant Ellis,[6] has suggested what would certainly appear to be a more logical development. They point out that Oriental carpets tend to move from an initial period of sophistication ('realism' would be a more appropriate word), through succeeding phases of abstraction (or degeneration) until the composition as a whole and its individual elements become so abstracted as to be hardly recognisable for what, originally, they were. If this concept of the development of oriental carpet design is followed through, it has to be realised that even those rugs which Ellis would consider as being among the earliest surviving examples do not represent the composition at its earliest developmental stage, since it would be gratuitous to suggest that even these 'early' rugs are anything but semi-abstract; the compositional elements of dragons and other animals, leaves, flowers, etc., are, of course, more easily recognisable than on other, presumably later, rugs but even so we would hardly describe them as realistic.

Thus, to the obvious questions, when, where and by whom were the dragon rugs made must be added, "How did the composition come to be used in the first place?" As we can see it at present, there appears suddenly at the end of the 16th century a group of rugs which, even at their most sophisticated, are already in a state of compositional degeneration. Since no Caucasian rugs from an earlier generation have survived to demonstrate a clear development, it is assumed that the inspiration for the dragon rugs was not, in fact, an earlier group of Caucasian rugs at all, but the highly developed and sophisticated products of the Safavid Persian court manufactories. The dragon rugs represent a bold and powerful provincial rendering of the Safavid animal and 'vase' carpets, made, it is thought, in workshops established in Kashan and Kirman in central Persia.

The earliest writers attributed the dragon rugs to Armenia, a view which few subsequent writers have been prepared to endorse. The popularly held view for a number of years has been that the rugs were made in Kuba, a town in north-west Caucasia, but this idea has again been challenged by Ellis and others, who have pointed out that Kuba was not a major city until the mid-18th century and that, in any case, a more southerly origin, nearer to the present Persian border and within an area once under Safavid dominion, makes more sense. The city of Shusha in the Karabagh region has been suggested and is accepted here as being a more likely place of origin than Kuba. As to who wove the dragon rugs, we return to the theory put forward by Maurice Dimand[7] that the Armenian national, as opposed to the geographical, provenance is a strong possibility.

Some writers, most recently Serare Yetkin,[8] have suggested that the second major group of early Caucasian carpets, the 'floral' rugs, developed out of the dragon rugs, the zoomorphic motifs becoming, in the process, purely floral, with a 'transitional' type in the middle which retains vestigial dragon forms close in form to the medallions which appear on 19th and 20th century carpets attributed to Lenkoran (cf. nos. 186-191). If this view is followed, then it is interesting to consider the existence of one dated transitional piece, the Gohar carpet dated 1149 of the Armenian calendar (A.D. 1699/1700) and an even more floral carpet but, again, of Yetkin's transitional type in the Turk ve Islam Museum, Istanbul, dated 1156 A.H. (A.D. 1743).[9]

There is little reason to doubt the authenticity of either of these dated carpets (the date on the Gohar was suggested by Kurt Erdmann to be a forgery, something which did not seem the case when the piece came on the market in London in 1977).[10] No dated dragon carpet exists with the

---

6. Cf. Charles Grant Ellis, *Early Caucasian Rugs*, Washington, 1976, and the same author's review of Serare Yetkin's *Early Caucasian Carpets in Turkey* in *Hali*, vol. 1, no. 4, Winter, 1978, pp. 377-383.

7. Cf. M.S. Dimand and Jean Mailey, *Oriental Carpets in the Metropolitan Museum of Art*, New York, 1973, pp. 266-267.

8. Cf. Serare Yetkin, *Early Caucasian Carpets in Turkey*, 2 vols., London, 1978.

9. The Turk ve Islam carpet is reproduced in Yetkin, op. cit., plate 24.

10. Lefevre and Partners, London, 20 May 1977, lot 5. Reproduced also in Jean Lefevre, *et al., Caucasian Carpets,* London, 1977, p. 31. "The date

exception of the example in the Textile Museum, Washington, which is signed by Husayn Beg and which has a date which can be read in several ways although 1101 A.H. (A.D. 1689) seems the most likely; unfortunately, however, it seems that this latter piece is a copy made probably in the 19th century of a carpet, the date on which may have been either 1001 A.H. (A.D. 1592) or 1101 A.H. (A.D. 1689). In terms of the orderly progression of the dragon carpets, a date at the end of the 16th century would fit better than one at the end of the 17th, which would be exactly contemporary with the transitional Gohar carpet.

One other problem exists. There are a number of flat-woven carpets in the soumak technique extant, which are usually attributed to north-west Caucasia, either Kuba or Daghestan (although, again, probably attributable to the Karabagh). Many of the finest examples bear dates in the early part of the 19th century, including one in the Wher collection dated 1806[11] and another, sold by Nagel in Stuttgart, dated 1837. These rugs certainly seem to represent a more direct link, albeit a highly degenerated one, with the dragon carpets than do the so-called floral rugs. Since it seems fairly obvious that both the dragon and floral carpets drew their repertoire of motifs from a common source—the Safavid court carpets (which, in turn, drew heavily on Chinese and Mongolian motifs)— it is perhaps more useful to describe the Caucasian products as two distinct and mutually independent types, rather than to attempt an historical progression whereby one must be the antecedent of the other.

Finally, the suggestion that those dragon rugs with the most naturalistically drawn animals must be the earliest examples, and those with more abstracted forms must be the later degenerated versions, is as easily challenged as the old German theory; there exists, for instance, a group of animal carpets, probably from the second half of the 18th century and attributable to the south-west Caucasus, which have stylised, but nonetheless clearly recognisable animal combats and hunting scenes among trees and foliage which, again, are obviously later, provincial, renderings of Safavid models.[12]

The presence of these pieces demonstrates that Caucasian weavers were capable of producing well organised compositions with realistic animals (and based on Persian originals) long after the dragon rugs are considered to have all but disappeared, or at least to have entered into a period of extreme stylisation bordering on abstraction. Somehow, the question of variable abilities in weavers, some of whom may not have understood what in any case was an imported series of motifs, never seems to be considered.

The quality of the whole group of early dragon carpets—wool, colour, knot density, etc.—varies little from one piece to another. Some, such as the Graf carpet, have more crowded fields, and more varieties of fauna may appear in some examples. The majority of the best rugs have red grounds, a high number have dark brown and a dark blue or mid-blue is not uncommon; there is also an apparently unique white-ground example in the Wher collection, a very beautiful piece but with what would appear to be a late rendering of the dragon motif.

Structurally, the majority of examples have Z2S wool warps and wefts, the warps usually natural, the wefts often dyed one or more shades of red. Knot density tends to be around 1,250 to 1,400 per sq. dm (80 to 90 per sq. in.). A few examples may have cotton wefts, and one, from the McMullan collection now in the Metropolitan Museum, New York, has an all-silk foundation. All examples are Turkish knotted.

The compositional relationship between the dragon rugs and the animal and floral carpets of Safavid Persia is seen as strongly in several groups of Caucasian floral carpets, the earliest examples of which are attributed to the 18th century. Two of these groups, the carpets with the so-called *Harshang* and *Afshan* patterns, may be related to the 'Shah Abbas' or 'Herat' carpets which were produced not only in eastern Persia but also by Kurds and others in north-west Persia, in other words, in the areas of Azerbaijan and Karabagh which, until the 18th century, were parts of Persia. There are also several carpets extant with a composition of huge palmettes of varying shapes, flanked by enormous lanceolate leaves, provincial versions, quite obviously, of Persian 'vase' carpets.

There are also the groups referred to by Ellis as 'carpets with vine leaf palmettes' and 'sunburst' carpets, the so-

---

appears as a chronogram containing four letters separated by dots set at the end of the uppermost line." The full inscription, translated by Norayr de Byzance for F.R. Martin, reads: "I, the sinful Gouhar have made this with my own hands, may anyone reading this pray for my obtaining grace." De Byzance read the Armenian date as 1129 (A.D. 1679/80), although most modern scholars are of the opinion that the later interpretation of 1149 is more likely.

11. The Wher soumak carpet is illustrated in Ian Bennett (ed.), *Rugs and Carpets of the World*, Feltham, 1978, p. 254.

12. Two examples have been published: (a) McMullan Collection, Metropolitan Museum of Art, reproduced in Joseph V. McMullan, *Islamic Carpets*, New York, 1965, no. 46, and (b) the Wher collection, reproduced in Yetkin, op. cit., vol. 2, fig. 222. The McMullan and Wher carpets have very similar compositions, although the motifs of the Wher piece are better drawn. We ought, perhaps, to add the unique Caucasian silk hunting carpet in the Keir collection to this group.

called Kuba carpets with their large hexagonal or diamond medallions with four curving bar appendages, and the 'Shield' group, with repeated rows of large heraldic lotus palmettes. There are also some 'oddballs', including the animal and hunting rugs discussed above, the rugs which would appear to be Caucasian renderings of the Safavid 'Portuguese' carpets and what would appear to be the unique 'tree' carpet, well-known from its illustration in Schürmann's book and which was purchased by the Mayer Foundation, Jerusalem, at auction in London in 1977.[13]

A number of these groups continued to be made throughout the 19th century and well into the 20th, with an increasingly mechanical look to the composition. Note, for instance, the rugs reproduced as nos. 308, 310, 311 and 312, all of which are end of the 19th century or later, with the possible exception of no. 308, which is possibly first half of the 19th century, or even late 18th century. All of these later pieces, it should be added, are attributed by the majority of scholars to Kuba in northeast Caucasia, which might indicate that earlier examples, attributable to the end of the 18th century and beginning of the 19th, might also have been woven there. However, as Charles Grant Ellis has implied, the carpets with hexagonal or diamond medallions with four curved bars, which are known in the trade as Kubas, are in all probability, from the Shusha area in the Karabagh. It would seem as if only the *Harshang* and *Afshan* patterned rugs may have been produced in Kuba, almost certainly in workshops established in the latter half of the 18th century (a number are known with dates between 1790 and 1840). Again, Ellis prefers to attribute even these pieces to Shusha, although he does not suggest why there should be so little connection between those and Karabagh weavings of only slightly later dates.

The majority of early Caucasian 'vase', *Harshang* and *Afshan* carpets have all-wool foundations and knot counts of between about 800 and 1,200 per sq. dm (50 to 80 per sq. in.). A number, however, have either an all-cotton or a part-cotton foundation; all examples are Turkish knotted. An interesting carpet in the Keir collection with Harshang design is Persian knotted;[14] it is so close in design to the majority of Caucasian *Harshang* carpets that it is difficult to believe that it is a Persian product, although one feels it must be. It is interesting to note that the Keir collection also contains another apparently Caucasian oddity, a silk carpet with a central medallion and animals amid foliage, obviously based upon Safavid animal and hunting carpets.[15] This piece, too, is Persian knotted and is one of only two silk-pile rugs attributed to the Caucasus to have been published; the other is a Turkish knotted red-ground prayer rug attributed by Schürmann to Kazak and dated 1210 A.H. (A.D. 1795).[16] It may be that both the Keir carpets should be attributed to north-west Persia, but in any event, they demonstrate the pitfalls awaiting anyone seeking to make attributions based upon style alone.

One of the most interesting groups of early Caucasian carpets has a composition of 'shield' palmettes and has recently been the subject of a detailed examination.[17] The group is of interest for a number of reasons but principally for one compositional feature—a 'curled leaf' meander border identical to that found on a group of bird and animal-tree *asmalyk* now attributed to the Tekke Turkoman (the same design is also found on a small number of indisputably Tekke main carpets)—and for one structural feature — almost all examples are woven on silk foundations, an occurrence shared by a few 19th century north Caucasian prayer rugs and, as noted before, the unique dragon carpet from the McMullan collection now in the Metropolitan Museum of Art.

Traditionally, carpets of this type have been attributed by the majority of scholars, with the exception of Erdmann,[18] to the eastern Caucasus, possibly Shirvan or Kuba; current opinion seems to favour the Shirvan region. The presence of the curled leaf border on a number of these pieces is, perhaps, attributable to the presence of Turkoman nomads in the Caucasus from the mid-17th century and of specifically Tekke Turkoman from at least the early 18th century; the 'shield' palmette itself can be traced to a number of Persian and Turkish textiles, the earliest of which may be dated to the 14th century. As it appears on the Caucasian carpets, it is, in other words, a formalised, almost heraldic, rendering of the lotus palmette.

The carpets we have discussed so far constitute the classical rugs of the Caucasus; although their dating is controversial, and likely to remain so, the majority, it is believed, is datable to before 1800. They may also be assumed to have been manufactured in workshops

---

13. Two examples of the 'Portuguese' type are illustrated in Ellis, op. cit., plates 31 (Metropolitan Museum) and 32 (Textile Museum). The unique 'tree' carpet was first published by Ulrich Schürmann, *Caucasian Rugs*, Basingstoke, 1974, no. 2. Subsequently, it appeared on the London market and was sold at auction by Lefèvre and Partners, 20 May 1977, lot 4. It was published by Jean Lefèvre, op. cit., pp. 28-29 and by Richard Ettinghausen, *Ancient Carpets from the Collection of the L.A. Mayer Memorial Institute for Islamic Art*, Jerusalem, 1977, no. 10.

14. Cf. Friedrich Spuhler, *Islamic Carpets and textiles in the Keir Collection*, London, 1978, no. 69.

15. Cf. Spuhler, op. cit., no. 70.

16. Schürmann, op. cit., no. 7.

17. Robert Pinner and Michael Franses, "Caucasian Shield Carpets", in *Hali*, vol. 1, no. 1, Spring, 1978, pp. 4-22.

18. Erdmann, op. cit., describes two examples as 'Caucasian-North West Persian', implying, perhaps a Karabagh origin. He suggests that the composition was derived from Safavid Herat carpets.

established by the various Caucasian Khanates along the lines of Ottoman, Safavid and Moghul court manufactories; the very size of many of the carpets, as well as the intricacy of their designs, make it extremely unlikely that they could have been woven in either a nomadic or a domestic village environment.

In the 19th century, however, changing economic and political status throughout Persia, Caucasia and central Asia caused both the decline of aristocratic and royal patronage, the concomitant flourishing of tribal and village weaving (produced originally, of course, for domestic consumption), followed by an equally rapid decline due to wars, resettlement and the organised destruction of tribal autonomies; at the same time, there were established, first in Persia, and subsequently throughout Turkey, the Caucasus and India, commercial factories which tended to stereotype their products and to impose on native traditions the whims and stylistic dictates of alien markets—principally those of England, Germany and the United States. This commercialising of eastern weaving, together with the introduction of synthetic dyes and machine-spun yarns, hastened the decline already begun by political forces. Surprisingly, many tribal and village groups continued to withstand these pressures until well into the 20th century.

There is, of course, no sudden and neat dividing line between the carpets usually referred to as 'classical' and those called 'village' products. Following F.R. Martin, 1800[19] is the convenient date used to separate what many conservative collectors no doubt consider to be the sheep from the goats (as it is, roughly, for so many other areas of the applied arts). However, the activities of many 20th century collectors, most notably Joseph V. McMullan, have created a climate of opinion which believes village and tribal rugs worthy of at least the same consideration as the classical carpets and, while this may seem cynically as at least in part due to the lack of sufficient quantities of classical carpets to create a large and competitive market, it also reflects the growing involvement of many young dealers, collectors and writers with the anthropology and history of the tribal and village peoples. Needless to say, the contents of the present volume are, largely, a reflection of contemporary tastes and pre-occupations among western rug collectors.

Serious classification of Caucasian village weaving began only in the 1960s and the terminology of the subject used by both dealers and collectors in the west is based primarily on the work of the Soviet scholar Lyatif Kerimov whose book, *Azerbaijan Carpets*, published in Russian in Baku in 1961, was used as a base by the German writer Ulrich Schürmann for his 1965 publication, *Caucasian Rugs*. Schürmann himself acknowledged his debt to Kerimov in the Preface to his book, but also remarks that Kerimov lists some 123 distinct varieties of Caucasian village rugs, often without illustrating examples; Schürmann confines himself to well under half this number, although many of the names now taken for granted among specialists in Caucasian village rugs—Fachralo, Lambalo, Chelaberd, Chondzoresk, Lesghi, *et al*, were first publicised and made available (and very convenient) frames of reference by Schürmann.

However, Schürmann's own remarks about Kerimov's listings would imply that our knowledge of Caucasian village weaving is at best only fragmentary and at worst represents the particular 'readings' of one individual, readings which may be very inaccurate. Several Armenian writers have argued that many of the 19th century village rugs, not to mention the dragon and other groups of classical carpets, were the products of villages settled by Armenian weavers. Thus in a book published in France in 1949, and written by the Parisian dealer Albert Achdjian, we read the following:

"Apart from KOUBAH, the other villages which have given their names to antique Armenian rugs are: NOUKHI, ARGNI, KANTSAK, AGTZNIQ, PERGRI, LENINAGAN, DJANIG, VAN, MOGG, CHADAKJ, AGHTAMAR, AGHECHE, MOUCH, SIGHET, CARS, ANI, ZORK, INGOUZAN, ARDAMED, ACHDARAG, KHATCHAS, KANGOUNI, ABARAN, ARDACHAD, CHARMARCOU, GOGLYS, TVIN, TCHIRVEG, NORACHEN, SOURP, HAY-KHAN, VOSDAN, CHAPAKH, ARDZGONK, KHORONK, SILVAN, KANOUS, VART, LIDIK, ANTZAV, EGIN, NAKIDJEVAN, SASOUN, KASAK, ARDAHAN, KARABAGH, CHIRVAN, DZAGHGANTZ, ARMOUG, MANAZCHERD, GARIN, DZAGHIATCHK, PAIPERT, HAZARAG, KEREZMAN and GUESSARIA".[20]

Although I include this quotation primarily for its curiosity value, Achdjian was obviously rehearsing traditional Armenian wisdom about Caucasian and eastern Anatolian rugs, in which there is quite possibly more than a whiff of truth. Certainly, many more contemporary writers on Caucasian village rugs have tended to treat the Kerimov/Schürmann classification with considerable caution and have frequently ignored the more detailed provenances completely. However, it is useful to be able to distinguish the various compositional types of rugs quickly and easily and the many different names now in general use do, at least, have the virtue of conjuring up instant mental images. Suffice it to say that it is for this reason that they have been retained in the present book and also so that the layman may familiarise himself with the terminology used by the majority of dealers and auctioneers. It should not,

---

19. F.R. Martin, *A History of Oriental Carpets before 1800*, Vienna, 1908.

20. Albert Achdjian, *Le Tapis/The Rug* (bi-lingual edition), Paris, 1949, p. 54.

however, be taken necessarily as an endorsement of these places of origin although, in the absence of new, convincing, and accessible research from Soviet Russian fieldworkers and researchers, it seems unlikely that a better classification will become available in the foreseeable future.

DATES

The earliest surviving examples of Caucasian village rugs, to judge from dated pieces, would appear to be from the last two decades of the 18th century. It must be realised that the dates on many oriental carpets should be treated with considerable caution and there are certainly rugs with dates it is impossible to take seriously. On a number of examples, the second figure, which might have read '3' could, by the removal of two, or three knots, have been altered to a '2', thus deducting a century from the actual date; there are also a considerable number of rugs, such as the Husayn Beg carpet in Washington, which have inscriptions and dates copied from genuine old pieces. Finally, there are those rugs upon which old dates have been woven probably with the intention of deceiving gullible buyers; the fact that many such pieces still appear regularly in popular picture books is ample testimony of just how gullible many dealers and collectors in the west remain.

From available evidence, it seems that the oldest groups of Caucasian village rugs are certain varieties of Kazak, some of those with the 'pinwheel' design having dates in the last decade of the 18th century, some Karabagh carpets with westernised designs of flowers, also dated in the late 18th century, and some 'Daghestan' and Shirvan rugs, which date from the early 19th century. There are also the dragon soumaks dated in the first three decades of the 19th century. We should also note the remarks made by Kurt Erdmann in *700 Years of Oriental Carpets*[21] that, "The dating of carpets stopped with the First World War, and the date 1932 in a Daghestan in the Roseliushaus in Bremen is the sole exception which I have encountered." Of course, in the context of oriental carpets in general, this statement is inaccurate, there being many Baluch and other Persian nomadic and village weavings with dates in the 1920s and 1930s, also a few Turkish rugs and very many Caucasian pieces.[22]

Because of the dangers inherent in accepting many of the dates at face value, it is difficult to make totally objective statements about the development of Caucasian village rugs in the 150 year period between 1780 and 1930. What does emerge, however, is that in many respects change was relatively slow in the 19th century, but declined very rapidly after that. It it possible to look at two undated Caucasian rugs and, on the basis of colour, composition, drawing ability and overall texture, to suggest that one is considerably older than the other. But, invariably, along comes a rug with all the obvious signs of antiquity, only to be dated between 1890 and 1910. Erdmann himself makes this point in *700 Years* by illustrating a Kazak prayer rug of superb colour and design dated 1913 – "Without the inscription, it would have been dated several decades earlier." With certain groups, such as the so-called Kasim Usag type, the quality appears to change hardly at all between the earliest dated pieces, from the late 1860s, and those with dates in the 1910-20 period; only in examples with dates in the 1920s and 1930s do we notice a really marked deterioration in colour, composition and drawing.

Apart from the possibility of incorrect dating, there are several other points to be remembered when reading and transcribing dates expressed in Arabic numerals. The first is that dates are quite frequently written in mirror image, so that 1311 becomes 1131 (often, the date is simply written the wrong way round instead of in proper mirror image). In some cases the zero is omitted, so that 1310 becomes 131; this is particularly confusing when the zero occurs in the middle of a date so that 129 could be either 1209 or 1290 (i.e. A.D. 1794 or A.D. 1873); when not left out, the zero in a number is usually expressed as a dot, rather than a circle or a diamond. It is also worth noting that sometimes the date in the Christian calendar is expressed directly in eastern Arabic numbers. Rugs in which dates are written the wrong way round (figures, in Arabic writing, run from left to right, unlike letters, which run from right to left) are often assumed to be late copies of early rugs, the design having been copied from the backs of the old pieces; there may be some truth in this, but it remains unproven.

The Islamic calendar begins with year 1 of the Hejira, which marks the beginning of the Pilgrimage of the Prophet Mohammed from Mecca to Medina on 16th July A.D. 622. In addition, the Mohammedan year is marginally shorter than the Christian year, gaining one day in every 33.7 years. For a quick and rough method of transposing Islamic dates, add 583; for an accurate method, divide the Islamic date by 33.7, subtract the result and then add 622.

A.H. (Year of the Hejira)	A.D. Equivalent beginning on:
1178	1st July 1764
1179	20th June 1765
1180	9th June 1766
1181	30th May 1767
1182	18th May 1768
1183	7th May 1769
1184	27th April 1770
1185	16th April 1771

---

21. Kurt Erdmann, *Seven Hundred Years of Oriental Carpets*, London, 1970, p. 174.
22. Among Caucasian examples seen recently was a Chajli with poor colour and composition; this was dated 1347 A.H. (A.D. 1922). It was sold at auction by Rippon Boswell, London, 3 March 1979, lot 86.

A.H. (Year of the Hejira)	A.D. Equivalent beginning on:	A.H. (Year of the Hejira)	A.D. Equivalent beginning on:	A.H. (Year of the Hejira)	A.D. Equivalent beginning on:
1186	4th April 1772	1239	7th September 1823	1292	7th February 1875
1187	25th March 1773	1240	26th August 1824	1293	28th January 1876
1188	14th March 1774	1241	16th August 1825	1294	16th January 1877
1189	4th March 1775	1242	5th August 1826	1295	5th January 1878
1190	21st February 1776	1243	25th July 1827	1296	26th December 1878
1191	19th February 1777	1244	14th July 1828	1297	15th December 1879
1192	30th January 1778	1245	3rd July 1829	1298	4th December 1880
1193	19th January 1779	1246	22nd June 1830	1299	23rd November 1881
1194	8th January 1780	1247	12th June 1831	1300	12th November 1882
1195	28th December 1780	1248	31st May 1832	1301	2nd November 1883
1196	17th December 1781	1249	21st May 1833	1302	21st October 1884
1197	7th December 1782	1250	10th May 1834	1303	10th October 1885
1198	26th November 1783	1251	29th April 1835	1304	30th September 1886
1199	14th November 1784	1252	18th April 1836	1305	19th September 1887
1200	4th November 1785	1253	7th April 1837	1306	7th September 1888
1201	24th October 1786	1254	27th March 1838	1307	28th August 1889
1202	13th October 1787	1255	17th March 1839	1308	17th August 1890
1203	2nd October 1788	1256	5th March 1840	1309	7th August 1891
1204	21st September 1789	1257	23rd February 1841	1310	26th July 1892
1205	10th September 1790	1258	12th February 1842	1311	15th July 1893
1206	31st August 1791	1259	1st February 1843	1312	5th July 1894
1207	19th August 1792	1260	22nd January 1844	1313	24th June 1895
1208	9th August 1793	1261	10th January 1845	1314	12th June 1896
1209	29th July 1794	1262	30th December 1845	1315	2nd June 1897
1210	18th July 1795	1263	20th December 1846	1316	22nd May 1898
1211	7th July 1796	1264	9th December 1847	1317	12th May 1899
1212	26th June 1797	1265	27th November 1848	1318	1st May 1900
1213	15th June 1798	1266	17th November 1849	1319	20th May 1901
1214	5th June 1799	1267	6th November 1850	1320	10th April 1902
1215	25th May 1800	1268	27th October 1851	1321	30th March 1903
1216	14th May 1801	1269	15th October 1852	1322	18th March 1904
1217	4th May 1802	1270	4th October 1853	1323	8th March 1905
1218	23rd April 1803	1271	24th September 1854	1324	25th February 1906
1219	12th April 1804	1272	13th September 1855	1325	14th February 1907
1220	1st April 1805	1273	1st September 1856	1326	4th February 1908
1221	21st March 1806	1274	22nd August 1857	1327	23rd January 1909
1222	11th March 1807	1275	11th August 1858	1328	13th January 1910
1223	28th February 1808	1276	31st July 1859	1329	2nd January 1911
1224	16th February 1809	1277	20th July 1860	1330	22nd December 1911
1225	6th February 1810	1278	9th July 1861	1331	11th December 1912
1226	26th January 1811	1279	29th June 1862	1332	30th November 1913
1227	16th January 1812	1270	18th June 1863	1333	19th November 1914
1228	4th January 1813	1281	6th June 1864	1334	9th November 1915
1229	24th December 1813	1282	27th May 1865	1335	28th October 1916
1230	14th December 1814	1283	16th May 1866	1336	17th October 1917
1231	3rd December 1815	1284	5th May 1867	1337	7th October 1918
1232	21st November 1816	1285	24th April 1868	1338	26th September 1919
1233	11th November 1817	1286	13th April 1869	1339	15th September 1920
1234	31st October 1818	1287	3rd April 1870	1340	4th September 1921
1235	20th October 1819	1288	23rd March 1871	1341	24th August 1922
1236	9th October 1820	1289	11th March 1872	1342	14th August 1923
1237	28th September 1821	1290	1st March 1873	1343	2nd August 1924
1238	18th September 1822	1291	18th February 1874	1344	22nd July 1925

A.H. (Year of the Hejira)	A.D. Equivalent beginning on:	A.H. (Year of the Hejira)	A.D. Equivalent beginning on:	A.H. (Year of the Hejira)	A.D. Equivalent beginning on:
1345	12th July 1926	1369	24th October 1949	1393	4th February 1973
1346	1st July 1927	1370	13th October 1950	1394	25th January 1974
1347	20th June 1928	1371	2nd October 1951	1395	14th January 1975
1348	9th June 1929	1372	21st September 1952	1396	3rd January 1976
1349	29th May 1930	1373	10th September 1953	1397	23rd December 1976
1350	19th May 1931	1374	30th August 1954	1398	12th December 1977
1351	7th May 1932	1375	20th August 1955	1399	2nd December 1978
1352	26th April 1933	1376	8th August 1956	1400	21st November 1979
1353	16th April 1934	1377	29th July 1957	1401	9th November 1980
1354	5th April 1935	1378	18th July 1958	1402	30th October 1981
1355	24th March 1936	1379	7th July 1959	1403	19th October 1982
1356	14th March 1937	1380	25th June 1960	1404	8th October 1983
1357	3rd March 1938	1381	14th June 1961	1405	27th September 1984
1358	21st February 1939	1382	4th June 1962	1406	16th September 1985
1359	10th February 1940	1383	25th May 1963	1407	6th September 1986
1360	29th January 1941	1384	13th May 1964	1408	26th August 1987
1361	19th January 1942	1385	2nd May 1965	1409	14th August 1988
1362	8th January 1943	1386	22nd April 1966	1410	4th August 1989
1363	28th December 1943	1387	11th April 1967	1411	24th July 1990
1364	17th December 1944	1388	31st March 1968	1412	13th July 1991
1365	6th December 1945	1389	20th March 1969	1413	2nd July 1992
1366	25th November 1946	1390	9th March 1970	1414	21st June 1993
1367	15th November 1947	1391	27th February 1971	1415	10th June 1994
1368	3rd November 1948	1392	16th February 1972		

STRUCTURE

The majority of Caucasian pile rugs have woollen warps and wefts and a wool pile tied with a symmetric knot (also called the Turkish or Ghiordes knot). Very few — indeed only the two rugs in the Keir collection mentioned above have been published — have asymmetric (Persian or Senna) knotting and only two published rugs have silk piles. A significant number of Caucasian rugs may have either all- or part-cotton foundations and a few rugs of specific types— e.g. the 'Shield' group—have wool piles knotted on all- or part- silk foundations.

In the construction of the majority of Caucasian rugs, there is a depressed warp caused by the wefts being stretched tight over alternate warps; between each row of knots, there will be two or three wefts (weft 'shoots').The exceptions are Kazak rugs, in which all the warps are of even tension, thereby sitting on one level; they are also multi-wefted.

In the course of our discussion of the various types and groups, we will frequently have recourse to expressions such as 'Z2S' or 'Z3S'. In the preparation of single strands, wool is spun (i.e. twisted) in an anti-clockwise direction; to give it greater tensile strength, two or more strands are then plied (i.e. twisted together) in a clockwise direction. Thus 'S' and 'Z' are commonly used rebuses in the vocabulary of textile structure for clockwise and anti-clockwise respectively; the wool and silk used in all oriental carpets is constructed in this manner, with the exception of the Egyptian 15th century Mamluk carpets, the later Cairene court carpets and certain 19th century Turkish silk rugs. 'Z2S', therefore, means that, in the manufacture of the wool used to create all or part of the rug, two single strands have been spun in an anti-clockwise direction and plied in a clockwise one, and so on for 'Z3S', 'Z4S', etc.; because the wool of Mamluk and Cairene court carpets is constructed in the opposite manner, the description of the warp of a Mamluk carpet might read 'S2Z'.

DYES

The colours of oriental carpets were obtained originally solely from vegetable, natural mineral and insect sources. In the 1860s, however, there began the introduction of synthetic dyes and also the more wide-spread use of the various shades of red and pink-red called cochineal. Synthetic dyes slowly ousted the use of natural colours and now there are few oriental carpets employing vegetable colours. It has to be said that the attempts by some governments in the East to fight against synthetic colours, even to the extent of harsh economic sanctions and mutilation of the dyers and weavers caught using them, had little effect; the weavers themselves delighted in the brilliant mauves, purples, pinks, reds, oranges and greens which began to appear in their rugs, first used sparingly and preciously (initially synthetic dyes were very expensive) but later, as the dyestuffs became cheaper and more freely available, in greater quantities. Sadly, many of the early dyes faded badly and quickly, changed colour and ran badly when wet; many later chrome-based dyes, while faster and more water resistant, were nevertheless harsh and unmellowing. One has only to see an otherwise attractive Caucasian rug spoiled by the inclusion of one ghastly orange or fluorescent pink to understand why many collectors will avoid pieces containing synthetic dyes whenever possible. There are, admittedly, many dealers and collectors who would argue, with some justification, that the abhorrence of serious collectors for pieces containing synthetic dyes has been carried perhaps a little too far, but faced with the possibility of buying two very similar pieces, one of which has purely natural dyes and the other one or more synthetic colours, even they would agree upon which of the two it is advisable to buy.

One other point which some dealers might make, however, and one which is certainly true, is that many tribal and village groups, especially nomadic tribes such as the various Turkoman and Baluch peoples, often took far longer to use synthetic colours than other more settled groups; thus, although many carpets contained quite substantial quantities of synthetic dyes by the last two decades of the 19th century (this is especially true of Persian city weavings and Turkish village rugs), other pieces by different peoples, probably much later in date, have no synthetic colours. There is in my collection, for instance, a Baluch rug dated 1343 A.H. (A.D. 1924) which has no synthetic dyes, while I own several other Baluch weavings which probably date from between 1880 and 1900 which contain small quantities of synthetic dye, usually the early aniline Fuchsine; this was originally a bright mauve which fades to white, ivory or tan. As an added comment on dated rugs, we illustrate a slit-tapestry rug of a type attributed by some scholars to eastern Anatolia, by others to Azerbaijan and by others to as far east as Daghestan, which has a date in the 1830s but contains an early synthetic dye, Fuchsine, which was not invented until the 1850s and probably not used by Oriental weavers until the 1870s!

Kazak

Star Kazak and Swastika Kazak

Numbers 1 and 2 are related very closely in origin. The first is of the type usually called in English 'star' Kazak and the second 'swastika', although its interlocking design can be interpreted as a version of the star; some of the second type have the swastika motifs standing in greater isolation on a less busy field. However, as with descriptions of Oriental carpet designs generally, the term 'swastika' is more one of convenience than reality; pieces of this design can often be found described in the literature as either 'eternity symbol' Kazaks or 'pinwheel' Kazaks.

Star Kazaks are usually of more square format than the present example. This rug bears the Islamic date 1244 A.H. (A.D. 1829); several extant star Kazaks bear dates in the last decade of the 18th century and first three decades of the 19th century— indeed, very few, if any, other groups of Caucasian carpets can boast so many examples dated so early. The majority of these early dated star Kazaks have blue cotton or wool wefts, while obviously later examples have wool wefts, either dyed red or natural brown. Some experts would argue, however, that this structural difference is not a matter of chronology; they suggest that there are two distinct groups of star Kazaks, one, with the blue wefts, the result of a settled, urban production, and the other of a more nomadic, village tradition. Although this may be partly true, there is no doubt that there are no star Kazaks which are either very early in appearance or which bear early dates which do not have blue wefts, usually cotton and occasionally wool. The swastika Kazaks invariably have an all-wool structure.

The knot count on both types will usually be between 900 and 1,000 per sq. dm. (58 to 65 per sq. in.), although the early cotton-wefted star Kazaks can sometimes go above this and late examples, frequently with synthetic dyes, may often fall considerably below my bottom limit. Old star Kazaks tend to have a clearly drawn design on a white field, with a predominant use of light colours, especially green and purplish-mauve.

1 Very fine old piece dated 1244 A.H. (A.D. 1829) with a beautiful range of colours including a pale green and a light purplish-mauve. The closest parallel in earlier carpets to the design of this piece is, surprisingly, a group of 17th century Moghul Indian carpets which, in turn, echo the geometric interlock of 15th century Mamluk carpets from Egypt. If one compares the present piece to the Moghul rugs with interlocking star compositions, such as that illustrated as no. 47 in Spuhler, König and Volkmann's *Alte Orientteppiche*, the resemblance is really quite startling. It should be noted that the date on this piece is written in reverse; this phenomenon is considered by some experts as an indication that the date is not to be believed. An explanation frequently put forward is that obviously late rugs with early dates, either written correctly or in reverse, are copies of early dated rugs (there is some evidence for this, as I have shown in the introduction). Certainly, the dates woven in Caucasian village rugs, especially if in reverse, should be treated with some caution, but there can be little doubt that the present example is a very good early piece, almost certainly woven in the first half of the 19th century.
252 x 152 cm

STAR KAZAK KAZAK 19

Kazak Motifs

Some of the typical motifs found on various types of Kazaks. The number by the drawing indicates the rug from which it was taken. Clearly these can only be considered as general motifs; the interpretation by individual weavers varies widely within the overall format.

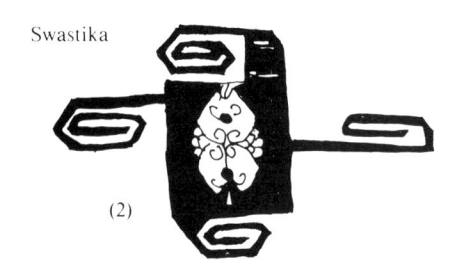

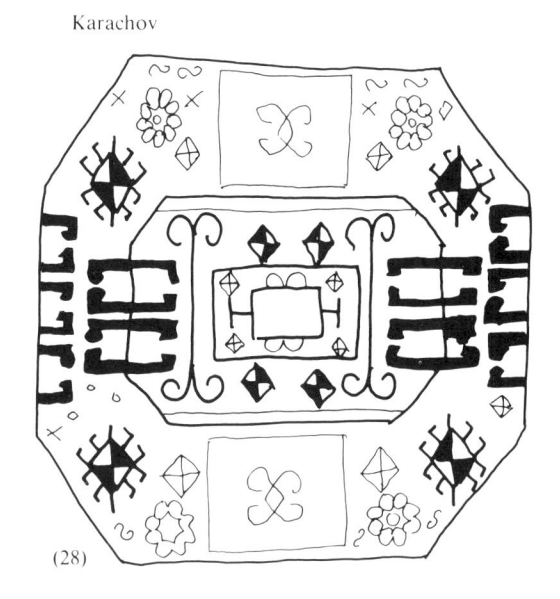

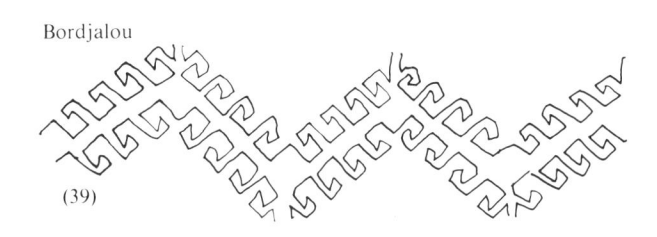

Swastika
(2)

Karachov
(28)

Bordjalou
(39)

(40)

Fachralo
(22)

2 Swastika Kazak. This piece has the pale, almost pastel, colours often found on early examples of this group. However, the ornate reciprocal border composition is considered by some experts to be a fairly late feature. The bright yellow of the two central palmettes (and seen also in other minor details) is a most unusual colour. There seems little doubt that the swastikas themselves are highly stylised zoomorphic motifs. They would seem to be related to the motifs found on some early Turkish carpets, such as the borders of a 'Lotto' rug of about 1600 in the Budapest Museum (*Alte Anatolische Teppiche aus dem Museum für Kunstgewerbe in Budapest*, no. 3). Possibly mid- to late 19th century.
 225 x 181 cm

2

3 An unusual prayer rug with swastika motifs. The inscription in the arch, 1122, cannot be used for a reliable date. I have not seen another example of this type. Probably mid- 19th century. 131 x 102 cm

4 Another unusual prayer rug with natural ivory field and borders. The single large medallion relates this piece closely to the following group of Lori-Pambak rugs. This is one of three published examples of this type —the other two (Charles W. Jacobsen, *Oriental Rugs*, pl. 152, Peter Bausback, *Antike Orientteppiche*, p. 159) have square white fields, in other words are not prayer rugs. All three have almost identical colour arrangements; the present rug and the Jacobsen piece have versions of the leaf-and-calyx border, the Bausback rug a simple zig-zag-and- cruciform design. An example illustrated by Raoul Tschebull, "The Development of Four Kazak Designs", *Hali*, vol. 1, no. 3, seems to be the same piece as that illustrated by Jacobsen. Tschebull links this piece to other examples of the so-called Lori-Pambak group and implies that examples of this type are late in date. Second half of the 19th century.
141 x 110 cm

Lori-Pambak

To Lori-Pambak, a village in the west central Caucasus, is attributed a group of colourful rugs, many of which have a distinctive quatrefoil medallion, clearly seen in nos. 5 and 8. This medallion is probably derived from an early animal totemic symbol representing pairs of opposed animals and birds. Vestigial remains of this can be seen most clearly in the medallion of 5, where the ends of the medallion at top and bottom can be read as two pairs of facing birds with crested heads.

Most Lori-Pambak rugs will have an ivory wool warp and red wool weft, both Z2S. The selvedges, as on the majority of Kazak rugs, will have two bundles of two warps wrapped in red or in polychrome bands. Knot counts vary from about 700 to 1,000 per sq. dm (45 to 65 per sq. in.).

5 Probably later than at first glance it might seem, even though it has the most clearly delineated birds in the central medallion of any of the Lori-Pambak rugs illustrated here. The drawing in the main white-ground border has lost almost all contact with the meandering floral vine found on early pieces. Tschebull (op. cit.) illustrates a very similar example, no. 29, which he suggests is the second stage of the composition's development, no. 29 being dated to the equivalent of A.D. 1897. So close is the Tschebull rug to ours that it is difficult to believe that ours could be much older.
232 x 178 cm

Further Kazak motifs

Lori-Pambak 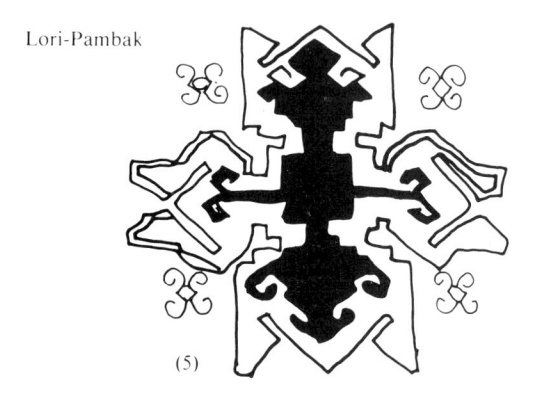
(5)

Shikli 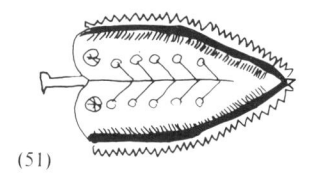
(51)

Hooked Polygon 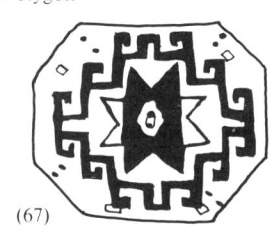
(67)

Tree of Life 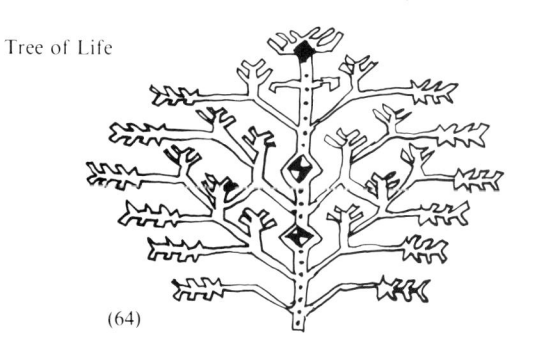
(64)

Tile Pattern 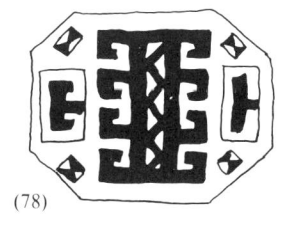
(78)

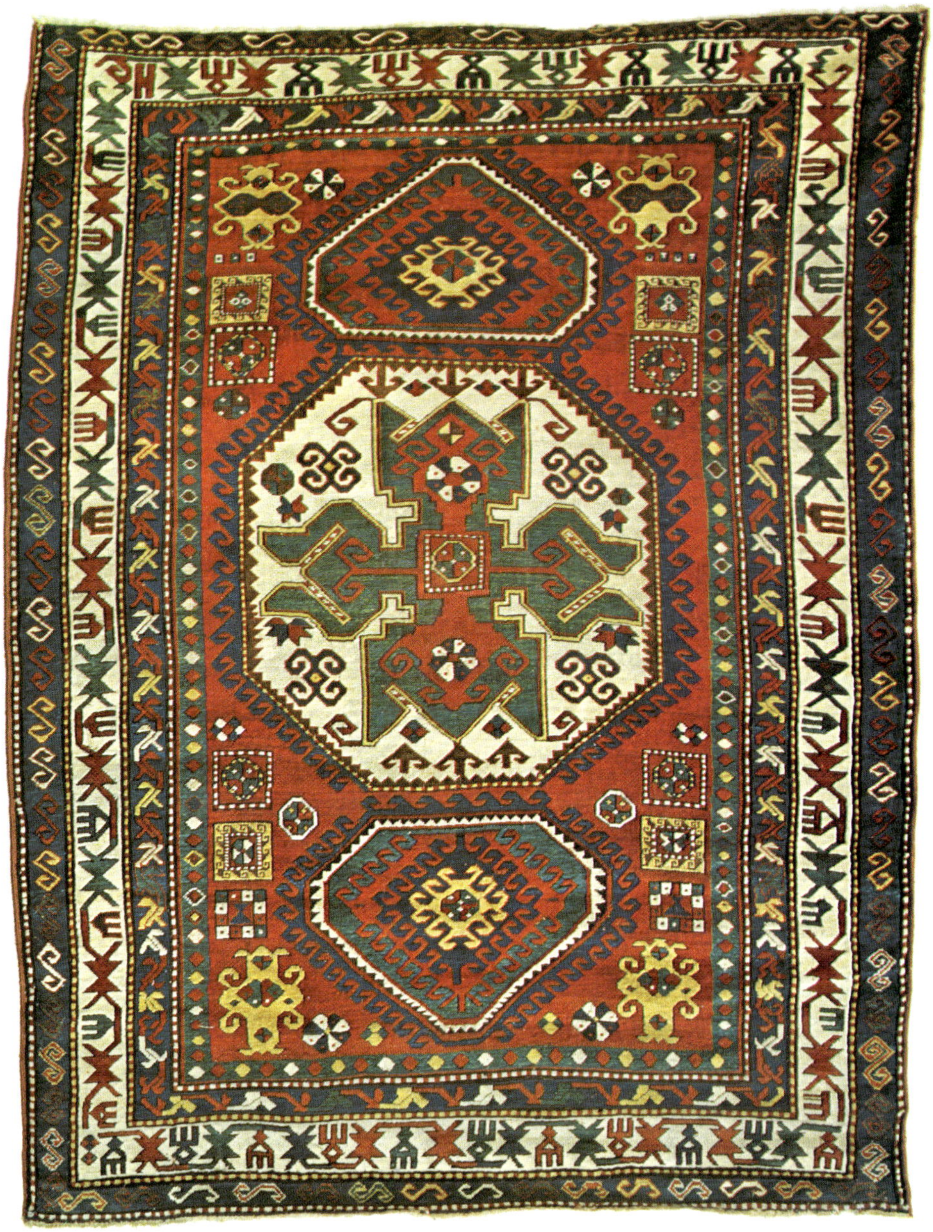

6 Unusual large double-ended medallion with the main Lori-Pambak motif contained within it. The birds' heads still retain their crests, although this piece is very stiffly drawn and possibly even later than 5. Many such pieces have harsh synthetic colours. Late 19th century.
231 x 156 cm

7 A number of Kazaks are found with triple medallions but few, such as this example, with two. Skeletal Lori-Pambak motif but the birds' heads nicely crested. Probably late 19th/or even early 20th century.
233 x 171 cm

8 A handsome, if perhaps late, example. With 5, this is the best-known Lori-Pambak composition. Raoul Tschebull, in his essay 'The Development of Four Kazak Designs' (*Hali*, vol. I, no. 3, pp. 257-261), illustrates a very similar example (fig. 30) which is dated 1911; the borders of that piece have a somewhat cruder composition than that seen on the present rug and the illustration, being in black and white, does not allow us to compare the colour range to the extremely beautiful polychromy of our example. However, the birds on both pieces have lost their crests and the general simplification of the design suggests that it is a late development. Late 19th/or early 20th century.
236 x 175 cm

8

Triple-Medallion Kazaks

The triple-medallion design has given its name to a well-defined group of Kazak rugs which were probably produced all over the south-west Caucasus. The medallions are usually two blue and one white, or vice versa, and the field colour red. The motifs within the outer medallions of all the pieces illustrated here, with the exception of 11, show a clear affinity with the quatrefoil medallions of the Lori-Pambak rugs. The quality of these pieces is usually high and, in the absence of such obvious pointers as woven dates or synthetic dyes, it is difficult to distinguish differences in age. The foundation is usually all wool, the warps of grey or brown, the wefts one of various shades of pink or red. It is interesting to note the coarseness of no. 12, which is probably the latest of the examples illustrated here; Tschebull (op. cit.) suggests that pieces such as this may have been woven under contract arrangements with rug merchants. The best, and presumably, oldest triple-medallion Kazaks may have knot counts as high as 1,200 per sq. dm (77 per sq. in.), dropping down to around 600 (38) in very coarse examples.

10 Another triple-medallion Kazak, but a distinctly more handsome example than the previous rug. In his *Hali* article, Raoul Tschebull makes the following observation about this group: "The development of the Triple Medallion Kazak pattern presents a number of problems. As far as I am aware, the pattern does not appear in western Turkey, is rarely found in dated pieces and the rugs on which it does appear show no clear structural trends, other than a tendency towards larger sizes in the 19th century." He goes on to suggest that such rugs were woven all over the south-west Caucasus. Our rug has very similar field and border compositions to Tschebull's fig. 10, which he suggests is the earliest type; however, the crowding in the field seen on our rug is typical of a specific type, two examples of which, nos. 9 and 11 are published here. All three have the "arrow block" motifs in the white ground medallions. The colouring is rich and varied, and there are no obvious synthetic dyes. Probably late 19th century.
219 x 147 cm

9

9 Triple-medallion Kazak with rosette borders, another frequently encountered design. The large rosettes in the main border and the overall composition have affinities with east Turkestan rugs. The blocks of arrows in the white ground medallions are often found used as border motifs. Rugs of this type were made in the second half of the 19th century and into the early 20th century.
203 x 136 cm

11 (*overleaf*) This is of the same type as 9, but a better example, a fact made obvious by comparing the borders.
250 x 185 cm

12 (*overleaf*) A colourful, but rather crudely drawn example. The presence of two human figures in the upper right-hand side of the field is an amusing and unusual feature. Also of interest are the four yellow ground octagons containing four C-like motifs facing in opposite directions; a similar decorative device is associated with a specific group of Yomut Turkoman main carpets, sometimes called the Ogurjalis or C group. The "arrow block" motifs have moved from the white ground medallion to the border. Late 19th or early 20th century.
200 x 164 cm

TRIPLE-MEDALLION KAZAK 29

11

TRIPLE-MEDALLION KAZAK

'Sewan' Kazaks

These Sewan Kazaks (13-19) with a single large cruciform medallion, represent another well-defined group from the south-west Caucasus. The medallion is found in three main forms — wing-sided and arrow-head ended (17, 18, 19) or square-sided and squared-octagon ended (14, 16) or straight-sided and arrow-head ended (13, 15). They come in a variety of textures, the knot count range being about the same as for the triple-medallion Kazaks. The foundation is all wool; warps may be grey or brown, although late pieces, including examples bearing the Islamic equivalents of 20th century dates, usually have uniform ivory warp and weft. Wefts may be blue (on pieces usually thought to be early), light brown, dark brown, pink, red or ivory. It should be noted that although the German name for this group is 'Schild- (shield) Kazak', it is not related to the 'Shield' carpets described in the Introduction.

13 Although the composition of this piece is complex, it is crowded and stiff. It is interesting to note how the fan-tailed motifs, seen at the centre of the design facing in opposite directions, can be related to the zoomorphic motif found on a certain type of dragon *sileh* rug (cf. our 478). It seems likely that rugs with medallions of this straight shape are fairly late. This rug is missing many of the most common motifs, such as the 'trees' in the corners of the medallion (see 15), and the wide white-ground frame has here become a simple ribbon motif or a very narrow white-ground frame. The overall look of the piece lacks the primitive and heraldic splendour, which makes so many rugs of the group among the most distinguished of all Caucasian village weavings. Late 19th or early 20th century.
195 x 115 cm

SEWAN KAZAK

14 'Sewan' Kazak with stylised animals and bold reciprocal arrow-head guards, and with the medallion surrounded by latch-hooks, commonly called 'running-dogs'. The outer border is close in design to those found on some Caucasian kilim. The straight-sided, octagon-ended medallion is not as commonly encountered as the wing-sided medallion. On this piece, however, the weaver has badly miscalculated the size of the space available and has had to curtail the octagon at one end. The hook-edged motif within the central small white-ground decahedron (with its bottom point cut flat) is, according to Kerimov, called the 'wedding table'. This suggests that rugs of this design were once woven for a specific festive occasion, i.e. a wedding. Probably second half of the 19th century. 237 x 176 cm

15 A rug similar to 13 and with a somewhat similar series of borders. It has the same four animals in the centre, although in a different position, and similar fan-tailed ornaments, although here, they are of a more tree-like character. In the centre of the rug is seen a block of double T ornaments, associated in particular with a group of south Caucasian/north-west Persian flat-weaves. However, the arrangement of the motifs within the white-ground rectangle is similar to the treatment of the bars in the centre of Karachov rugs, to the white-ground rectangles on rug nos. 34-36 and also to the 'Surahani' group from Shirvan (cf. nos. 272, 274, 275). Late 19th or early 20th century.
170 x 116 cm

16 A fine example with well-proportioned medallion and a typical border design. An example similar in style to the present piece, once in the McMullan collection, is dated 1797, but is obviously considerably older than the present piece, as well as having a different palette of, predominantly, dark blue and red. The McMullan piece also contains a dark purple-brown colour which is considered a sign of an old Kazak. Raoul Tschebull illustrates a related rug in his *Hali* article (fig. 7), which he, too, compares to the McMullan rug. However, he points out that his piece has small details dyed with a mixture of madder and the synthetic red Ponceau 2R, which means that it must post-date the McMullan rug by almost a century (that is, if we accept the date on the latter). Second half of the 19th century.
220 x 157 cm

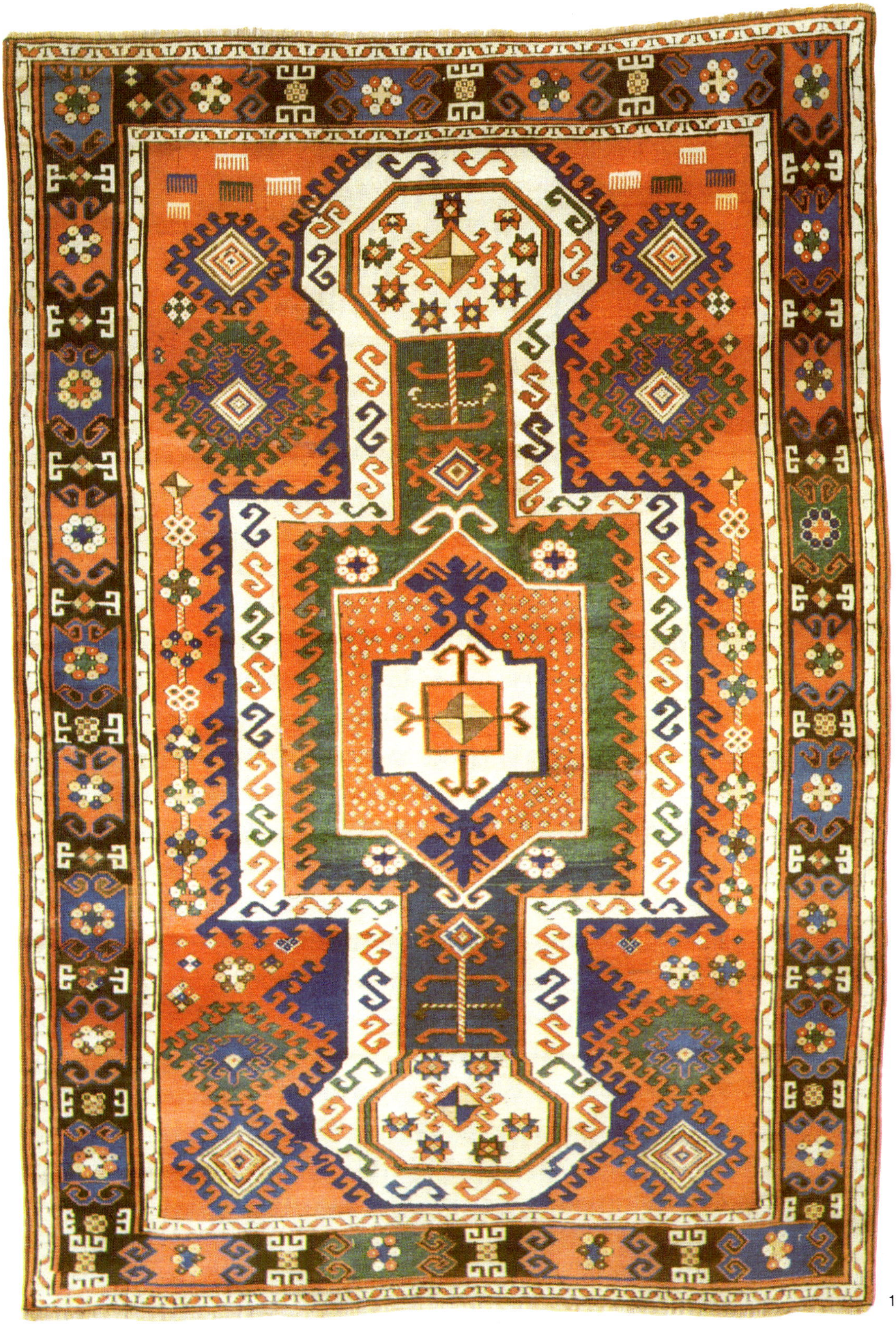

16

17 The most beautiful and powerful version of the 'Sewan' Kazak medallion. This rug has a boldly drawn example, with a plethora of double-headed animal figures and a particularly handsome pair of *medachyl* (reciprocal arrow-head) guards. Tschebull, in his *Hali* article, illustrates a somewhat similar example (no. 5), which he points out is very similar to a rug dated 1828. The motifs in the border of the Tschebull rug are identical to the beetle-like forms flanking the main medallion in the centre of our Lori-Pambak rug no. 8. However Tschebull remarks that rugs with cruder versions of this composition (and more coarsely knotted) are known with dates in the first decade of the 20th century. Late 19th or early 20th century.
206 x 178 cm

Various forms of the large central pattern found on Sewan Kazaks

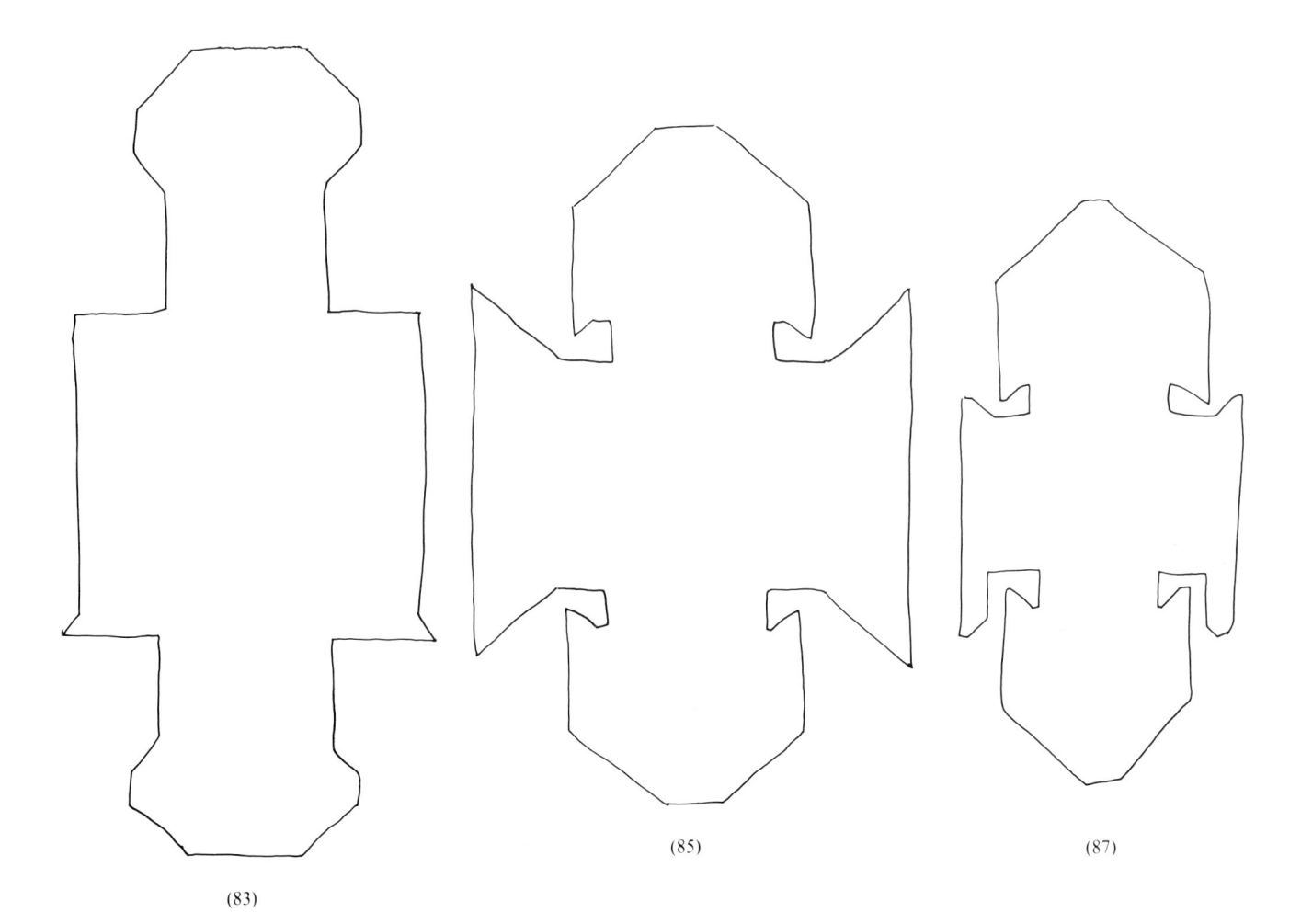

(83)   (85)   (87)

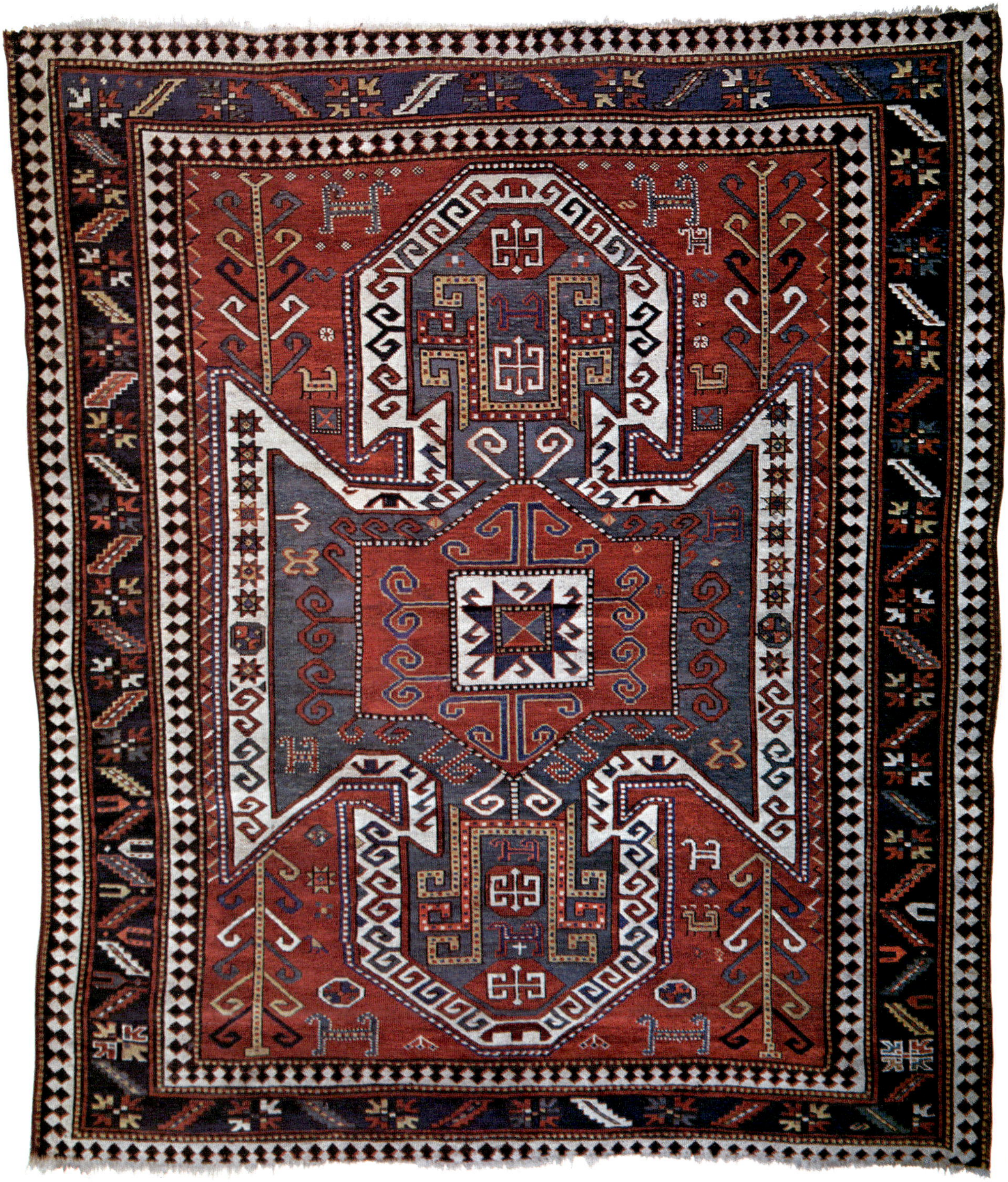

17

18 Very similar in design to the previous piece, but with a more beautiful and mellow colour range. Second half 19th century.
252 x 178 cm

19 Another example of the same group as 17 and 18, but with a stiff and unsatisfactory main border composition which harks back to that on no. 5. The centre of the rug, with its white rectangle, no longer has the peculiar 'marriage table' motif, but a double latch-hook ending in well-defined facing 'bird heads'. This motif is echoed at the top and bottom in the whiteground frame and its four indented parts. Notice how the medallion border ornamentation plays on the 'S' model. The colour is fairly attractive, but the piece is probably not as old as 18. Late 19th or early 20th century.
256 x 181 cm

20 An interesting hybrid between the Sewan Kazaks and the following group of Fachralo Kazaks. Note the Armenian inscription at the top of the field. Probably first quarter of the 20th century.
199 x 116 cm

21 Rugs of this type are often described, probably erroneously, as 'opposed niche' prayer rugs. Note the umbrella border which is often seen as a guard design and is found in a different style on Turkoman weavings, as well as on those of several Persian tribes, particularly the Afshar and Baluch. A somewhat similar, but earlier, rug of this type is illustrated in Raoul Tschebull's *Kazak* (pl. 8). Late 19th or early 20th century.

Fachralo

Fachralo is a town north of Lori-Pambak and just south-west of Bordjalou. It has given its name to a number of usually small, boldly designed and brilliantly coloured Kazak rugs but, although this has proved a useful descriptive adjective in the rug trade, it is one used by experts on Caucasian weaving with caution. Modern research also favours the spelling Fekhraly. Structurally, all the pieces are fairly similar. The foundation is all wool; the warp is usually ivory or ivory mixed with one or more shades of natural brown, the wefts one or more of various shades of orange-pink, pink or red. They have the usual western Caucasian selvedge of two bundles of two warp threads wrapped in red; occasionally some of the selvedge may be wrapped in pink, brown or even blue. The ends are usually missing, although remnants of loosely S-plied plain weave may be present, either in pink or red. Most examples have six colours — red (field), blue, green, yellow, dark brown, ivory. Knot counts are in line with previously described groups, falling as low as 550 per sq. dm (35 per sq. in.).

22

22 A typical Fachralo design with a rich red field with an inscription in the top part of the field. Probably late 19th century.
249 x 180 cm

Fachralo Prayer Rugs

Examples ascribed to Fachralo are the most frequently encountered of Kazak prayer rugs. In design they are usually similar, with a green or green-blue *mihrab* sitting on a red field. Within the *mihrab* there is one principal medallion consisting of one decagon within another; the inner figure is usually red and the outer ivory or white, although on a few examples this colour scheme is reversed (e.g. 24). On the majority of Fachralo rugs, whether of the prayer design or not, the outside medallion at top and bottom has rows of latch-hooks, ending at the points with double hooks; this motif is often echoed within the central decagon (cf. 24, which also has double hooks on the outside at the four compass points but no latch-hooks at top and bottom). These double hooks are highly stylised vestigial traces of ancient totemic bird figures and on Turkoman rugs, with which they are particularly associated, are known as *kotchak*.

Fachralo prayer rugs are almost always small, around 5ft. by 4ft. (152.5 x 122 cm) and there are some which are almost square, usually around 4ft. (122 cm). As with all Kazaks, one looks for boldness of drawing, vivid colour, fine glossy wool and a good spatial sense to the design. It is also worth reiterating that, while one has to be careful with pieces bearing dates (cf. 24 again), rugs bearing late dates (1900-1920) indicate that the quality of weaving and design in this area of the Caucasus remained very high throughout the late 19th and early 20th centuries.

23 Attractive Fachralo prayer rug with a well-spaced medallion. The bright tonality is typical. Second half of the 19th century.
133 x 108 cm

24 A very good Fachralo prayer rug; this has the alternative *mihrab* form, without the more normal indent at the base seen on 23, 25 and 27. The floral motifs surrounding the *mihrab* are often found on Fachralo prayer rugs. Like 23, this piece has a simplified version of the typical Fachralo border seen on 20, 25 and 27, often described as 'leaf-and-calyx' or 'leaf-and-wineglass'. Dated 1311 A.H. (A.D. 1894).
150 x 130 cm

25 Good Fachralo prayer rug of typical design. It is possible that some of these rugs are not 'Fachralo' but prayer rugs of the 'Sewan' Kazak group. Last quarter 19th or first quarter 20th century.
152 x 114 cm

26 This rug has a white-ground border containing a meander and cross design, which is less usual on Fachralo prayer rugs, although it is known from a number of published examples; it is a border which, in a slightly different form, appears on a number of Baluch rugs attributed to the Adraskand Valley, south of Herat, in Afghanistan. In a more sophisticated form, it appears on a Caucasian floral rug in the Textile Museum, Washington, illustrated by Charles Grant Ellis in *Early Caucasian Rugs* (p. 68) and attributed by him to late 18th/early 19th century Karabagh or Shirvan. A very similar prayer rug with identical borders is illustrated by Raoul Tschebull in *Kazak* (pl. 22), although this latter piece has the 're-entry' shaped *mihrab* like our nos. 23, 25 and 27. Probably last quarter 19th century.
129 x 108 cm

FACHRALO PRAYER RUGS   KAZAK

27 A slightly larger than average Fachralo prayer rug; the long hooks coming off either side of the main medallion are often encountered and link these pieces with the Karachovs. The floral minor borders flanking the main border are unusual; the somewhat overcrowded nature of the ornamentation suggests that this may be a late piece, as does the probability that a synthetic orange dye was used in some of the field ornaments. Early 20th century.
162 x 127 cm

Karachov

The town of Karachov (sometimes rendered Karatchoph) is southeast of Lori-Pambak, between Karaklis and Idjevan. It has given its name to a group of Kazak rugs with bold, majestic designs, the most characteristic of which resemble certain Turkish rugs, notably the Cannakale Bergama group, which, in turn, hark back to one of the most important groups of Classical Turkish carpets, the so-called ' Large Pattern Holbeins', which can be traced through European painting back to at least the 15th century. The well-known Karachov version consists of a large central white-ground octagon, flanked at the four corners of the field by four white-ground squares; the main field colour may be blue, green, blue-green or red. A second and less well-known group consists of pieces with either three, four or five medallions arranged along the vertical axis, the medallions being both polygonal, resembling the Yomut Turkoman 'Kepse' *gül*, and rectangular or square. The polygonal medallions almost always have red grounds and the rectangular ones white; the main field colour is usually green or blue.

The structure of these pieces varies considerably, the only firm rule being that the knot is symmetric and the foundation wool. Probably more Karachovs survive than any other group of Kazak rugs; they were obviously woven in considerable quantities in the late 19th and early 20th centuries, probably for export to the West. Although the knot density does not differ significantly from previously described Kazak groups, some examples are fairly tightly woven, with knot counts of between 1,150 and 1,300 per sq. dm. (75 to 85 per sq. in.), although around 900 (60) is also often found. The sides are usually made of two bundles of two warps, occasionally three bundles of two, wrapped in pink wool; the wrapping alternatively may be in multi-coloured bands. The ends are usually remnants of red S-plied plain weave. Warps are usually ivory, grey or brown wool, or mixtures thereof, and the wefts red or ivory. Such colours are not, however, invariable.

Writers on rugs—and this is a point which applies to all the groups illustrated in this book—tend to disagree about the stylistic symptoms of a late or early weaving. In general, we are considering rugs which were woven within a span of about 100 to 120 years. One would expect the earliest pieces to be well drawn and with a good sense of space. With later rugs, many of the fine details become lost or clumsily formalised, the space becomes more cramped and we find crudity mixed with clutter. It is difficult to make accurate chronological assessments of these or any other rugs—it is largely a question of instinct and experience.

28 This is an absolutely typical Karachov, exhibiting a balanced composition based upon the inter-relationship of many squares of differing sizes clustered about a 'skeleton' design, having a large white-ground central octagon which sits within an implied square, formed by triangular corner pieces. These dotted corner pieces are not 'reinforced' by outlining, as in all the following examples: this non-outlined type is usually found on what would appear to be the oldest examples and may, therefore, be a useful guide to establishing relative ages within the group. Balancing this central arrangement of motifs are four medium sized square medallions in each corner of the field which add strength to the composition as a whole by being of the same ground colour as the central large octagon, i.e. white. Invariably these flanking white-ground squares contain rows of stars, almost always three by three rows but, occasionally, as in our 31, two by two, and very often these stars are found being used as a design motif within the central octagon. As regards minor ornamentation, other typical features seen on this piece are the hooked 'bars', with either single or double hooked endings 'growing' inwards from the sides of both the octagons and from the sides of the field immediately opposite the octagon. These are balanced by the hooked bars surrounding the four flanking white ground squares. The main border design of this rug, with its series of 'Greek' 'double T' motifs, is in one form or another more usually encountered on Karachovs than on any other group of Kazak rugs, although, as can be seen from the following examples, a wide variety of the 'calyx' border designs also appears. Second half 19th century.
251 x 163 cm

29 (*overleaf*) An even more attractive example than the previous piece, with a superb green ground and most attractive yellow-ground main border. This rug has one or two unusual features of design, most obviously the central medallion which is a more 'upright' octagon with a double-sided arrangement of red and the white latch hooks to give the impression of an octagon within an octagon. Because of the way in which the octagon is drawn, the triangular corner pieces look distinctly awkward, although they still manage to give the intended impression of a square surrounding the central octagonal medallion. The richness of colour, most obviously demonstrated by the bottle green of the field, is further enhanced by the sparkling white of the central octagon and four principal flanking squares, the gold yellow of the main border, with its unusual motif, the brilliant red and white reciprocal *medachyl* guards, the rich, clear red used for many of the minor motifs in the field, and the similar use of a most attractive shade of light blue, the latter a colour not often found on Kazak rugs. Although this is a piece of quite respectable age, the various elements of the composition have a certain crudity of draughtsmanship and the composition itself, with its horizontal arrangement, is a little lacking in subtlety—this may have something to do with the unusually elongated nature of the rug's shape which does not accord particularly well with the basically square nature of the composition. I would be inclined to consider it slightly later in date than the previous piece. Last quarter of the 19th century.
234 x 146 cm

30 (*overleaf*) Another typical Karachov. The composition differs from the previous two in the arrangement of the central motif; here the square, which on the previous two has been implied by the presence of triangular-shaped corner pieces, is actually drawn in full. Another difference is the presence of three small octagons of equal size placed in a vertical row within the central medallion. The yellow-ground main border, with its laterally opposed latchhook edged triangles (forming an implied yellow zig-zag) is well drawn. However, it is a little out-of-keeping with the restrained and sombre mood of the field composition which has a somewhat stiff appearance. Last quarter 19th century.
218 x 175 cm

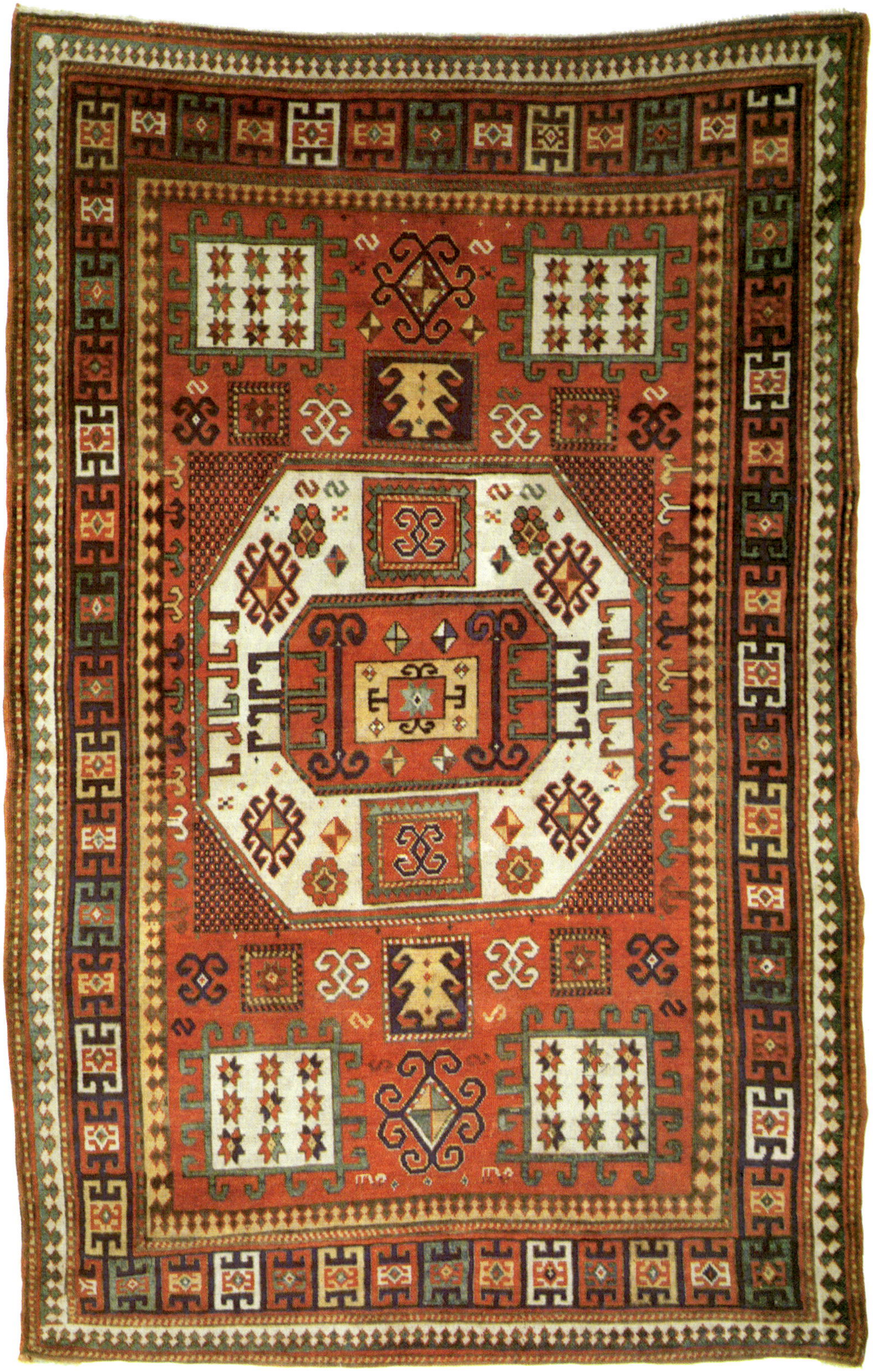

28

29

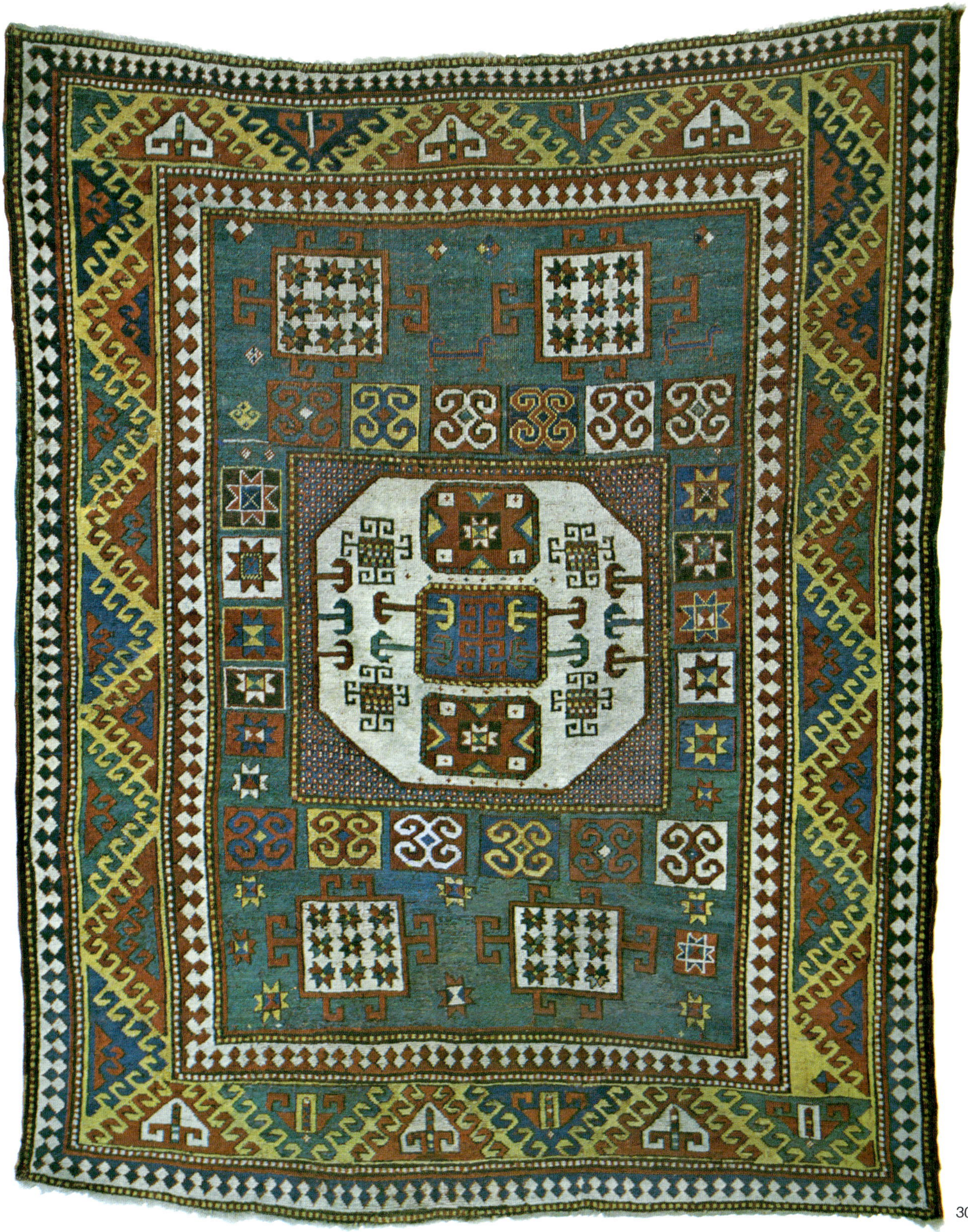

30

31 Another piece of similar vintage to the previous two, although possibly a little later. The attractive yellow-ground main border has an interesting variant of the famous leaf-and-calyx design, the 'calyx' in this instance being replaced by a stem containing three 'C'-like motifs; this 'completes' the 'transition' from one motif to the other which can be seen in its first stage in the border of the Fachralo Kazak no. 20, which has the usual stylised rendering of the 'calyx', on the stem of which, however, is one 'C'-like motif. Like the previous two pieces, this rug has a field composition which, although of the 'classic' Karachov type, somehow lacks the excitement, the splendidly barbaric, heraldic qualities of the best old pieces. The noteworthy feature, however, is the presence of small cruciform medallions in each corner of the white-ground octagon. Although similar to the motifs found in a similar position on the previous piece, these examples are more delicately drawn and have *kotchak* finials at top and bottom. Note the lack of a main border and outer guard at the top of this rug; this amount of loss would be very costly to have replaced—assuming that one could find a skilled restorer willing to undertake the task. Both the loss and the problems and costs inherent in rectifying it would have a very marked effect on the price of this or any similarly damaged rug especially if, as in the present case, it is not a rug of the highest quality. As a word of advice to private owners, this is not the sort of piece to offer privately to a dealer, as the latter will use such an obvious and serious drawback as the loss of the whole of the top border as a weapon with which to beat down the price to 'rock-bottom'. Such a piece is far more likely to fetch an equitable price at auction. Probably late 19th century.
206 x 153 cm

32 This rug shows yet another variant of the 'leaf-and-calyx' border, the calyx in this instance being replaced by a block of four inward pointing arrows; an identical variant border can be seen on the Karachov no. 17 illustrated in the Hamburg *Kaukasische Teppiche* catalogue, or on two of our Sewan Kazaks, nos. 17 and 18, and on a triple-medallion Lori Pambak illustrated by Schürmann in *Caucasian Rugs*, no. 15. This rug has the inter-relationships caused by the stars of the flanking squares being found also in the central octagon, which is a feature of many Karachovs (although, among those we illustrate, found only on this example). Although this piece shows a greater movement in the arrangement of the field motifs, the slightly uneven shape of the rug, seen particularly clearly in the top border, combined with a distinct crudity of draughtsmanship, argue for a date at the end of the 19th century. This example is of a slightly smaller and squarer format than the other examples we illustrate. Last quarter 19th century.
195 x 175 cm

33 This is a rug on which the 'folk' element is pushed to the limit. The great beauty and subtlety of the colours and the marvellous rich, glossy wool contrasting with the extreme crudity, some might say ineptitude of the drawing, exemplified by the lopsided rendering of the central octagon, and seen also in its reduction of the usual *medachyl* guards to a series of tiny rectangular blocks of red, yellow and white on a dark blue ground. The logical explanation for this exaggerated mishandling of the draughtsmanship is that this piece was made by an apprentice weaver without either the experience to know instinctively how large each motif should be in order to fit the whole composition into the allotted space, or the ability to weave any but the simplest motifs. This would also explain the simple 'arrow-block' border composition. It is worth noting here that, although the relationship between this particular Karachov design and the well-known 'large pattern Holbein' composition is particularly strong, there is also an affinity between the way in which the motifs are used on Karachov rugs and on a specific group of well-known Baluch bag-faces, which have a central octagon and square medallion within which are four stylised animal motifs which on the Karachovs have become further stylised into a series of geometric arrangements. Despite the poor draughtsmanship of the present piece, both its colour and its wool still suggest a comparatively early date. Late 19th century.
214 x 147 cm

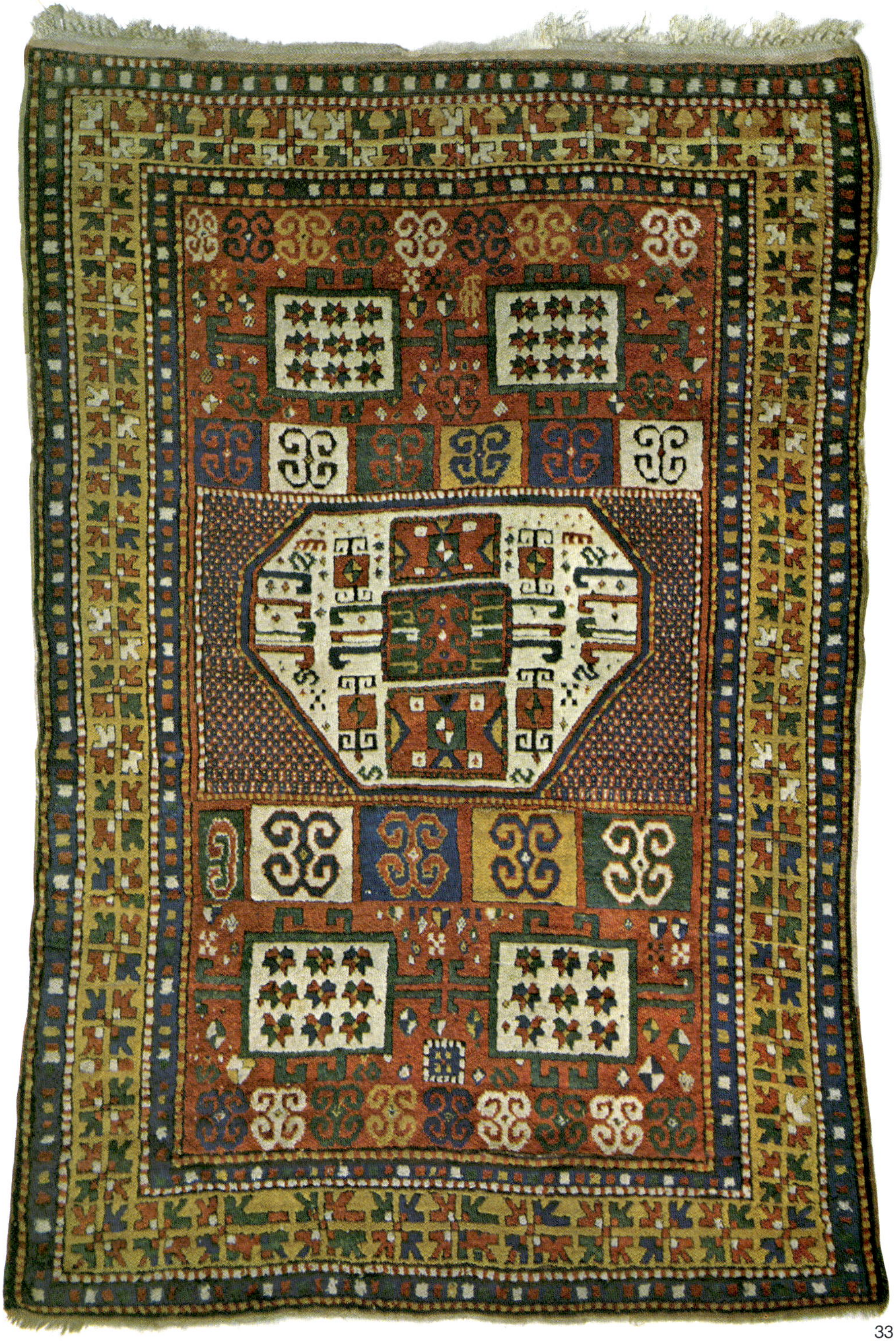

33

34 This rug and the four following examples have the alternative form of Karachov composition which is considerably less common than the previous 'large pattern Holbein' type. The majority of examples, such as this piece and the following two, have the main field composition contained within a dotted frame arched at either end. On this example and no. 36, this 'field within a field' arrangement is merely implied by the presence of two dotted arch-shaped bars at either end of the field, with no change in the ground colour. On no. 35, however, the frame is continuous, so as to face a large, elongated, dodecahedron medallion with a contrasting ground colour, green, to the colour of the main field—red. On no. 38, the 'frame' has become rectangular and the clearly defined 'two-field' system has become merely implied by a series of border 'frames' of differing outline. Only no. 37 of the rugs we illustrate has a series of completely 'freestanding' motifs, with no attempt to suggest an inner division of the field; unlike the other examples, no. 37 also has only one sort of medallion of polygonal shape as opposed to the attending squares and polygons of the remaining pieces. However, it retains the alternating red and white palette of the main medallion. Despite the visual appeal of no. 34, created in part by the use of tiny red, white and yellow stars in the field, the overall palette is a little dark and muddy, and the main ivory-ground border has a series of particularly heavy, unsuitable motifs which detract from the field composition. Of interest, however, are the motifs in the four corners of the 'outer' field, which appear in more simplified form on the following two examples; they would appear to be quite obvious, if highly stylised human figures, the only motifs, indeed, which retain a clearly recognisable animal base in a composition made up of what are almost totally geometricised medallions. Circa 1900.
240 x 125 cm

35 This piece, with its well-defined 'two-field' composition has more mellow colours than the previous piece and would seem quite obviously to be an older rug. It is difficult to establish the relationship between this particular Karachov composition and that of the more usual 'large pattern Holbein' type: is one the result of a simplification of the other? This seems unlikely in view of the fact that both types were made concurrently; in addition, neither shows a greater degree of 'realism' which one would expect if dealing with a logical progression from a source close to the original to one much further removed. However, in the use of minor ornamentation, the overall arrangement of various polychrome geometric medallions on a red or blue-green (or green) field, the two groups are quite obviously in a close degree of relationship to each other as well as to the other groups of 'Kazak' rugs. It seems probable that, like the ' Lori Pambaks', 'Sewan Kazaks' and 'Bordjalou' rugs, or rather the specific designs conveniently known by these titles, the two types of 'Karachov' designs were woven by different groups living in fairly close proximity to each other who, like the weavers of the other groups of Kazak rugs, composed and drew their own particular versions of a design which over the course of centuries, had become 'split' or 'developed' into various closely related geometric versions, all of which seem to betray a common ancestry, although what that ancestry might be, beyond a series of totemic images with an immediate religious, political and a sociological relevance, it is now difficult, perhaps even impossible, to determine. Within this specific 'second group' Karachov designs, the most interesting, because different, feature is the polygonal red medallion which is found in many different versions, including the five different ones we illustrate. Although this may be an amalgam of one or two medallions seen in different forms on the 'large pattern Holbein' type of Karachovs, it is probable that it is a motif which shares a common ancestry with the motif found on certain Yomut Turkoman rugs and bag faces called the 'Kepse' *gül*; Such a relationship seems especially likely when looking at the Kazak versions found on our 36. The present rug has clear, bright colours, a well-balanced composition and good drawing; it is probably the earliest example of this type we illustrate. Third quarter 19th century.
225 x 137cm

36

37

36 Another attractive piece with red polygons asymmetrically drawn. Stiff umbrella borders but well constructed field. It has a wide range of colours, including aubergine. The overall appearance of the rug suggests that it is later than the next piece. Without examination of this piece I would not wish to attribute a date to it. However, pieces which look similar have been found to be early 20th century
260 x 130 cm

37 Something of an oddity, with a vertical row of red and white polygons but no squares. Charming field ornaments including animals and stylised human figures; well drawn border. Dated in western numerals 1888, and with a crudely rendered Armenian inscription. The *abrashed* sea-green field is an unusual and most attractive feature.
260 x 142 cm

38 A well drawn piece with the appearance of good age. Note the unusual treatment of the latch-hook meander border on the long sides. The reciprocal running dog guards are not often found on these rugs, the reciprocal arrow-head being favoured. Both the colour and the composition of the main border, with its latch-hooked polychromed panels, forms a link with the next group of Bordjalou Kazaks. It should be noted that the composition itself consists of opposed half-diamonds with latch-hook ends on a white ground, not a running white latch-hook meander on a polychrome ground, as is often stated. Probably late 19th century.
202 x 118 cm

39 Typical Bordjalou composition with latch-hook field design echoed in the borders. Late 19th or early 20th century.
230 x 136 cm

40 An example with a contrasting rectangular compartmental field; note the tiny bird figures in the border.
235 x 166 cm

Bordjalou

Bordjalou is the most northerly town associated with the production of Kazak rugs. If the most striking features of Kazak rugs are their thick, lustrous wool, brilliant polychromy and a strength of design which might almost be described as barbaric, then the archetypal Kazak is the extraordinary latch-hook bordered Bordjalou. However, rugs attributed to this area come in a variety of designs and there are some extremely beautiful prayer rugs. There is also a widely differing colour tonality between rugs of very similar design—compare, for instance, 41, 42 and 43. The rugs have an all-wool foundation, the warps usually one or more of various shades of brown, the wefts often a mixture of pinks, reds and browns. Selvedges are usually two bundles of two warps wrapped in red, although the wrapping can be in polychrome bands. The ends (which are rarely present) are either red or blue plain weave.

41 This is a beautiful and most unusual example, which in many respects seems different from the other rugs illustrated in this section. Most notable is the field, with its niche-shaped and dotted panels at either end. The brilliant blue ground is a feature seldom encountered on rugs of any type from this area, and taken with the heraldic-looking medallions scattered upon it, the throne-like nature of the end panels and the large flower heads of the minor borders, give the piece a distinctly Chinese appearance. The boldly drawn main border has some extremely beautiful colours, notable among which are a dark chocolate brown and a light mauve. This latter colour appears on a comparable rug illustrated by Raoul Tschebull in *Kazak* (pl. 24), a piece which also has the same somewhat unusual structure—loose and very shaggy. Tschebull remarks of his rug: "The coarse weave and large amount of aubergine dye are not typical Kazak characteristics, and the rug could have been made in another part of the southern Caucasus or in eastern Turkey." To compensate for the lack of the vivid sky-blue seen on our piece, the Tschebull rug has a brilliant and most unusual shade of dark turquoise. Second half of the 19th century.
216 x 140 cm

42 The strange pattern, with its predominant light green, yellow and unusual light brown in the border, makes an interesting contrast with 41 and 43. The outer guard with its star pattern is rare. The similarity between this piece and several types of Anatolian village rugs is striking. Rugs of this type often have long curly wool pulled to the right. This is an exceptionally fine example. Probably second half of the 19th century.
270 x 142 cm

43 On this piece, the borders are the dominant feature, a characteristic of many Bordjalou rugs. This example has light, almost pastel, colours but, although well-drawn, is probably late; the T-meander outer border design is rarely encountered and has a very archaic flavour. Probably last quarter 19th century.
196 x 159cm

43

44 This piece has two opposing, boldly drawn, reciprocal arrow borders in dark brown and white, and in red and navy blue. This border is often found on prayer rugs (cf. 45, 46, 47), and this version is generally considered to be a geometric and degenerate rendering of the beautiful fleur-de-lys border found on old Turkish and Caucasian rugs. Compositionally, the use of three borders of almost equal weight is unusual on such pieces. It is interesting to compare it to the very similar series of borders seen on the 'swastika' Kazak, no. 2. Probably last quarter of the 19th century.
185 x 137 cm

45 This is an extraordinary rug of a design not encountered before. The borders are typical as are the two rows of three hexagonal medallions at the top and bottom of the field, medallions which can be often found used as an all-over field pattern (they appear also on 46, 47 and 49). The large decagonal medallion is, of course, more often associated with Fachralos, and the four stylised birds with fan-tails resemble those which are among the principal identifying features of a group of Shirvan rugs called Akstafa (cf. 214, 215 and 216). The field is of a beautiful brick red, with a marked *abrash* in the centre and at the base. The different coloured bands of selvedge wrapping can be clearly seen. Although this rug may well date from the last quarter of the 19th century, its quality is self-evident.
215 x 159 cm

44

BORDJALOU KAZAK 61

45

62 KAZAK — BORDJALOU PRAYER RUGS

46 Although the borders are well-drawn, this prayer rug has crudely rendered field designs, which are also badly spaced. The colours are a little pallid (note the dark blue *abrash* seen clearly in the lower third of the inner guard border). Late 19th or early 20th century.
205 x 129 cm

47 Even if this prayer rug was not dated (1313 A.H., A.D. 1895/6), one would have no doubt that it was a late example—indeed, one might have dated it even later. The white and dark brown reciprocal border is very crudely drawn, as are the field ornaments, which are squashed into a *mihrab* which is too large for the overall composition. The colours are extremely pale and wishy-washy.
114 x 118cm

48 A well drawn and beautifully spaced rug, which is unusual for its white ground (it is worth noting that any white-ground Oriental rug of age and quality has a special place in the hearts of collectors). This piece employs one of the main Kazak border designs which is not, however, found very often on Bordjalou rugs. The medallions seen on the red field are almost identical to those seen on the Lori-Pambak rug no. 8, and indeed some authorities might not wish to categorise it as Bordjalou at all. Probably late 19th century.
134 x 105 cm

49 On the evidence of the photograph only, a collector would be unwise to assume that this rug is much older than 47. The running dog border, being simpler, is a more satisfactory solution than the botched-up trefoil of 47 and, although the drawing of the field ornaments is hardly superior, the spacing is much better. The colours are deeper and richer, with the field of the *mihrab* a vivid shade of blue. The difficulty of dating this rug is another good example of the fact that even late Kazaks can often be boldly coloured and well designed, even though they may lack the imagination and finesse of early examples. 19th century.
116 x 87 cm

49

Shikli Kazaks

This group of rugs is the least known of the various Kazak types; examples seem to appear quite rarely on the market in London and New York. There are three main designs, the one most often found being represented by the following five examples; this has a central hexagon with four two-sided cornerpieces and three large palmettes at either end of the field. The second type has two large hexagonal medallions with flower-like ends on an open red field, with three half-hexagonal arrow-headed medallions down each side of the field; occasionally there are palmettes at either end. Two examples of this type, one with a most unusual blue-ground floral border, appeared in a sale held by Fritz Nagel on 12 November, 1977 (lots 199 and l99a). The third design is the rarest; it is a variation on the first, with three arrow-headed hexagons vertically arranged, with the usual corner pieces and four palmettes.

Shikli rugs have strong affinities with certain groups of Persian tribal rugs—Kurdish and Afshar in particular—and one tends to think of them as being late and atypical examples of alien influence on native Kazak weaving. The name 'Shikli' derives from one of the 111 provinces listed by the Russian scholar L. Kerimov, who was primarily responsible for the attributions to specific locations of many groups of Caucasian carpets, attributions which many authorities today tend to treat with some caution.

Shikli rugs may have either an all-wool foundation or a mixture of wool and cotton. The warps are usually of undyed brown or beige wool, the weft either of wool or cotton or a mixture of both, the wool either natural brown, or dyed blue or red, the cotton either unbleached or dyed the same colours. Some of these pieces are unusually finely knotted for Kazaks (examples with a part-cotton foundation tend to have a higher knot count); one piece I have seen with two orange-red and one blue-red palmettes at either end and with what appeared to be a particularly harsh synthetic orange dye, had a knot count of 2,000 per sq. dm (129 per sq. in.). This piece also had a red field, whereas most rugs of the central medallion type have dark blue fields.

50 A typical Shikli design in every way except for the light blue colour of the central medallion. Note the many animals, including camels, on the field. One of the oddest features of this group is the series of dots, dashes, brackets, letters and other characters and symbolic motifs woven, apparently haphazardly, on to the white ground field of the medallion. The fact is that each group of 'symbols' seems to be very carefully worked out and no two pieces appear to be the same. This piece is unusually long. Probably late 19th century.
300 x 151 cm

51 A much better drawn and spaced example than 50; the palmettes are more obviously leaf shaped, without the rather ugly arrow-head endings. The main white-ground guard composition is a more finely drawn version of that seen on the Lambalo Kazak, no. 59, and the inner red guard has the diagonal and cross composition discussed in connection with the Fachralo prayer rug, no. 26. Note the alternate blue and red wrapping of the selvedges. The central medallion contains a variety of clearly recognisable tiny birds and S-shaped motifs which may be related to the dragon *sileh* motifs (cf. 475-478). Probably late 19th century.
213 x 137 cm

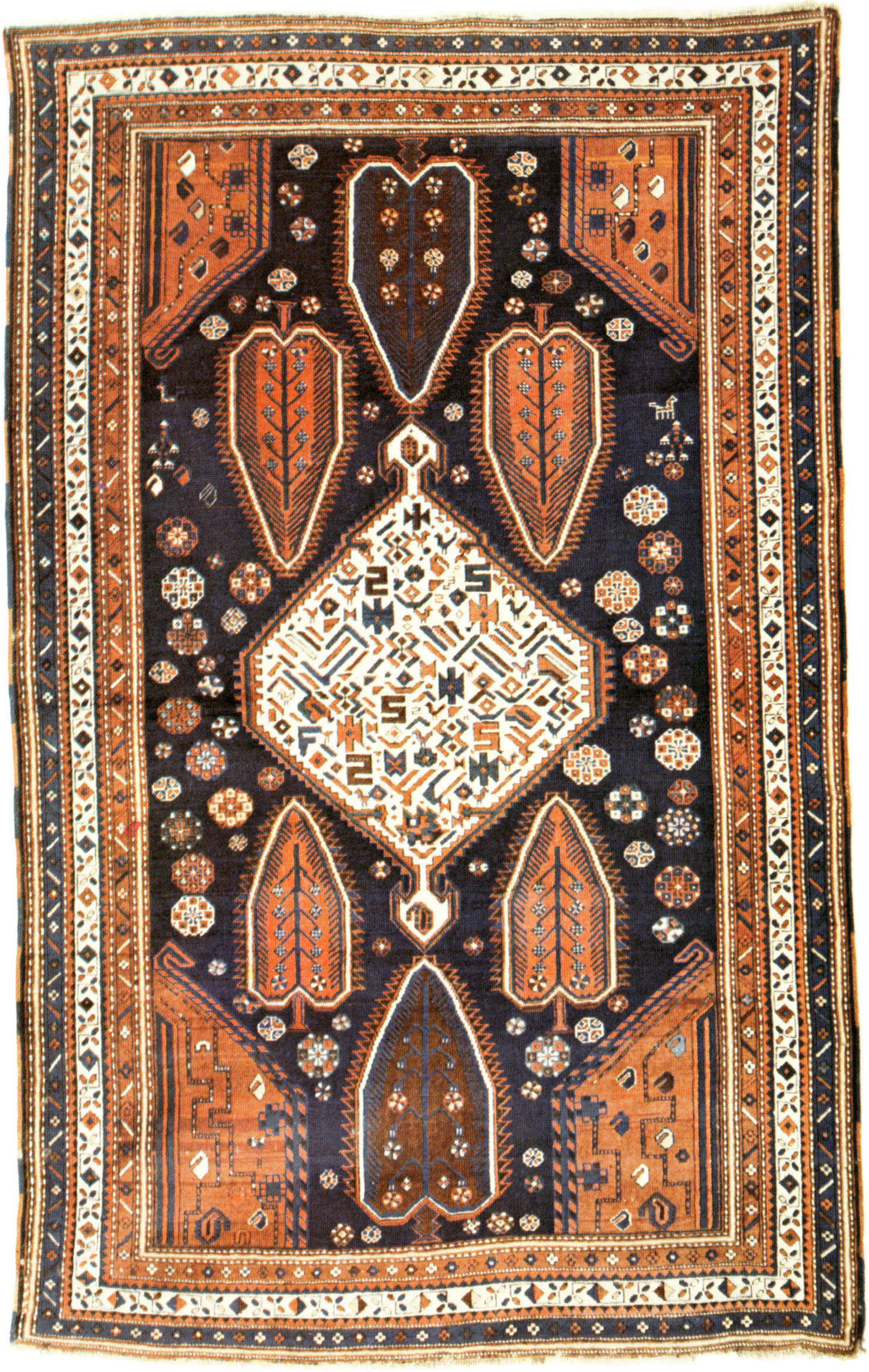

51

52 Very similar to 50 but with a better spatial sense. The motifs within the central medallion are also better spaced and more stylised than those of the previous piece. Probably early 20th century.
259 x 124cm

53 A charming small piece, probably of the same age as 51, with which it has many points in common, including the motifs within the central medallion.
206 x 140 cm

54 Another well-drawn example with its field ornaments and borders drawn in the same manner as 50 and 52, and probably of the same period.
231 x 142 cm

55 An unusually uncluttered example, with two very beautiful guard borders with a stylised floral meander. However, the overall appearance of the piece is a little stark, especially when compared with the next two examples, and lacks the riot of detailed ornamentation which makes these rugs so attractive. Late 19th or early 20th century.
204 x 119 cm

56 A distinctly more attractive example; it has a variation on the leaf-and-calyx border, with the inclusion of stylised floral sprays, which I have never seen before. A beautifully drawn and spaced composition, although there is no evidence from the illustration to demonstrate that it is older than 57.
313 x 105 cm

Shulaver Kazaks

The majority of Shulaver Kazaks, like the three examples illustrated here, are long and narrow; usually the field design is formed from a narrow section of a diamond lattice. Most of the known examples do not seem particularly old and it is, therefore, no surprise that the typical example illustrated as no. 57 is dated 1328 A.H. (A.D. 1910/11). With their bright colours and variety of small scattered motifs, Shulavers have a cheerful, almost festive, look.

These rugs tend to be tightly knotted, with a short, fairly hard wool. They have a stiff handle, unlike many other Kazaks, which are soft and floppy. Shulaver itself is a town about 40 kilometres to the east of Fachralo. Rugs of this group, because of their tough wool, tend to wear well and are popular as furnishing pieces in the West.

57 A colourful example of typical design but spoiled by what appear to be ugly synthetic colours, seen most clearly in our illustration in the badly faded central medallion, as well as in the upper orange medallion and the bottom sugar pink medallion. Dated 1328 A.H. (A.D. 1910/11).
360 x 108 cm

Lambalo Kazaks

Like the Shikli rugs, the Lambalo pieces represent another somewhat atypical Kazak group; in design, they seem more closely related to Talish rugs from the far south-east Caucasus, or those from Gendje, mid-way between Lambalo and the south-eastern coastal town of Lenkoran. Most examples have a red field which in some cases is left empty except for one or two tiny ornaments (cf. 59). Lambalo rugs are loosely knotted— between about 650 and 900 per sq. dm (42 and 58 per sq. in.). The warp is usually of natural brown wool and the weft usually red wool or sometimes white cotton. Most examples which appear on the market do not seem very old, the earliest dated pieces being from the 1870s.

58 Although the drawing is a little crude, this rug has beautiful colours, especially the unusual light green of the field (with a dark green *abrash* at the base) and the mauve which appears among the main border medallions. It may therefore, be older than is suggested by the drawing, the somewhat cramped design and, for a Lambalo, the unusual geometric ornamentation. It is interesting to compare the treatment of the field with that of the Bordjalou Kazak, no. 41. Second half 19th century.
222 x 125 cm

59 A typical Lambalo design. The inner border has a particularly attractive pattern of large flower heads. The white-ground border with its charming floral meander and the outer blue-ground border with its alternate flower-head pattern are also characteristic features. Note the pair of facing birds in the open red field, a typical conceit for this type of rug. The treatment of the field is similar to that of Talish rugs—compare, for instance, no. 178. Second half of the 19th century.
214 x 135 cm

60 Although the field on this rug is reduced to a minor element of the overall composition, it shares many features with no. 59, especially the border design. Probably late 19th century, though some examples seen by this author date to the early 20th century.
210 x 119 cm

61 Like 59 and 62, this piece has a distinctly Talish look, although the borders are typical for a rug of the so-called Lambalo group. The floral meander in the white-ground border is related to the more realistic version often encountered on east Caucasian rugs (cf. our 250-252, for examples), but in this form is closer to the rendering found on some south-west Persian tribal weavings. The version seen on the east Caucasian rugs we have mentioned is close to that found on old Baluch rugs from east Persia, and still one of the most popular border designs among Baluch weavers. Probably late 19th century, but again some seen are probably later.
187 x 121 cm

62 Again we see the white-ground floral meander border of 59 and 60. The one white and two dark blue medallions strategically placed on the rich tomato-red field create a strong dramatic effect, and this is a fine example of Lambalo weaving, even though it could possibly be no older than the turn of the present century.
495 x 193 cm

LAMBALO KAZAK 75

Tree or Garden Kazaks

This group is one of the best known and most eagerly collected types of Kazak weaving. Tree (sometimes called tree-of-life) or garden Kazaks come in two distinct varieties, both of which are illustrated here. The first (no. 63) has one large all-over tree; among 19th and 20th century tribal and village weavers, perhaps only one other group, the Baluch, produced rugs with a single large tree used in a comparable way. A similar device is also found on some east Turkestan rugs and there is also a very rare group of Ersari prayer rugs, probably from Afghanistan, which has an overall composition of a single tree and a colour combination very similar to the Baluch single tree prayer rugs. The second, and by far the most common, type has a design of small shrub-like trees, resembling coral branches, which are either flanked by (no. 64) or flank vertical row(s) of octagons or squares. Examples are known with three (e.g. no. 64), six (Raoul Tschebull, *Kazak,* no. 39) or eight (Joseph V. McMullan, *Islamic Carpets,* no. 47) trees. The ground colour of all known examples is red.

This tree-shrub design is derived from 16th and 17th century Safavid garden carpets; those with directional designs of trees and flowering shrubs from the more angular and stylised Kurdish versions woven in the 18th and 19th century. A direct link between Caucasian and Persian weavings of this type is afforded by the unique early 18th century blue-ground Caucasian tree carpet now in the Mayer Foundation, Jerusalem Museum (Lefevre, *Caucasian Carpets,* no. 4).

The tree of the present group is always drawn in much the same manner and has the double headed bird motif at the base; an almost exact equivalent of this particular rendering of the bird-tree combination is found on a very rare type of Baluch rug (i.e. Victoria and Albert Museum no. T. 195-1922, illus. Jenny Housego, *Tribal Rugs,* plate 25), while the tree design itself is also found on some Balkan kilims (Ulrich Schürmann, *Teppiche aus dem Orient,* no. 97), on north-west Persian carpets of the *Bid Majnun* design and on certain Luri weavings from south-west Persia (i.e. Formenton, *Oriental Rugs and Carpets,* p. 176).

Chronologically, tree Kazaks present a problem. Most of the known examples date from the second half of the 19th century to the end of the second decade of the 20th. The earliest date on a tree rug known to me is 1866 (our no. 160) and the latest, which appears on the example illustrated here, 1917 (our 64). There is not much discernible difference between them, except in the use of colour, 64

63 This is one of the most characteristic treatments of the Kazak tree pattern and also one of the most effective. It is noticeable that while the pairs of animal or bird figures at the base of the trees are clearly recognisable on the multi-tree rugs, on these single-tree examples they are reduced to a mere bracket which also appears at the top of the tree facing in the opposite direction. The rug has the diagonal and cross composition in the minor borders. Probably late 19th century.
216 x 172cm

TREE OR GARDEN KAZAK

having a harsh synthetic orange. No. 64 also has the same ugly border found in another late piece, Tschebull plate 39, dated 1890. By contrast, an example sold at Parke-Bernet in 1978, dated 1322 A.H. (A.D. 1904/5), had an attractive geometric flower-head border, identical to that found on some north-west Persian Kurdish rugs. The 1866 piece has an unusual white-ground umbrella border. A long rug, shown in Munich in 1978 (Spuhler, König and Volkmann, *Alte Orientteppiche*, no. 53) claimed in the catalogue to be from the first half of the 19th century, has the same border as the 1905 rug. The McMullan rug, with its eight trees, is beautifully drawn and has a most unusual plain green border with red serrated edges on white; it may well be the oldest of the group.

All the analysed examples have a wool warp and weft, the warp being 3 or 4ZS ivory and brown wool, the weft 2ZS dyed red. The selvedges are two bundles of two warps wrapped in red. Average knot count about 900 per sq. dm (58 per sq. in.).

64 This is, without doubt, the ugliest example of a Kazak tree rug it could be one's misfortune to encounter. The drawing is crude (although not much cruder than many undated examples which are often optimistically catalogued as 'early 19th century') and there is a particularly bilious (probably synthetic) orange in most of the minor ornaments. The degeneration in quality can be seen not only in the use of this harsh dye but also, most obviously, in the ugly main border composition and the generally rough look of the piece. The rug is dated 1335 A.H. (A.D. 1916/7), which is about its only point of interest. Note, however, the presence of 'S' motifs on the middle tree.
243 x 162 cm

Miscellaneous Kazak Rugs

The following rugs have, in most cases, an all-over design of geometric medallions, either hooked octagons or hooked diamonds. Like other Kazak rugs, they are the descendants of a long tradition, in many cases the designs being almost identical to those seen on rugs illustrated in 15th century European paintings.

65 A famous, and ubiquitous, design of eight hooked crosses (called 'Memlinc gül'). Compare the design of the outer border with that of the main border of the Karachov no. 28. The composition of the main border is most attractive. Probably second half 19th century.
170 x 140 cm

66. The large medallion in the centre of this rug relates to the Fachralo group, although the daisy-like flowers of the guards are, perhaps, more characteristic of east Caucasian weaving. The motifs within the central medallion obviously have strong zoomorphic connotations. Probably second half 19th century.
218 x 171 cm

66

67 Very popular Kazak design with the Memlinc güls within octagons in a single vertical row. The hooked cruciform medallion has been named after the 15th century Flemish painter Hans Memlinc, as it is present in carpets from several of his works. As well as in many other Caucasian areas, pieces of this design were also woven in Anatolia, and it is generally assumed that the rugs which appear in Memlinc's paintings, and those in the works of other 15th and 16th century Flemish and Italian painters, were probably Turkish rather than Caucasian. This theory, however, remains unproven. Probably second half 19th century.
209 x 119 cm

68 A beautiful piece with lovely colours, including an extensively used light green, brick red and yellow, although the execution of the design is a little clumsy. Compare the double-S border of the stencil type with 28 (Karachov) and 64. Probably second half of the 19th century.
183 x 127 cm

68

69

70

69 This is a very interesting rug, with what would appear to be an exceptionally beautiful colour range and a very ornate composition. The main border composition is a particularly fine and ornate reciprocal arrowhead and trefoil, of a type rarely encountered. A version of it, more fleur-de-lys like in character, can be seen on a palmette rug at Colonial Williamsburg, illustrated by Ellis in *Early Caucasian Rugs* (pl. 30), and attributed to late 18th/early 19th century Karabagh; this same border also appears on a fragment with large palmettes and lanceolate leaves in the Mosque of Lala Mustafa Pasa at Ersurum and on a carpet with medallions and trees in the Turk ve Islam Museum, Istanbul, dated 1156 A.H. (A.D. 1734). Both these latter rugs are illustrated by Yetkin in *Early Caucasian Carpets in Turkey* (plates 42 and 24 respectively). A far less accomplished version can be seen on a good old 'Lenkoran' rug illustrated by Raymond Benardout in *Caucasian Rugs* (p. 63 and on another 'Lenkoran' illustrated

by Schürmann in *Caucasian Rugs* (pl. 57), the latter being slightly more sophisticated. These latter two pieces are, of course, attributed to the Talish weaving area and it is worth noting that Schürmann illustrates a 'Talish' rug (pl. 56), which has a design of three large diamonds sitting on a conjoined diamond shaped field with half diamond side-pieces, which has a quality of drawing and polychromatic richness not dissimilar to the present piece. Although it may not be particularly early, this rug, both for the drawing of its well conceived composition and for its excellent colour, is an outstanding Caucasian village rug. Its attribution to the Kazak area is not certain and it is interesting to note that we illustrate a rug with an identical border, no. 140, which is attributed to Erivan, the capital of Soviet Armenia. The treatment of the border composition on these two pieces is, of course, similar to the beautiful *medachyl* borders seen on old Anatolian rugs—for instance, the two 'Transylvanian' rugs illustrated in Dall'Oglio's

69 continued
edition of Végh and Layer's *Turkish Rugs in Transylvania,* (plates 11 and 12). The running latch-hook composition is also found on Turkish rugs, particularly in the wide borders of examples attributed to Ghiordes, but also on examples of the Transylvanian type (e.g. the piece in the Fine Arts Muesum, Budapest illustrated in *Alte Anatolische Teppiche aus dem Museum für Kunstgewerbe in Budapest,* no. 11). Both our 69 and 140 would seem to be from the same area, as does 115; all three were probably woven by Armenians and could have been made in eastern Anatolia. Probably second half of the 19th century.
234 x 108 cm

70 Close in design to 67 and with the same blue-green field. The variation in the calyx motif in the top and bottom borders is an unusual feature. Probably second half of the 19th century.
284 x 116 cm

71 An example very closely related to no. 68 in both design and colour. The checkerboard diamond poles are particularly beautiful; the use of half medallions is rarely encountered and this is one of the few Kazak rugs of this type in which the weaver wished to show the field design quite unequivocally as a section of an endless repeat. The green-red diamond reciprocal border is another noteworthy feature and this example also shows the same crude drawing as 68. A number of very similar rugs were woven by Kurds in east Anatolia. Second half of the 19th century.
193 x 143 cm

84 KAZAK COMPARTMENTED

73 This is an unusual composition. The border relates the rug to Karabagh pieces. The rug has attractive colours and probably dates from the second half of the 19th century.
210 x 114 cm

72 A very unusual piece in which the field is divided into horizontal bands in the manner of kilim designs; the S-like ornaments jointed by a straight line, possibly stylised bird figures (the design is often called bird-on-pole), are very closely related to those found on Yomut Turkoman weavings, especially *asmalyk* (camel flank hangings). The overall arrangement of the composition, however, is also reminiscent of certain Baluchi Kilim, although it is interesting to compare it with the composition of the tiny bagface we illustrate as no. 484. Probably late 19th century.
278 x 112 cm

74 A colourful rug, but crudely drawn and cluttered in design. Note the pale pink *abrash* in the top half of the field. Closely related to Karachovs. In main ornamental details and in colour this piece seems closely related to the previous example. Second half of the 19th century.
207 x 160 cm

74

75 This rug does not seem to form part of the same group as the majority of the examples illustrated in this section. It is probably not very old and seems more comparable to rugs such as our 200, which may be from the Moghan weaving area or even further east. The design is stiff and too regimented. Probably early 20th century.
242 x 123 cm

76 The hooked cruciform is here the principal medallion containing a smaller multi-layered hooked octagon. Note the umbrella design in the inner border and compare the checkerboard diamond poles to those of 71. The rug is close in appearance to east Anatolian rugs. Probably second half of the 19th century.
202 x 154 cm

75

COMPARTMENTED　　KAZAK　87

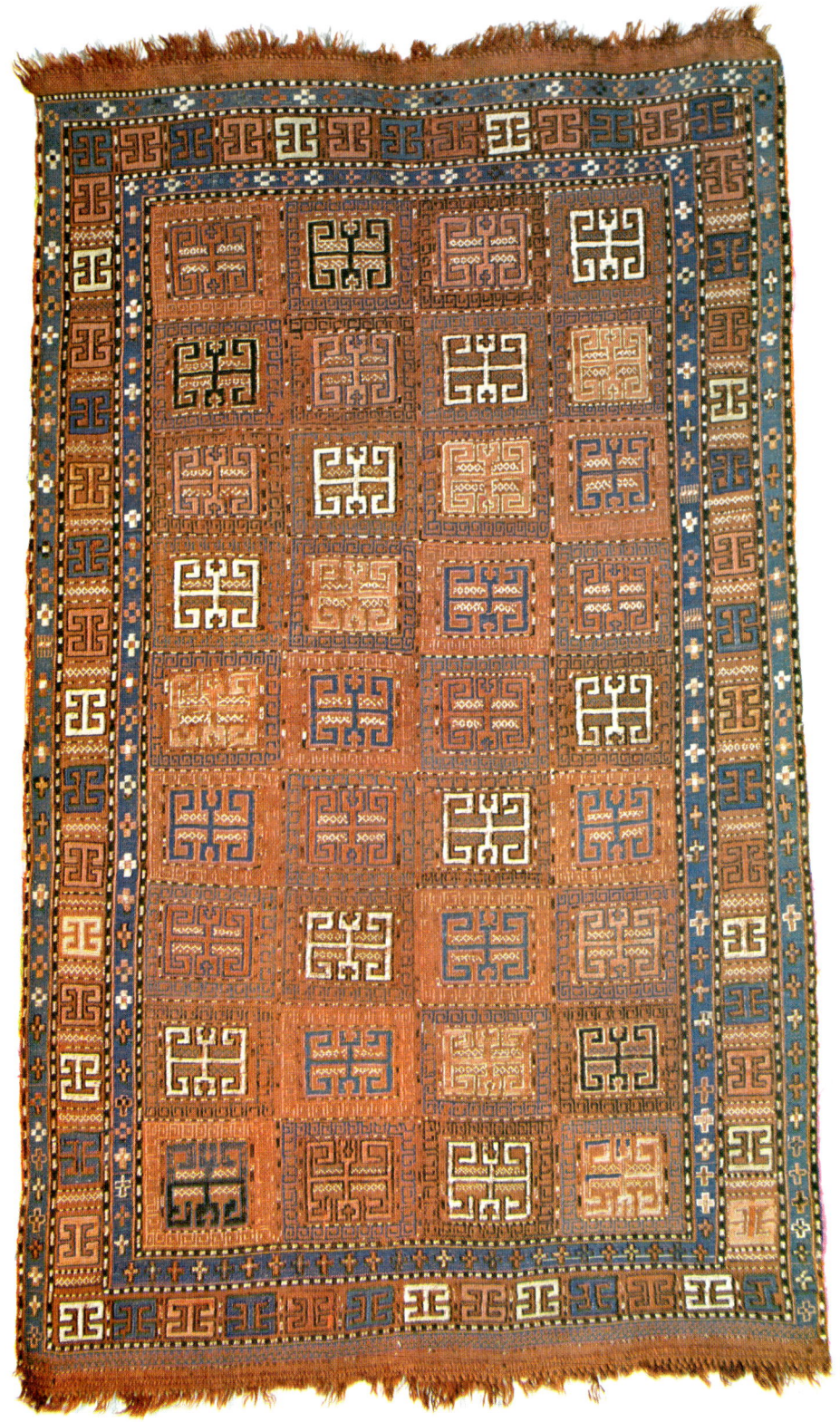

77 The first flat-woven, as opposed to pile-knotted, rug encountered in this book. This brocaded example is probably quite coarse. Its predominantly red colour is not particularly attractive and bespeaks a comparatively recent date. A well-known Caucasian border design, probably a highly simplified version of the so-called Kufic border, is here used not only in the border itself but also as an all-over field design within a square lattice composition. The double-E design without a square lattice seems to be a very old all-over composition. It is seen, for instance, in medieval European paintings as the pattern for what appear to be tiled floors (i.e. in a late 15th century miniature of *The Annunciation* in a Book of Hours in the Bistumsarchivs, Trier, illus. *Marienbild in Rheinland und Westfalen,* 1968, no. 223). This group of rugs is discussed in detail in the flat-weave section, nos. 454-459. Probably late 19th century.
172 x 111 cm

78 A very attractive piece with splendid colour. Like the majority of the pieces in this miscellaneous group, it has a wool warp and weft, the latter dyed pinkish-red. The border composition and the motifs within the octagons are variants of the double-T design which is found on a wide variety of south Caucasian/north-west Persian pile-knotted flat-woven rugs and also on some examples from east Anatolia. Compare this rug with 65, 68, 71 and 76 for similar treatments of a conjoined field composition. Probably second half of the 19th century.
218 x 155 cm

77

TILE PATTERN　　　　　　　　　　　　　　　　　　　　　　　　　　　　　KAZAK　89

78

Karabagh

Karabagh is the most southerly of the main Caucasian provinces, just north of the present Iranian border and once part of the north-west Safavid province of Azerbaijan. It had a large Armenian population and its capital, Shusha, is considered by some authorities, among them Charles Grant Ellis, to have been the possible place of manufacture of many of the great old groups of Caucasian weaving, in particular the dragon rugs. During the 18th century, Karabagh gradually came under the political domination of Tzarist Russia.

Many Karabagh rugs are close in style to north-west Persian Kurdish pieces and among the rugs illustrated in the following pages, we should note nos. 122-129 and nos. 134-137 fall into this category. Many of these south Karabagh rugs have cotton wefts and a floral lattice composition obviously influenced by Persian models. Indeed, the attribution of a number rugs to either Karabagh or north-west Persia is still a matter of controversy. Most of the pieces for which a Karabagh attribution is fairly certain have an all-wool foundation, the warps Z3S and the wefts Z2S; those pieces which have either cotton wefts or a mixture of cotton and wool are generally of the type which, from the design, could be either Persian or Caucasian, depending on one's point of view.

79 The format of this piece, with a single large cut-sided medallion, is a little unusual, as can be realised by a perusal of the following examples. In colour, however, it is typical, with the medallion ground colour blue-green and the field red. The stylised animal figures at either end of the field are not particularly common features, although a number of Chondzoresk rugs with them is known, including no. 80 in this selection. The border design, the so-called crab pattern, is the one most frequently encountered on rugs of this group. Late 19th/early 20th century.
187 x 115cm

Chondzoresk

Attributed to a village and its environs in the north-west part of Karabagh, this distinctive group of rugs was, and to a certain extent still is, known as cloud-band Kazak. The adjectival description refers to the worm-like configurations within the principal medallions, which are assumed to derive from Chinese sources, as does the Swastika-like medallion found within the centre square.

The origin of this design presents something of a problem; most of the examples known would seem to date from the end of the l9th century and beginning of the 20th—indeed the only dated examples I know bear dates in the first decade of the 20th century; as is demonstrated by no. 84, however, which is dated 1902 (in a strange mixture of western Arabic and Roman numerals by an Armenian) and is a very handsome piece, high standards were maintained into the present century. But as with so many distinctive groups of Caucasian rugs, there is no apparent precedent; unlike the following Chelaberd and Kasim-Usag groups, the development of which out of dragon and floral rugs of the 17th and 18th centuries can be clearly traced, the Chondzoresk pieces illustrated here are of a type which, despite all the appearance of the culminating stage of a long history, have no clearly identifiable antecedents.

80 Many features of the design, most notably the stylised animals, relate this somewhat gloomy piece to the previous example. Two features are worthy of note—the curled leaf motifs, which can be seen above the animals at the base of the rug, are similar to parts of the design found on Swastika Kazaks, while the motif between these animals, an heraldic figure resembling the Russian double-eagle, is obviously related to the following group of Chelaberd rugs and yet may well represent a pair of addorsed dragons. Late 19th/early 20th century.
210 x 98 cm

81 A well-designed piece with, for this group, an unusual border related to that found on some Caucasian kilim. The filler ornaments of *boteh* and stylised animals are also unusual as is the ivory ground of the centre medallion. The composition of the rug, although not particularly rare, is interesting; on many examples (see also no. 85), there is a fractional medallion at the top, bottom or at both ends, which gives the impression that the composition is an endless repeat. Late 19th/early 20th century.
216 x 114 cm

82 I know of no other example with the eight-pointed stars of this piece. The overall composition perhaps relates this group more closely to Anatolian models, a relationship which, from the study of other examples does not spring so forcibly to mind as with some of the Kazak rugs with geometric motifs. Late 19th/early 20th century.
275 x 127 cm

83 Unlike the somewhat cramped compositions of the previous examples, this rug has a well-spaced field and generous borders. It has a particularly pleasing array of colours which include a light green, a light blue and purplish-brown, the last, as we have noted before, being often considered as an indication of an oldish piece. Some of the filler ornaments again suggest an affinity with Anatolian village rugs. Late 19th century.
204 x 149 cm

84 This piece is another illustration of how dangerous it is to make dogmatic statements about the age of Caucasian rugs. It has a generously designed field, well drawn borders, including a not particularly usual reciprocal diamond guard and interesting field ornaments (although what was probably intended to be a Swastika within the central medallion seems to have gone a bit wrong). Although the overall drawing is a little crude, I have little doubt that if it were not for the date, 1902, the form of which suggests an Armenian weaver, this piece would be considered by many people as at least a quarter of a century earlier.
268 x 141 cm

85 In design, this is the least satisfactory of the Chondzoresk rugs reproduced here. The latch-hook side pieces which serve both as outlines to, and fillers between, the medallions are unusual, as is the tight umbrella border and the continuous ribbon motif in the guard stripe. An almost identical rug, sold at auction by Phillips in New York on 16 June, 1978 (cf. *Hali,* vol. 1, no. 2, p. 195) ,was signed and dated 1900 in Armenian. Late 19th/early 20th century.
259 x 110 cm

86 A handsome carpet, with an interesting tonal contrast between the green central medallion and the outer dark blue medallions. The floral-meander main border, with its unexpected pale blue ground, is unusual for this group, although it is one of the most ubiquitous Caucasian/Persian border designs. The four small hexagonal medallions with their pale yellow grounds contain designs which can not only be related to Lori-Pambak medallions, but also to the minor *gül* of Tekke Turkoman main carpets, the so-called *Kurbaghe gül.* The format is unusually long and narrow and, despite its interesting range of colours, this rug is probably not particularly old. Late 19th/early 20th century.
276 x 115 cm

84

CHONDZORESK   KARABAGH

85

86

Chelaberd

This group of rugs is popularly misnamed in the carpet trade 'sunburst-' or 'eagle Kazak', although its attribution to Karabagh is not now seriously disputed. The interpretation of the main medallion as a stylised rendering of the Russian coat-of-arms of a double-headed eagle is understandable, albeit wrong.

Unlike the previous group, the development of the Chelaberd design can be seen through a number of extant rugs, the earliest of which may date as far back as the 17th century. In brief, the design has evolved out of the so-called dragon rugs with their overall lattice of broad serrated leaves flanking animal figures and palmettes. On some of these early dragon rugs, such as that in the Burrell Collection, Glasgow Museum and Art Gallery, a pair of dragons can be seen flanking a central palmette, the latter the obvious prototype for the principal medallion of the Chelaberd rugs, a medallion to which the American scholar, Charles Grant Ellis, refers as a 'sunburst'. On the fragment of one dragon rug in an American private collection (cf. Ellis, *Early Caucasian Rugs,* plate 8), half a typical Chelaberd medallion can be seen. The majority of the earliest rugs on which the full-blown Chelaberd medallion appears are obviously somewhat later and degenerated versions of the dragon rugs, datable in the main to the mid-18th century. The greatest number of them can be found illustrated in the two-volume monograph by Serare Yetkin, *Early Caucasian Carpets in Turkey* (plates 25, 26, 27, 32, 45, 46, 49, figs. 153, 182, 183 and 185). There is also the well-known rug in the Siesta Collection, Milan (Ellis, op. cit. fig. 17), which has, among other motifs, fractionalised Chelaberd medallions in the four corners and one whole medallion in the centre. The carpet formerly in the Barbieri Collection, Genoa (Ellis, op. cit., fig. 15) has a very geometrically rendered medallion in the centre.

The present group of Chelaberd rugs, the name originating from a village slightly to the south-east of Chondzoresk, dates from the second half of the l9th century and beginning of the 20th. Their fairly certain attribution to the south Caucasus, especially when coupled with the attribution of the following group of Kasim-Usag rugs to the same area, is some circumstantial evidence that the earliest dragon and floral carpets, which many scholars had attributed to Kuba in the north-east, were also woven in the south. As with so many groups of 19th century village rugs, it is difficult to establish a chronology—one must look for quality of drawing, a sense of spatial values in the composition and clarity of colour.

One of the earliest dated examples known of the Chelaberd group is the rug in the Fisher Collection, Virginia Museum of Fine Arts, Richmond, U.S.A., which bears the Armenian inscription 'Domiksel U. Arpegov' and the date 1850, the Russian name referring either to the weaver or, more likely,

87

continued on p.98

87 A typical example of the medallion and bars type, with the usual colour format. However, we should note the presence of a bright light red field, the yellowish-green of the central cross and the attractive light blue elements within the central red diamond The majority of the Chelaberd rugs do not have animal figures but this example has attractive pairs of animals facing different directions above and below the main medallion which, because they are all standing the same way up, make the design directional (i.e. the design has only one correct way to be viewed), an unusual compositional feature. There is also a pair of stylised birds on the dark blue field area within the bottom leaf bar. Probably an early piece in relation to the majority of examples illustrated. Second half of the 19th century.
232 x 126 cm

88 Long rugs of the Chelaberd design are not particularly common and this example, over 15 feet in length, is most unusual. It is also exceptionally beautiful, with some brilliant colours, including the light blue seen at the topmost part of the field, gold-yellow, used predominantly in the flower-heads, and the rich emerald green of the crosses. The main border composition is a geometrical floral meander of a type not often encountered on Caucasian rugs and associated principally (although in a slightly different form) with south-west Persian tribal weavings. The field composition itself is most interesting; on examples such as 87, 89 and 90, the central medallion is flanked at either end by upward and downward pointing bars (stylised leaf forms) which enclose a half medallion. The fact that the medallion *is* halved suggests an endless repeat design, a concept confirmed by the present piece, in which the bar-and-medallion composition at either end of no. 87 is seen in its whole form in the centre of the rug, with half medallions at either end. Other unusual features, seen at the lower end of our illustration, are the male and female human figures and the beautifully drawn *boteh* below them; these figures seem to be wearing Azerbaijan festive costume which suggests that this piece was woven to commemorate a special event, probably a wedding, an interpretation enforced by the fact that the rug is dated. The style of *boteh is* also very Persian in character. All these stylistic features suggest that the rug may have been woven in the southern Karabagh, perhaps even in north-west Persia. The date itself is 1297 A.H. (A.D. 1879/80), the lateness of which is surprising in view of the piece's splendid quality, but one which allows us to place many examples (which are often given optimistically early attributions) confidently in the last two decades of the l9th and the first two of the 20th centuries.
462 x 124 cm

Chelaberd continued
to the recipient. This rug has a bright yellowish-green, seen in some of the present examples, has one and a half medallions and a white-ground floral crab border. Its early date rather spoils the theory that the earliest group of Chelaberd rugs is that on which a central medallion is flanked at either end by outward pointing bars, which are the highly degenerated remains of the serrated leaf lattice of dragon rugs (cf. our examples, nos. 84, 85 and 86).

In colour and structure, all the pieces are very similar, although, as we said earlier, clarity of colour—especially the presence of bright, lightish hues—is indicative of an earlier date than the many dark and gloomy examples which abound, a large number of which will have synthetic colours. The medallions consist inevitably of a green or blue cross on a white ground, with a central red diamond; on the examples with leaf bars at either end there will be dark blue areas within. The field colour is always red. The warp and weft are of wool, the warp usually white and the weft red; knot counts tend to be around 800 per sq. dm (52 per sq. in.). On good old examples, the pile is thick and high.

89 Although the same basic design as no. 87, this rug has many features which indicate a later date. The overall palette is darker and the colour range more limited. The design is much more cramped and the comb-like drawing within the leaf bars has become stiff and unattractive. Although there are no obviously synthetic colours, there can be little doubt that this piece is considerably younger than 87. Probably late 19th century.
246 x 160 cm

90 An attractive piece, with the best compositional spacing of the 'medallion and bars' Chelaberd rugs we illustrate. The field is a bright red and the colours generally are clear and pleasing. Probably late 19th century.
215 x 138 cm

89

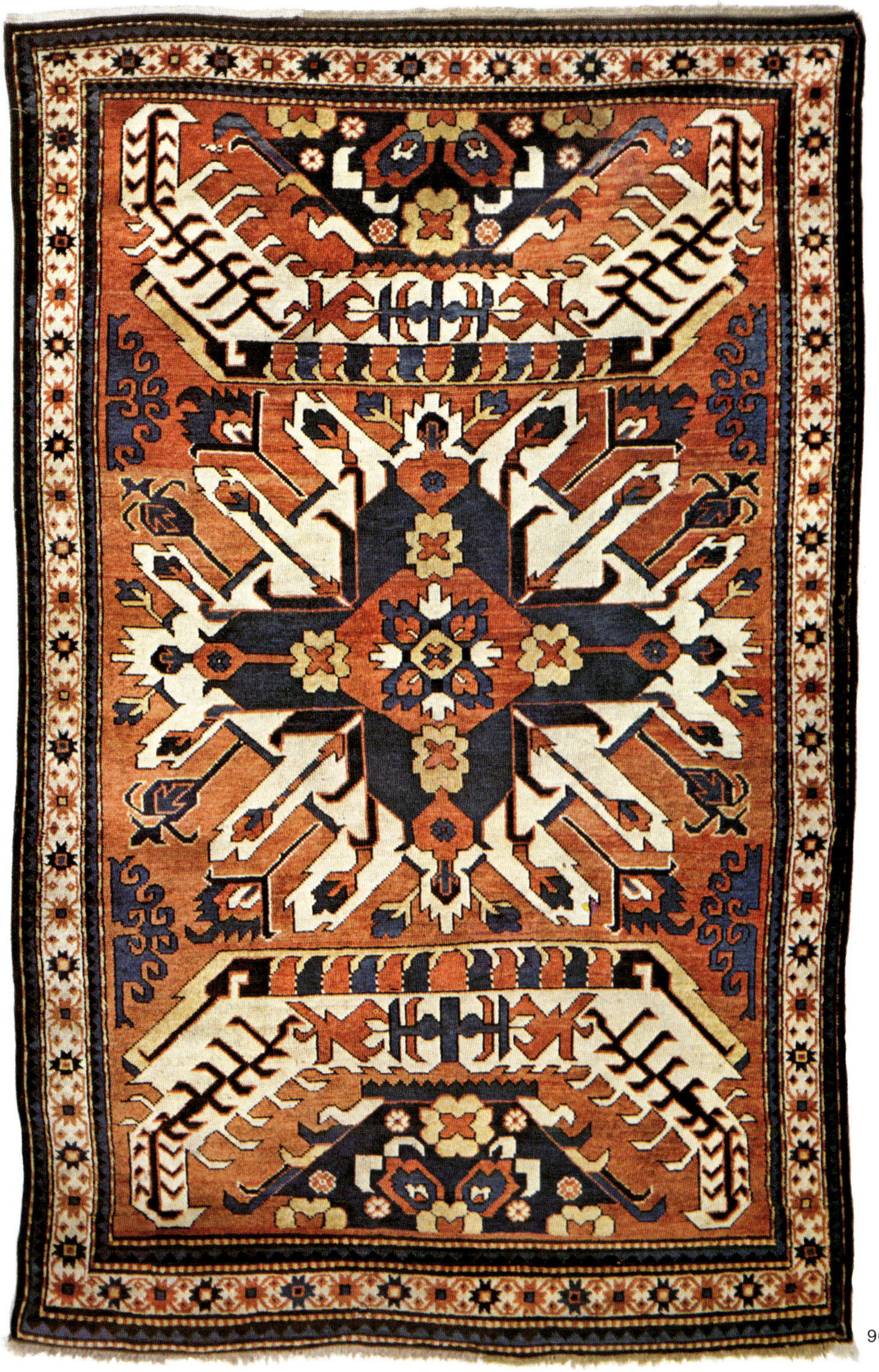

90

91

92

91 This piece represents another compositional type within the Chelaberd group, in which the field is divided into two compartments by means of a band; usually the two resulting areas are of roughly equal size with one large medallion in each, although on the Fisher rug, for instance, the bar divides the field into 1: $1^1/_2$ areas, with medallions of 1: $^1/_2$ dimensions in each. In terms of drawing and spatial arrangement, this rug does not have the look of much age (the red in the centre of the medallions looks synthetic); it has one very unusual feature—the light blue depiction of a man in the upper right-hand corner. There are also other strange zoomorphic figures among the filler ornaments in the rest of the rug. Note the dark blue border. Early 20th century.
216 x 125 cm

92 (detail) On this piece the central bar is a continuation of the border. The overall effect of the design is a little stilted and mechanical and the piece has the feel of a mass-produced object with little individuality. Late 19th/early 20th century.
205 x 135 cm

93 A third compositional type, with more than one medallion and no bar dividing the field. Many of the comments made about the previous piece apply to this example, the design of which is absolutely regular, with none of that amusing idiosyncrasy one finds on the best village rugs woven in a genuine domestic tradition. The narrow zig-zag panels at either end of the field are unusual. Late 19th/early 20th century.
218 x 147 cm

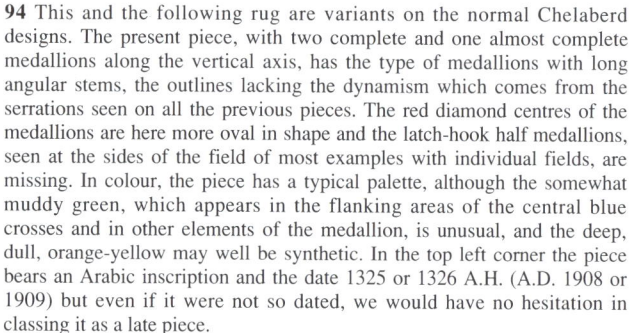

94 This and the following rug are variants on the normal Chelaberd designs. The present piece, with two complete and one almost complete medallions along the vertical axis, has the type of medallions with long angular stems, the outlines lacking the dynamism which comes from the serrations seen on all the previous pieces. The red diamond centres of the medallions are here more oval in shape and the latch-hook half medallions, seen at the sides of the field of most examples with individual fields, are missing. In colour, the piece has a typical palette, although the somewhat muddy green, which appears in the flanking areas of the central blue crosses and in other elements of the medallion, is unusual, and the deep, dull, orange-yellow may well be synthetic. In the top left corner the piece bears an Arabic inscription and the date 1325 or 1326 A.H. (A.D. 1908 or 1909) but even if it were not so dated, we would have no hesitation in classing it as a late piece.
273 x 153 cm

95 This rug is something of an oddity. The field has a marked *abrash*. The dark blue border has a latch-hook design which I have not seen on any other Chelaberd, or, indeed, on any other pile-knotted Caucasian rug; it is closer to the type of border one finds on certain kilim, both Caucasian and Anatolian. The medallions themselves show a greater expanse of white than is usually found, but the most interesting feature is the way the flanking strips to the crosses end, not in the *kotchak* forms of all the other examples we illustrate, but in curled forms. It is unwise to be dogmatic about a piece from a particular group with so many unusual features; however, the rug is almost certainly late, and may well be from the Kazak weaving area. Probably first quarter of the 20th century.
317 x 135 cm

96 Again an oddity; the overall effect is bold and there is a brilliant colour range of clear reds, blues, yellow and green. Each of the exceptionally large medallions contains an unusual myriad of small floral ornaments and there are also several small bird and animal figures which, as in no 87, make the design directional. The octafoil floral motifs are echoed in the white-ground border; this border design is most unusual for Chelaberds but is often encountered on north-west Persian Kurdish pieces. Another fascinating element of the design is the way the four major stems at the diagonal corner of the medallions end in dark blue motifs resembling crab's claws. This may well be a residual and highly stylised rendering of the dragon motif; there is also something disturbingly zoomorphic about the narrow dark-blue (top medallion) or yellow (bottom medallion) stem which ends in motifs which resemble ducks' heads with widely opened beaks. Late 19th/ early 20th century.
233 x 144 cm

Kasim-Usag

According to Ulrich Schürmann, this group was woven by Kurdish tribes in Karabagh, although in structure they are not distinguishable from the Chelaberd rugs, with which, quite obviously, they share the same design history. A number of floral carpets, datable to the 18th century, exist which show a compositional design of a central medallion bracketed at top and bottom by two inward pointing bars —e.g. Museum of Fine Arts, Boston (Ellis, pl. 17). On some examples the two brackets have joined to form an octagonal frame to the medallion (e.g. Yetkin, vol. II, no. 164). These rugs, in turn, are related to the rugs with *outward* pointing brackets at either end and especially to that most controversial of rugs, the Gohar carpet, which bears an Armenian inscription and a chronographic date equivalent to A.D. 1679/80 or A.D. 1699/1700, the later date being the most likely.

The closest parallel to the 19th century Kasim-Usag rugs is an 18th century carpet in the Turk ve Islam Museum, Istanbul (Yetkin, vol. I, pl. 28). This had the two large white brackets pointing inward at either end, although, as one would expect on a piece of this date, these brackets still retain strong traces of the large lanceolate leaves from which they, and the straight-sided bars of the Kasim-Usag rugs, derive. On the vertical axis, there are two octagonal medallions with frames containing motifs similar to those found on the Kasim-Usags, with a large central Chelaberd-type medallion, forming an interesting link between the Chelaberd rugs and the Kasim-Usags. Two other examples of similar type are also illustrated in Yetkin (vol. 2, figs. 163 and 164).

The earliest weavings closest in composition to the present group of carpets are not, in fact, pile-knotted pieces, however, but a group of exceptionally beautiful small silk embroideries; these are dated in most books to the 17th century. These, in turn, should be compared to a group of squarish, pile-knotted carpets probably dating from the early 19th century; the latter often have blue cotton wefts and extremely soft and lustrous wool.

Most of the present group must be dated to the last quarter of the 19th century and the first third of the 20th. It is interesting to note that almost all the known dated examples seem to fall into the period 1900-20 (cf. nos. 98 and 100) and the similarities between these late examples are so great that commercial workshop production is a possibility. Most have Z2S wool warps and dyed Z3S red-brown wool wefts. Knot counts are fairly high, averaging around 900 per sq. dm (58 per sq. in.).

97 The same type as no. 99. This piece has somewhat muddy colours and an unusual gold-yellow ground border with zig-zag leaf design. Many of its colours tend to confirm a Kurdish origin. Late 19th/early 20th century. 217 x 135 cm

98

98 This piece is, in design, far more closely related to the 17th century embroideries than any other of the rugs illustrated here. The white bars are more interestingly drawn and have not been reduced to the more usual straight-sided forms. Similarly, there is no central cruciform medallion, only two thin bracket bars at either end. The motifs within the white bars are more free and there is a wealth of well-constructed ornamentation throughout the field. It bears a date, or rather two dates; the upper one reads 1293 A.H. (A.D. 1876/7), which would make it one of the two earliest recorded examples of its type. However, the lower date seems to read 1282 A.H. (A.D. 1865/6), although the twos are both reversed. The presence of two conflicting dates on one piece does not mean, of course, that both should be disbelieved automatically. In addition, the existence of another rug of this type with the date 1293 A.H. is another source of suspicion (cf. no. 100). Nevertheless, this rug has many positive features.
205 x 138 cm

99 Dated 1335 A.H. (A.D. 1916/7), this example affords us a good yardstick with which to measure the others. The format is typical, with a huge central cruciform medallion with a red ground and a white ground medallion in the middle, and two large inward-pointing
continued on p. 107

99

106 KARABAGH   KASIM-USAG

99 continued
white-ground bars at either end of the field on a dark blue ground. Several dyes within the piece are probably synthetic, including a deep orange-yellow and an apparently faded grey-green. Some of the angular latch-hook ornaments within the white bars and the four grey-green figures which flank the central white medallion seem to retain zoomorphic vestiges, especially the latter which may be all that remain of the original dragon figures. The elements which appear in the spade-shaped medallions at top and bottom of the large cruciform are closely related to the main motifs of the Chelaberd rugs. The floral crab border is as often found on these rugs as on the previous group.
248 x 132 cm

100 Although obviously of the Kasim-Usag group, this piece is an unusual hybrid. It lacks the general format of the previously illustrated examples and has two and two-thirds white-ground medallions, of the type found normally within a large red-ground cruciform on the vertical axis. It lacks the inward pointing bars at either end of the field, although the diamond-head arrangement of latch-hook bars at either side of the field between the medallions is typical of the arrangement of side-pieces and central medallions on a large number of extant 18th century floral carpets from the south Caucasus. The border design will be familiar from its consistent appearance on Kazak rugs. First quarter of the 20th century.
241. x 147 cm

101 Except for the unusual yellow-ground border, which echoes the colour of the two narrow bars within the field, and the fact that this piece has only an implied cruciform medallion, the overall composition is typical. There is a wide range of colours. Both in design and colour it is extremely close to a Kasim-Usag rug illustrated by Michael Franses in *The World of Rugs,* 1973 (no. 15), which bore the extremely early date of 1293 A.H. (A.D. 1876). However, there is so little obvious difference between this latter piece and our no. 99, which is exactly 41 years younger, it would seem there was little, if any, degeneration during this period. Probably late 19th century.
224 x 124 cm

101

108 KARABAGH — TRIPLE MEDALLION

102

103

102 Although the centres of the medallions contain unusually naturalistic floral motifs—most of the others contain either a star within a square or a crab lozenge—some of the colours mark this out as a late example. The inscription at the top of the field, cannot be read. Note the animals at top and bottom, unusual features for this type. It seems as though the rugs of this group are connected with the Sewan Kazak group (e.g. nos. 17-19), for on late versions of the latter, the same floral palmette as appears in the centre of each of the three medallions on this rug, is found in the centre of the medallion 'complex' in the space occupied by the white rectangle on the piece we illustrate. It is, of course, much the same palmette as also appears in the centre of the Chelaberd medallions, is related to those on the so-called Erivan rugs we illustrate (nos. 140-143), and is found on two so-called Gendje rugs (153-154). Like all the rugs of this design, this piece has a red field. Probably first third of the 20th century.
234 x 129 cm

103 This piece, with its rather mechanical drawing, has star motifs within the medallions. The white motifs at top and bottom of the central rectangle in the medallions seem reminiscent of the 'Dragon and Phoenix' motif, which is often rendered in such highly stylised forms as this. Late 19th or early 20th century.
213 x 145 cm

Rugs with Three Medallions

These rugs have medallions which bear an obvious relationship to those found on Chelaberd rugs but which have become even more highly stylised, and some would say degenerate descendants of the 18th century floral carpets of the southern Caucasus. They are also related to Sewan Kazaks (cf. 102) and a number of authors have suggested that the medallions are derived from Turkoman *güls* with which, certainly, they would seem to have some affinity. In handle and structure, these pieces are indistinguishable from Kasim-Usags and are considered by most carpet dealers to be part of the same group: In some publications, however, they also appear as Lenkoran or Saliani, both names indicative of a south-east coastal origin.

104 This rug has the typical design for the group but the pale lime-green in the top of the lower two medallions may have faded. Late 19th or early 20th century.
210 x 137cm

110 KARABAGH   TRIPLE MEDALLION

105 In every way typical except for the presence of an extra fractional medallion at the top of the field, which converts the design from a self-contained entity to part of an endless repeat. It is of considerably finer quality than the previous two examples. Probably last quarter of the 19th century.
193 x 116 cm

106 A variant on the type, with four and three-quarter medallions on the vertical axis. Probably last quarter of the 19th century.
270 x 112 cm

107 This is an attractive and unusual variant of this design, and one which resembles the rug illustrated by Schürmann in *Caucasian Rugs,* p. 51, although it lacks that piece's richness and variety of colour. The four geometric motifs which flank the two central octagons are, of course, similar to the motifs occupying the same positions in the previously illustrated examples of this group; here, however, their zoomorphism is more apparent as is their relationship to the swastikas on the eponymous group of Kazak rugs. The central floral star can, in turn, be linked with the very similar motifs on Chelaberd rugs, the main border composition is unusual (although it appears on the following rug and is also found on examples of the Sewan Kazak group) and in overall appearance, this rug seems closer to Anatolian prototypes than the previously illustrated examples. Probably early 20th century.
200 x 103 cm

105

TRIPLE MEDALLION
KARABAGH 111

106

107

Prayer Rugs

Although the tradition of weaving prayer rugs was strong in the 19th century throughout the Caucasus (despite the fact that there is ample evidence that a large proportion of pile-knotted rugs, especially in the southern and central regions, was the work of Christian Armenians), one rarely finds examples described as Karabagh, possibly because an attribution to this region is actually a little speculative. Indeed, there would probably not be universal agreement about the attribution of the following three pieces.

108 An interesting piece with a striped field containing *boteh* within an angular meander. The drawing of the *boteh is* similar to that on the Chelaberd no. 88. The unusual border composition can be seen on no. 107. Note the similarity of the strange totemic motif in the arch of the *mihrab* to that which appears on no. 110 as well as on the Shirvan (no. 228), the Marasali (no. 229) and most especially on the Kuba (no. 326), which also has a somewhat similar treatment of the spandrels. Another rug with parallel vertical divisions, in each of which is a vine meander identical to this with small flowers rather than *boteh* and with a more floral version of the main border composition, is illustrated in the Frankfurt exhibition catalogue *Kaukasische Teppiche*, 26. Probably late 19th century.
157 x 187 cm

109 Within the field of this piece is an interesting array of hour-glass leaf motifs. A similar prayer rug is illustrated in Roy Macey's *Oriental Prayer Rugs*, where it is described as Kazak. It is interesting that identical hourglass motifs are found on rugs woven by the Baluch and Bal'huri tribes of eastern Persia; their presence on prayer rugs, according to the German authority, Dr. Dietrich Wegner, is symbolic of the Tree of Life. A similar composition is, of course, often found in the borders of Caucasian rugs, where it is popularly referred to as the 'crab' pattern. Probably late 19th century.
152 x 92 cm

110 A related example dated 1280 A.H. (A.D. 1863) is illustrated by Peter Bausback in his *Antike Orientteppiche*, 1978 (p. 215). I cannot help feeling a more north-easterly attribution to be likely. Probably last quarter of the 19th century.
123 x 105 cm

110

114 KARABAGH — BOTEH RUGS

111

112

111 Rugs with diagonal rows of *boteh* can be found throughout the Caucasus and Persia. In the Caucasus itself, the best known *boteh* rugs are from the Baku district in the central east coastal area, one particular group of which is known as *boteh-hila* in the carpet trade. The present rug and the three following examples present some problems of attribution. The vivid polychromy of this piece, while not untypical of Karabagh rugs, is found also on Saliani pieces from the Baku district, and the design itself is close to the latter group's rugs. However, we should note the somewhat sugary pink, which is a particular feature of many Karabagh weavings. Baku/Saliani rugs differ from most Karabagh pieces in having cotton or mixed wool and cotton wefts. In style, this example is almost identical to the rug illustrated in Schürmann (op. cit., no. 91). Probably late 19th century.
319 x 89 cm

112 The drawing of the *boteh* and the blue ground of this piece, as well as the striped border, are also features of some east Caucasian rugs, and the rug may be compared to the *boteh* illustrated in Schürmann (op. cit., no. 86). Probably late 19th century.
295 x 113 cm

113 Another rug the design of which is similar to east Caucasian versions.
295 x 109 cm

114 An attractive rug which, when it was sold at Nagel's in 1976, was catalogued as a Gendje. Certainly the border and guards suggest a south or central Caucasian origin and the town of Gendje, situated at midpoint between Kazak, Karabagh and Shirvan, acted as a melting-pot for many different styles, as well as being an important marketing centre. Probably late 19th century.
265 x 122 cm

115 We have encountered the type of latch-hook decoration seen on this and the following two examples on Bordjalou Kazak rugs (cf. nos. 39, 44) and on other Kazak rugs not attributed to any particular village (e.g. nos. 69, 75, 76). This piece has a particularly interesting reciprocal border design made up of seemingly tiny squares forming arrow-heads; this is a format derived from kilim border patterns, the technique of which makes the weaving of diagonal lines very difficult. A wide range of colours makes this an attractive piece. Probably second half of the 19th century.
266 x 122 cm

116 The conjoined latch-hook diamond pattern is well-known in Kazak weavings, as well as in those of the Baluch, e.g. *Hali Vol.* III, no. 2, p. 145. Raoul Tschebull, in *Kazak* (plate 26), illustrates an example of some age which has blue wool wefts. Latch-hook diamond patterns are also found in rugs attributed to Moghan (196, 201-203), Shirvan (227) and Dagestan (417-419). The present piece does not seem particularly old. Late 19th/early 20th century.
247 x 121 cm

HOOKED DIAMOND MEDALLION

KARABAGH 117

117 This rug in my view is almost certainly a Kazak of the Bordjalou group and not a Karabagh; it is catalogued as the former by Peter Bausback in *Antike Orientteppiche* (p. 174). Its ivory ground is unusual and it has some beautiful colours – particularly a rich green. The large floral palmette borders are another rare feature, although it is worth noting that a long *boteh* rug with identical border palmettes in the Victoria and Albert Museum is attributed to Talish by Michael Franses and Robert Pinner in their discussion of the Museum's Caucasian rugs, *Hali*, Vol. III, no. 2, p. 162, figure 17. The latter rug was not new when it entered the South Kensington museum in 1880 and is one of the most handsome examples of Caucasian village weaving we have encountered so far. It seems likely to be of good age, probably dating from the third quarter of the 19th century. The piece has light brown wool warps, darker brown wool wefts and is quite finely knotted – 1,400 per sq. dm (90 per sq. in.).
218 x 142cm

118 KARABAGH | SMALL SHIELD PALMETTES

118

119

118 This piece and the two following rugs again are not easy to attribute and may well be from the Kuba or Shirvan regions. This is particularly true of the present piece with its tightly knotted all-over design, which is uncharacteristic of the bolder medallion forms of south Caucasian weaving. A prayer rug with a somewhat similar field design will be found illustrated in Roger F. Gardiner, *Oriental Rugs from Canadian Collections* (no. 30). This is attributed to Baku, c.1900, and has a wool warp and weft. The small shield-like medallions which form an all-over pattern on this rug are, however, familiar from the appearance of almost identical motifs on several groups of Kazak rugs. Raoul Tschebull, in *Kazak* (plate 27), illustrates a Sewan Kazak with a similar white-ground border (and in his essay 'The Development of Four Kazak Designs', *Hali*, Vol. I, no. 3 he remarks that Sewan Kazaks with this border are probably among the oldest of their type). It also appears on our no. 8 (Lori Pambak, surrounding

continued on p.119

SMALL SHIELD PALMETTES

KARABAGH 119

118 continued
the main green medallion), no. 24 (Fachralo prayer rug, surroundmg the *mihrab*) and no. 48 (Bordjalou prayer rug, surrounding the /*nihrab*). No. I 18 has a wide range of colours but what appear to be some traces of synthetic dye, blue overcast selvedges and the remains of blue flat-woven ends, may Indicate a more northerly, perhaps Kuba, origin. Probably late 19th/early 20th century.
327 x 153 cm

119 A rug with an all-over desigll ol shield-like palmettes. Its design is related to the famous group of rugs mentiolled in the Introduction, probably dating from the 18th century, which have an all-silk foundation and a design of rows of shieldlike lotus palmettes flanked by bo~eh-like medallions. It is interesting to note that the overall composition is similar to that of a group of Afshar rugs from southwest Persia. Probably late 19th century, though some examples have been seen which are early 20th century.
196 x 106 cm

120 Here, the field is divided into three vertical bands, coloured red, blue and red. The shield-like lotus palmettes form an obvious link with the previous piece but the overall appearance is different. A closely related rug, with field divided Into red and blue bands, is illustrated by Jean Lefevre, *Caucasian Carpe~s* (no. 39), where the connection between it and a similarly decorated group of Ersari Turkoman carpets is made. The Lefevre rug, however, has differently shaped medallions which resemble open-winged moths pinned to a board, and does not have the clearly drawn deer and birds of the preserit rug. Another rug with insectlike medallions and the field divided into three vertical stripes, with each medallion in an alternately red or yellow panel, is illustrated by Jenny Housego, Tribal Rugs (plate 81), and is attributed to the Kurds of Khorasan in north-east Persia. Although the interpretation of the medallion on 121 as a lotus-palmette is widely accepted, it is impossible not to notice how the downward-pointing arrow-heads seem to form two animal heads facing each other. Perhaps we are dealing with a residual animal-and-tree image. Probably late 19th century.
204 x 121 cm

120

121 This carpet contains motifs and designs common to a wide range of south Caucasian and Persian tribal weavings. In many respects it looks more Persian than Caucasian. If we compare it to the details of the carpet reproduced as figs. 17-19 in A. Cecil Edwards' *The Persian Carpet,* we can see an almost identical use of the Herati pattern as an all-over field design, and the identical floral meander found within the pale green-yellow guard stripes of this piece appears in fig. 17 in Edwards' book, a Qain carpet which, because of the lack of a diamond lozenge within the Herati pattern, can be attributed with some certainty to Khorasan, the most easterly Persian province. The floral meander we have mentioned is one of the most ubiquious designs on Persian rugs and pile-knotted artefacts, being seen on many Kurdish pieces from south Caucasus and north-west Persia, on Qashqa'i, Luri and other tribal weavings from Fars in south-west Persia and on the products of the Baluch and other tribes from east Persia and Afghanistan. This is an interesting piece which, if it is from Karabagh, shows the strong influence of Persian design. It has many of the hall-marks of a workshop-made piece produced from a cartoon in the late 19th or early 20th century for export. Its length —over 14 feet —has led it and similarly proportioned rugs to be called 'gallery carpets' or 'runners'.
430 x 100 cm

'HERATI' PATTERN

KARABAGH

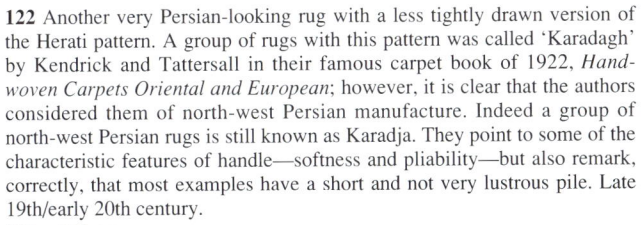

122 Another very Persian-looking rug with a less tightly drawn version of the Herati pattern. A group of rugs with this pattern was called 'Karadagh' by Kendrick and Tattersall in their famous carpet book of 1922, *Handwoven Carpets Oriental and European*; however, it is clear that the authors considered them of north-west Persian manufacture. Indeed a group of north-west Persian rugs is still known as Karadja. They point to some of the characteristic features of handle—softness and pliability—but also remark, correctly, that most examples have a short and not very lustrous pile. Late 19th/early 20th century.
212 x 114 cm

123 An unusual prayer rug on which the Herati pattern has become stylised and elongated. The centre minor border contains a chain-like angular vine meander, which can also be found on many Persian tribal weavings, especially those of the Qashqa'i and Luri from south-west Persia. Probably late 19th century.
152 x 93 cm

124 A piece which bears a striking resemblance to certain north-west Persian village rugs, particularly those of the Bidjar area, several of which have a 'broken' floral lattice. Its colour range is somewhat unusual—it might even have received a chemical wash. However, the two central medallions are apparently dyed with cochineal. The carpet could be north-west Persian, although it is clearly related to the group of Lampa-Karabagh. A rug of similar design is illustrated in the Frankfurt *Kaukasische Teppiche* catalogue no. 30. This has *boteh* borders similar to that on a rug in the V. & A. (T.309-1920, see M. Franses and R. Pinner, *Hali*, Vol. III, no. 2, p. 101, fig. 14). Early 20th century.
257 x 108 cm

125 This stylised lattice design, with its small white flowers, is known as the *mina-khani* and is found in various forms on the rugs of many tribes in Persia, particularly those of the Kurds and Baluch. The handling of the design on this rug and the minor border strongly suggest a Kurdish origin and although the large 'S' in the main border is found on several types of Caucasian rug, it is also found on Kurdish and other Persian tribal pieces, especially those from around the Veramin area in north Persia (from whence rugs with the *mina-khani* design also come; cf. Housego, op. cit. plate 82 for the border). Possibly late 19th century.
280 x 115 cm

126 Like the previous piece, this prayer rug has a highly stylised and rigid version of the *mina-khani* design in the field. Its white-ground borders contain an angular vine meander of a type associated in particular with south-west Persian tribal weaving but which is also found on Kurdish rugs from further north. Again, except for the *mihrab* arch itself, the piece has a distinctly un-Caucasian look, and is possibly the work of Kurds. Late 19th/early 20th century
150 x 89 cm

127 Following Ulrich Schürmann, who in turn followed Kerimov, Lampa-Karabagh is the name given to a group of rugs woven on the Caucasian/Persian border. This rug is typical of the group, and other characteristic examples can be seen as nos. 132-134. Note the border composition, which is a somewhat crude version of that seen on east Caucasian rugs such as nos. 250 and 252. Probably late 19th century.
314 x 127cm

127

128

128 A beautiful and clearly drawn, though highly stylised, version of the *mina-khan*i design on a rich red field, with an abundant use of two striking shades of light blue; normally, the appearance of a somewhat unusual orange colour in the flowers and borders might suggest the presence of a synthetic dye but the use of a vegetable dyed lightish brown-orange is characteristic of rugs woven either by Kurds or within their sphere of influence. Two examples of this bold *mina-khani* are illustrated by Kendrick and Tattersall (op. cit., plates 149 and 150), and we should note the similarities between this rug and our blue ground rug no. 125. Another fine example is illustrated by Inge Lise Jensen in *Kaukasiske Taepper en Dansk Privatsamling* (no. 19); this blue-ground piece is described, probably erroneously, as Shirvan. The attribution of 128 to the Caucasus is a little doubtful —a north Persian/Kurdish origin seems more likely. Probably late 19th/early 20th century.
281 x 135 cm

Carpets with 'European' Designs

Many groups of Caucasian and Persian carpets, usually woven in the second half of the 19th century, have floral designs clearly derived from western prototypes and woven, it is presumed, for the western market. In the Caucasus, two of the most famous groups are the Karabagh 'Russian' floral carpets (nos. 130-132) and those pieces, the majority of which are attributable to Seichur, which have pink-white cabbage roses on a green or blue ground (e.g. nos. 384-386). Of these, the Karabaghs are the most clearly derived from European, and specifically French, sources. It is assumed that the earliest examples (if not the later ones) were made on commission for the occupying Russians, who found them an inexpensive substitute for prohibitively costly Aubusson and Savonnerie imports. Although the majority of examples which have survived would appear to date from the late 19th century, there are a number of extant examples bearing dates in the late 18th and early 19th centuries —for instance, Schürmann, op. cit., plate 41, dated 1799, the European date being expressed directly in Islamic numerals (a date not noted by Schürmann in his text); Albert Achdjian, Le Tapis (p. 85, dated 1806), which has a purely Caucasian field design but a European inspired floral border; Jack Franses, European and Oriental Rugs for Pleasure (no. 14, dated 1809). Many of these pieces with early dates also have Armenian inscriptions and this Armenian connection has been taken by some authorities—e.g. Roger F. Gardiner (op. cit., pp.91, 172) —as indicating that the dates are authentic; however, a number of rugs

129 Fairly unusual design of repeated floral bouquets with a bird. It lacks the rococo spontaneity of many examples and may well be a late rug. Probably late 19th century.
580 x 110 cm

130 Many of the European floral Karabaghs are of large size, e.g. 129, and the small, charming, examples such as the present piece are comparatively rare. The design is clearly derived from Aubusson and Savonnerie models. Probably late 19th century.
195 x 153 cm

131 A number of floral Karabaghs have designs based around floral cartouches – e.g. Gardiner, op. cit., no. 41, Achdijan, op. cit., p.83. However, these tend to have a single longitudinal row of ovals and rarely multiple rows such as the present example. The design more closely resembles European tapestry-woven pieces and has the wide range of colours typical of Karabagh. Second half of the 19th century.
204 x 113cm

Carpets with 'European' Designs continued
of identical quality exist with dates much later in the 19th century—e.g. Ian Bennett, *Rugs and Carpets of the World* (p. 151), dated 1294 A.H. (A.D. 1877). Since the majority of these pieces was made for export either to Russia or the West, it is not inconceivable that a certain amount of false dating was carried on.

The majority have a blue field, although some, including the early example illustrated in Jack Franses' book, are red. They are woven with good quality wool, often with an ivory wool warp and weft. The knot count is variable but around 1,000 per sq. dm (65 per sq. in.) is the norm. They usually have a wide range of colours including bright yellows, pinks and blues.

132 A typical Lampa-Karabagh design. The bird forms can be compared with those found on many north-west Persian/south Caucasian flat-woven animal-trappings, often attributed to the Shahsavan tribe. The border composition is similar to that found on 127, which rug is very close in overall composition to the present piece. Some of the colours may be synthetic. Late 19th/early 20th century
340 x 146 cm

Lampa-Karabagh

Nos. 127 and 132-134 are examples of a well-known group of Karabagh rugs which have large medallions often, as in no. 133, of a markedly floral type, and flanked by fairly naturalistic birds (Jensen, op. cit., fig. 15 illustrates an unusual variant with stylised cypress trees instead of birds and a beautiful and apparently unique cypress tree border). Schürmann, op. cit., plate 42, illustrates a striking example with a large central floral medallion, two bar-like appendages and two human figures with what appear to be dogs. Murray Eiland, op. cit., fig. 151, illustrates a piece with a series of medallions of different shape on the vertical axis flanked by pairs of huge birds (eagles?). Another rug has floral medallions on the vertical axis with small bar appendages at either side of the field and four pairs of what could be either cockerels or peacocks; this example, which has an Armenian inscription, is illustrated in Albert Achdjian's *Le Tapis* (plate 85). A fourth example in recently published literature is that in Luciano Coen and Louise Duncan's *The Oriental Rug* (no. 44); the medallions and bar on this piece are close to those on Schürmann's example, although they are arranged in series down the rug's 19 foot length, while the cockerel birds are close to those on the Achdjian piece but more elaborate.

In all cases, except the Coen and Duncan rug, where they are slanted diagonally upwards, the sides of the field are decorated with short, inward-pointing prongs. These rugs are obviously closely connected with the previously described group of European influenced pieces— some such as the Achdjian and Coen/ Duncan rugs have European roses either in the borders or the field. As we noted in our discussion of the 'European' pieces, some of these Karabaghs have what appear to be almost unbelievably early dates — the Achdjian example, for instance, is dated A.D. 1806 and that in Murray Eiland 1212 A.H. (A.D. 1797). Structurally, most pieces seem to have an all-wool foundation, although the Schürmann example has mixed wool and cotton wefts. The Eiland and Coen/ Duncan pieces have knot counts of 1,255 per sq. dm (81 per sq. in.) and 1,240 per sq. dm (80 per sq. in.) respectively.

133 I have not examined this piece and the poor quality of the reproduction makes it difficult to be certain about its quality or age. There would appear to be some attractive colours in the field, particularly the green and a vivid light blue. The *boteh* border is an unusual and noteworthy feature, and should be compared with a similar border on an older rug with zig-zag designs in the Victoria and Albert Museum (cf. no. 136). Possibly late 19th century.
440 x 179cm

134 Exceptionally long and narrow rugs are often found with the Lampa-Karabagh design, of which this piece, approximately 19ft. by 3½ ft., is an example. There is a possibility that such rugs were woven for the Western market. In my view it could be as late as late 19th century.
572 x 109 cm

ZIG-ZAG MEDALLIONS

135 This and 136 represent a well-known group of Karabagh rugs with a continuous series of conjoined diamond medallions with zig-zag outlines. This rug, with its somewhat more elongated design, is the most typical; two published examples are those in the Victoria and Albert Museum, London (illus. Kendrick and Tattersall, *Handwoven Carpets, Oriental and European*, pl. 142) and the Cincinnati Institute of Fine Arts (illus. Daniel S. Walker) *Oriental Rugs in Cincinnati Collections* (no. 18). A very similar example sold at auction by Rippon Boswell in London on 3 March, 1979 (lot 69) was full of synthetic colour and was obviously woven at some time around the 1930s. Late 19th/early 20th century.
560 x 103 cm

136 This type with the more regular diamond medallions is almost identical in design to a rug illustrated in Schürmann (op. cit. no. 32) and to another in the Joslyn Art Museum at Omaha, Nebraska (cf. *A Rich Inheritance*, p. 43). All have a similar cruciform arrangement of motifs within each zigzag diamond, an arrangement which resembles the Yomut *kepse gül*. A huge variant, 21 ft. long, is illustrated by Murray Eiland, op. cit. pl. XLV, but this piece has an unusual look and Kufic borders; it seems more closely related to a rug which Schürmann illustrates in his book (pl. 80) and which he calls Surahani from Baku (although his piece has a cotton weft as opposed to the all-wool foundation of the Eiland rug. The Joslyn Museum rug has natural brown and white wool warps and dyed red wool wefts; Schürmann no. 32 has natural brown and white wool warp and wefts. The V. & A. rug mentioned in connection with 135 has a white wool foundation but the Cincinnati piece has cotton wefts. Knot counts seem to vary between 750 and 1,250 per sq. dm (48 to 81 per sq. in.). The V. & A. rug has a most unusual *boteh* border, while our 136, the Schürmann rug no 32 and the example in Cincinnati all have identical borders of a type usually associated with northwest Persian Bidjar rugs (cf. Bacharach and Bierman, *The Warp and Weft of Islam*, no. 57 for an identical border on a Bidjar rug of typical design). The Schürmann rug has an unusual ground colour for a border, a pale lime green. It is unlikely that any of these pieces pre-dates the last quarter of the 19th century, although Schürmann dates his example to c.1800. It is worth noting, perhaps, that the *boteh* border of the V. & A. rug is drawn in a style very close to that of certain Afshar rugs; A. Cecil Edwards, in *The Persian Carpet*, illustrates a number of north-west Persian rugs very closely related to these south Caucasian examples. Cf. also no. 124.
278 x 115 cm

135

136

137 A crowded design on the usual dark-blue field. Some of the colours, particularly the orange shades, look as if they may be synthetic. Most such pieces have a brown wool foundation and a low knot count – around 600 per sq. dm (39 per sq. in.). Late 19th/early 20th century.
275 x 125 cm

138 The comments I have just made apply to this piece also, although it has a more lively look to the field. Note the relationship of the border composition on this and the previous piece to those on nos. 107 and 108. Late 19th century, though some examples have also been made in the early 20th century.
299 x 138 cm

Goradis

Goradis is the most south-easterly of the known Karabagh weaving towns, to which is attributed a group of rugs all of which have designs of large angular *boteh* with leaf appendages at the end. Schürmann, completely erroneously, refers to these as 'scorpions'. Structurally, there is some indication that these rugs were not woven in one area, since some have an all-wool foundation and others, such as the example illustrated by Schürmann himself, op. cit., plate 38, have cotton wefts. The piece illustrated in Schürmann has more elegant, floral *boteh* than those found on the examples we illustrate; it is not, however, particularly early, being dated 1299 A.H. (A.D. 1882). This is one of the groups of Karabagh weaving which do not relate to those of Kazak and which seem to demonstrate a much closer Persian influence. It may be that the differences in their structure are accounted for by the fact that some were woven in the Caucasus and others across the border in north-west Persia. There is also a possibility that some may have been woven by Kurds, as the designs seem to show that movement from flowing curvilinearity to geometric formalism which are associated with Kurdish interpretations of town workshop designs.

139 Most so-called Goradis rugs are a little gloomy. This piece, however, has an unusually bright range of colours, including a vivid light blue. Some of the pinks look a little suspect, although Karabagh rugs are well known for a wide range of rather unusual looking vegetable and insect reds and pinks. Possibly older than it looks. Late 19th century or conceivably 20th century.
341 x 123cm

Erivan

This town is now the capital of Soviet Armenia, Yerevan. It is situated just west of Lake Sevan and was founded in 782 B.C. by the Urartian King Argishti I, who called it Erebuni. Ironically, this is the only Armenian name of origin given to any of the south Caucasian rugs, despite considerable evidence that Armenians were responsible for much of the 19th century weaving in the area and very possibly for much that went before; some authors, such as Albert Achdjian, suggest that just about every rug woven in the Caucasus was the work of Armenians. Some scholars today would argue an Armenian origin for the dragon rugs and one inscribed Armenian rug, the Gohar, was made at the end of the 17th century if the date is to be believed. However, the Erivan attribution of this particular group of rugs, while the three Karabagh rugs 132-134

140 The composition of this piece is similar to that of 132. There are many amusing small animals and birds among the infill ornaments but the overall impression given by the piece is one of good age. In many respects, however, it is atypical; its border system is particularly interesting and should be compared with 69. These two rugs may well have been woven in the same area. Probably late 19th century.
315 x 160 cm

141 This piece again has the same medallions as the Karabagh group and although the conjoined octagonal format of the field is unusual, the sides have the same inward-pointing prongs we commented upon before. Only the absence of the large birds between the medallions makes this piece different from the main Karabagh group. Late 19th century/early 20th century.
325 x 112 cm

ERIVAN **131**

142   143

Erivan continued
are, by implication, attributed to an area many miles to the southeast, does not make logical sense. Rather, it seems that the Erivans and the type of Karabagh we are now discussing form part of one and the same group, to which might be added the Shikli-Kazaks 50-54. All have either all-wool foundations, or wool warp and mixed wool and cotton weft, and in palette and handle are very similar. The sort of weavings known currently in the trade as 'Erivans' are almost all post-1920 commercially-made small rugs in a variety of designs.

142 A very similar piece to the previous one and all the same points apply. It has a date, 1906, written by an Armenian upside-down to the design (all the tiny birds in the side half-diamonds are upside-down when the date is the right way up!).
340x 114cm

143 A far more open and simplified design than on the previous pieces. The slightly weird colours are characteristic of the group and one might compare this example with the rug illustrated by Peter Bausback, *Alte und Antike Meisterstücke Orientalischer Teppichknüpfkunst,* 1973 (p. 31). Late 19th century, possibly early 20th century.
330 x 128 cm

Gendje

The town of Gendje was called Elizabethpol under the Tzars and is now known as Kirovabad, the principal town of the Soviet Socialist Republic of Azerbaydzhanskaya (Soviet Azerbaíjan). It is almost centrally placed between the Caucasian weaving areas of Kazak, Karabagh and Shirvan and acted as an important marketing centre to the rugs of those places and produced its own weavings in a style which shows the considerable influence of the major areas surrounding it.

If you ask any dealer exactly how he knows a rug to be Gendje, the answer, in all probability, will be somewhat vague. There is no particular style, as can be seen from the rugs we illustrate in the following pages. Many of them illustrate a lattice design which seems derived from both Kazak and Shirvan rugs, some have the *boteh* design popular in Karabagh and Moghan, while others exhibit geometric designs close in feel to Kazaks.

One particular border design which is considered characteristic of Gendjes consists of a continuous series of conjoined octagons — this can be seen on nos 151 and 155; conjoined octagons are also found as a field design (cf. nos. 151-158). Perhaps the only generalised statement which can be made about the rugs attributed to Gendje is that they rarely exhibit the bold large medallions associated with Kazaks, the weavers apparently preferring small, jewel-like, polychromatic ornamentation. When the designs are those which apparently depend on Shirvan models, they are almost always rendered with some degree of naïvety, some would say coarseness. In my experience, any attractive Caucasian rug in bright colours but with a slightly coarse drawing style and in a design reminiscent of one of the major types, is often called Gendje simply for the sake of convenience. It is an attribution to be treated with considerable caution.

In colour, Gendje rugs tend to be bold, with an abundant use of light, bright shades—aquamarine, gold, yellow, emerald green and so forth, and a lavish use of ivory wool. In other words, they tend to have a more shimmering, polychromatic, look than many of the rugs from the south Caucasus. In texture, they are often shaggy but with a somewhat dry look, typical of rugs made from poor grade wool.

Structurally, they differ very little from Kazak rugs—indeed, so close are they that distinctions are often arbitrary and even unnecessary. There is only one major difference about Gendje rugs as a group: out of 22 rugs attributed to Gendje which I examined in 1978-79, six or approximately 27% had cotton wefts. Of the nineteen for which I have knot counts, eleven had between 600 and 950 per sq. dm (39 to 61 per sq. in.), four between 950 and 1,400 per sq. dm (61 to 90 per sq. in.) and three between 450 and 600 per sq. dm (29 to 39 per sq. in.). Only one went over 1,550 per sq. dm (100 per sq. in.). Thus the majority of Gendje rugs are fairly coarse, although no more so than the majority of Kazaks.

145

144 A somewhat unusual piece with which to start, although the vertical band of somewhat elongated conjoined octagons suggests a Gendje origin. There is a wealth of amusing minor ornamental detail, including bird figures, and a typical Gendje use of colour. Compare the main border composition with those on nos. 107, 108 and 137. The tiny birds and other small ornamentation in the ivory ground half-diamond at the side of the field resemble north-west Persian tribal work. Probably late 19th century, but could conceivably be early 20th century.
267 x 109 cm

145 A colourful rug, the design of which strongly resembles Kazak pieces, especially from Fachralo. The field is red, unusual for a Gendje rug which almost always have dark blue fields. The attribution to Gendje rather than Kazak is probably justified by the widespread use of bright yellow and ivory, but is by no means certain. Probably late 19th century, though here again it might just be very early 20th century.
170 x 142 cm

146 This amusing and unusual piece has many motifs in the field which suggest that it might have been intended as a prayer rug; these include the small arched shape at the very top, which is flanked by two hands and a comb. The rest of the field has large shrubs (trees-of-life?) flanked by lotus palmettes, two of which have tiny birds either side (the totemic bird and tree symbol?) with a larger bird surmounting them. There are also male and female human figures, similar to those seen on no. 58, and a variety of small floral and geometric motifs. The series of borders — inner *medachyl* border, main white-ground 'stencil S' and outer zig-zag border— could be attributed to just about any area of the Caucasus, although a comparison with the borders of the Shirvans nos. 224 and 226 and the Kuba prayer rug no. 326 suggests that this attractive piece might be from further east, a suggestion, however, made less concrete by looking at the very similar border series which appears on the Karachoph Kazak no. 29. Probably late 19th century.
160 x 80 cm

147 Something of a puzzle rug. The *medachyl* border is probably the only obvious stylistic feature which suggests a Gendje origin. The red field, itself unusual for Gendjes, contains florettes, *boteh* and an amusing human figure accompanied by three camels. The border of crab florettes between brackets seems to be a degenerate and coarse descendant of the Kufic border design. Possibly an old rug, and certainly a most attractive one, although the main order design is decidedly clumsy. It is perhaps worth remarking that any rug which has so charming a field design as this will always have a ready market, even though its origin and the quality of manufacture may be in doubt. Note the similarity between the polychrome motifs of the minor borders to those framing the field of no. 69. Possibly Kazak, late 19th century.
207 x 113 cm

136 GENDJE

FLORAL LATTICE

148

149

148 Many rugs from Gendje have a bold, reciprocal arrow-head outer minor border called a *medachyl* border. The lattice design in the *mihrab* of this prayer rug containing stylised lotus palmettes is ubiquitous in the Caucasus but is particularly associated with Shirvan, Kuba and Daghestan. The cramped composition, somewhat loose drawing and vivid polychromy, as well as the obviously coarse knotting, all point to a Gendje origin. Note the *ad hoc* change from blue to white in the *medachyl* border and the way the inner guards cut across the main border at the base. Rugs of this type often date from the late 19th to the early 20th century.
138 x 99 cm

149 A very unusual little rug, with a series of borders not often encountered. The floral lattice can be compared to those on 148 and 150, although the use of square blocks between the lattice is not often found on Caucasian rugs, being associated in particular with the floral lattice rugs of the Baluch. The design is more often found on east Caucasian rugs. Late 19th/early 20th century.
144 x 113cm

FLORAL LATTICE
GENDJE 137

150 Another typically colourful, polychromatic Gendje rug with a coarse shaggy weave and loose drawing—a piece which is distinctly nomadic in feel and related to 148 both in quality and design. A good look at this piece will enable someone new to the subject to gain something of the almost instinctive ability to spot a Gendje shown by expert dealers in Caucasian village rugs, although the attribution remains very subjective. Probably late 19th century.
170 x 117 cm

151 Rugs with a single vertical row of large octagons containing geometric floral motifs are associated in particular with the Kazak group—cf. no. 70 for instance. The division of the field into horizontal blocks of colour is unusual although the running octagon border is, as we have noted, a design especially associated with Gendje rugs; its attribution to Gendje rather than to Kazak must, however, be considered unproven unless there is any marked structural idiosyncracy. The motif within the octagons seems clearly related to the principal motif of the Lori Pambak group of rugs, but is also not dissimilar to the ornament found on some south-west Persian tribal rugs and often called the Qashqa'i emblem. The piece has an attractive range of colours, including light blue; the one small animal to the left of the top field panel adds an amusing note. Second half of the 19th century.
212 x 140 cm

152 Many of the comments made about the previous piece apply to this rug's overall design. The border design is associated particularly with the Gendje and Talish areas (although compare the field rosettes of the Kazak no. 60). This rug does not have a divided field composition, and has a greater wealth of minor field ornamentation than 151, including many animals and birds. The 'running dog' minor borders are a fairly uncommon feature, although they are encountered occasionally on Kazak rugs (e.g. 38 and 39). In the top left-hand corner is an almost illegible Arabic inscription and a date which appears to be 1301 A.H. (A.D. 1883/4), which is quite acceptable.
253 x 144 cm

140 GENDJE

The two rugs illustrated on this page show how it can be extremely difficult to make positive attributions when examples show characteristics of more than one area.

153 Like the following piece, this rug has similarities to both Kazak and Karabagh weavings. In this instance, however, the case for a Kazak attribution is, perhaps, stronger. The attractive series of borders is almost identical to that seen on 55, both in design and colour; the spacing and boldness of design in the field is also characteristically Kazak and, of course, the small latch-hook diamonds flanking the series of conjoined octagons, although not exclusive to the Kazak area, are found on many examples attributed to that region. Like the similar motifs on the next example, however, the rosettes in the centre of the octagons can be related to those on Chelaberd rugs and also to those seen on Karabagh rugs with triple medallions, such as 102 and 107; the conjunction of bright pink and red is also a Karabagh characteristic. Wherever the rug comes from, however, it is a striking example of Caucasian village weaving. Second half of the 19th century.
213 x 121 cm

154 A very attractive rug with a polychrome octagonal lattice on a dark blue field; such a composition is, of course, found on Kazaks, such as 78, and the zigzag leaf-and-calyx border is also typical of Kazaks. One fascinating design feature, however, is that within each octagon is a cruciform rosette identical to those found at the centre of the main medallions on Chelaberd or 'Eagle Kazak' rugs from Karabagh. The colour of this piece, combined with a certain eclecticism of design motifs, suggest a Gendje provenance, although both the Kazak weaving area and Karabagh are almost equally strong candidates. Late 19th century.
233 x 158 cm

153

154

142 GENDJE

155

156

155 Another lattice rug, with conjoined hexagons containing stars. In various forms, this is one of the most ancient of central Asian carpet designs and can be found on rugs depicted in European paintings of the 15th century, some of which, scholars have argued, may have been of Caucasian origin. The border design is typical of Gendje rugs; Murray Eiland, in *Oriental Rugs* (pl. 155b) illustrates an example with an almost identical field composition, reciprocal *medachyl* borders and cotton wefts, which is attributed to 20th century Talish. Late 19th century.
250 x 112 cm

156 An attractive rug, the main interest of which lies in the fact that it is dated 1876 in the top right corner by an Armenian weaver. It may be from the eastern Caucasus, the shrubs within the lattice being very Daghestan-like in appearance. But for the date, I would not have thought it so early, although it is very well drawn.
250 x 112 cm

157

158

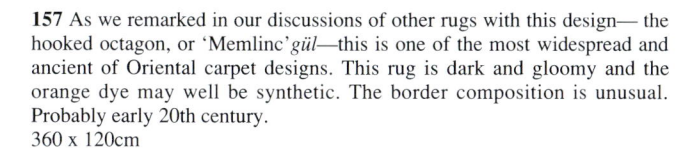

157 As we remarked in our discussions of other rugs with this design— the hooked octagon, or 'Memlinc' *gül*—this is one of the most widespread and ancient of Oriental carpet designs. This rug is dark and gloomy and the orange dye may well be synthetic. The border composition is unusual. Probably early 20th century.
360 x 120cm

158 A distinctly more attractive example than the previous piece and one which once again employs the hooked octagon or 'Memlinc' *gül* (so called after its appearance on rugs in paintings by the 15th century Flemish artist Hans Memlinc) most frequently associated, in the context of Caucasian rugs, with pieces attributed to Moghan (cf. 204-206). Once again the main guard borders have the distinctive vine meander seen previously on 55, 125 and 153, rugs catalogued as Kazak, Karabagh and Gendje respectively, and which can also be seen on the Talish rug 179. In colour, this piece resembles 155, although in some respects the latter seems more typically Gendje (if 'typical' is not a somewhat misleading adjective in this context). For the present rug, I prefer a more easterly attribution.
Probably early 20th century.
260 x 131 cm

159 For a full discussion of rugs with this design, see the two rugs catalogued as Kazak (63 and 64). The diagonal arrangement of the three trees is unusual but personally I can see no reason why this and 160 should be catalogued as Gendje rather than Kazak, although I am well aware that others may disagree. It is certainly one of the most handsome examples of its type but is not particularly early. Probably late 19th/early 20th century.
220 x 155 cm

160 Although there is little difference in the drawing of the trees, a comparison between this piece, with its beautifully drawn minor ornaments and border and clear colours, and 64, with its muddy colours, harsh synthetic dyes, stereotyped field ornaments and very clumsy border, is almost an object lesson in how to distinguish a good old piece from a fairly modern one. The age difference is just over 50 years and, although the degeneration is not as marked as that which has taken place between tribal and village rugs of the early 20th century and those which are produced today, we can see signs which are clearly symptomatic of the decline of an indigenous weaving tradition. In my opinion this rug is Kazak, a view supported by the English sale room catalogue when it was sold here. With its date of 1282 A.H. (A.D. 1866) it is the earliest documented example of the Kazak tree design known to me. The border design is found on a number of south Caucasian/north-west Persian flat-woven artifacts, but is also associated with certain south-west Persian tribal weavings, particularly those of the Afshar.
218 x 154 cm

'TREE OF LIFE' RUGS GENDJE 145

160

146 GENDJE — 'TREE OF LIFE' VARIATIONS

161

162

161 A similar array of birds and animals to 152. On a dark blue field, the design of this piece strongly suggests a totemic origin, with highly stylised birds and animals flanking the tree of life. The main border, with its stepped cruciform medallion apparently derived from kilim border designs, has been encountered before, e.g. the Chondzoresk Karabagh no. 81 and, in arrow-head form, another Karabagh no.115. There is, however, something a little unbalanced about the ratio of width to length – the piece is missing its guards at either end and even such a slight loss as this can make a considerable difference to a rug's equilibrium. I am not sure of the attribution, Kuba being a more tempting suggestion; certainly rugs of this design are usually attributed to this region and I see no reason why this piece should be considered of a different group to 313, which it closely resembles. However, I have seen rugs of this design which are certainly of south western origin— for instance the splendid Kazak example sold by Rippon Boswell in London in November 1980. Late 19th or possibly very early 20th century.
286 x 100 cm

'TREE OF LIFE' VARIATIONS

162 Another variation on the tree-of-life motif with an ascending design of shrubs related to 161 and 164, and also to 'Kuba' rugs such as 313 and 328. The origin of the design can probably be found in the all-over directional shrub carpets of Safavid Persia, a design which then spread to Moghul India. The design is on a red ground and we should not ignore the close affinity between these pieces and the 'Tree' Kazaks, an affinity seen particularly strongly in this example. Late 19th/early 20th century.
208 x 116 cm

163 An interesting and unusual design which is probably a highly stylised version of the tree of life. Trees of similar form are found on Yomut Turkoman asmalyk (camel flank hangings). Within the white branches we can see the repeated 'S' motif which is, perhaps, the most famous ornament associated with the Gendje rugs but not, of course, exclusive to them. Probably early 20th century.
240 x 130 cm

164 A piece with many design features which would normally be found on a rug with a north-eastern provenance. The colours, which are most attractive and include a striking light blue field, are again the factors which suggest a Gendje origin, although I am inclined to favour an attribution to the Shirvan/Kuba region. Probably early 20th century.
257 x 107 cm

148 GENDJE — BOTEH RUGS

165 Five rugs illustrate that most ubiquitous of Oriental carpet compositions, the overall diagonal *boteh* design. If we compare this example to the Karabagh no. 111, it will be immediately apparent that, in terms of design, there is little to distinguish one from another. No. 165, however, has the range of bright colours associated with Gendje rugs and also uses the interlocking border motif which is seldom, if ever, found in Karabaghs. Probably 19th century.
358 x 103 cm

166 Another *boteh* rug, the individual motifs being angular and hexagonal in form. Again the polychromy of the design suggests a Gendje rather than a Karabagh origin. Late 19th/early 20th century.
265 x 82 cm

167 An attractive rug with many animals flanking the *boteh* which are here of diamond form and arranged in horizontal rows with diagonal colour changes. The border design has clear affinities with that found on many Talish rugs although the minor borders as well as the overall tonality of the piece suggest that this might be a Kurdish rug, or one woven under strong Kurdish influence. Late 19th/early 20th century.
289 x 101 cm

168 Although the palette of this rug is not unpleasing the design itself is a little stiff. The inner and outer minor borders contain the same floral meander discussed in connection with the somewhat atypical Karabagh no. 121 and the main border design, a version of the leaf-and-calyx, is drawn in a manner which does not seem particularly characteristic of the Gendje version. It is possible that this piece may have been woven by Kurds from the Caucasian/Persian border area. Late 19th/early 20th century.
292 x 107 cm

165

166

BOTEH RUGS GENDJE 149

167

168

170 A rug with very attractive colours (note in particular the light greens and blues). The diagonal stripes contain small polychrome stars, a not unusual alternative to the Gendje 'S' motifs, although an attribution to Shirvan or Kuba may be possible. Late 19th century/early 20th century.
234 x 112 cm

169

170

169 To the majority of people experienced in Caucasian rugs, a design of diagonal stripes of contrasting colours, each stripe containing small repeated floral or geometric ornamentation, is the one they would suggest if asked to name what a typical Gendje rug looked like. This piece is fairly unusual in its filler ornaments consisting of myriad tiny dots, but is otherwise typical of a late Gendje rug. Probably early 20th century.
260 x 120 cm

171 A typical long Gendje rug with contrasting stripes containing 'S' motifs. The crab border is also found on Kazak weavings. The piece has superb colours and bears a date which may be interpreted as 1264 A.H. (A.D. 1847), surprisingly early but not unbelievable. The colour range and motifs are similar to those on Shahsavan tribal rugs from Moghan.
378 x 112 cm

172 The field design is similar to that of the previous piece but here we have the stepped cruciform kilim border. In colour it has that predominantly pink look which is characteristic of some Karabagh rugs. Although the colours are mellow, and the piece seems of good age, it is unlikely to be as old as 171; like that piece, however, this, too, has a 'tribal' look about it and may also be by the Shahsavan tribe, although possibly from further south, near the Persian border.
263 x 100 cm

DIAGONAL STRIPES GENDJE 151

171

172

Talish

The Talish weaving area is the most south-easterly district to which Caucasian rugs are attributed. It was originally part of the Safavid province of Azerbaijan and now forms part of the Soviet Socialist Republic of Azerbaydzhanskaya. The principal town is the port of Lenkoran, about 40 miles north of the present Iranian border, to which are attributed a specific group of Talish rugs with characteristic medallions.

Most Talish rugs have a long narrow format. The composition, called *met-hane*, consists of an open dark blue – more rarely red or green – field with an inner frame of either a continuous zig-zag meander or a *medachyl*. The field is usually surrounded by a white-ground main border flanked by two red minor borders and, quite often, an additional outer border. The most characteristic main border design consists of a series of large rosettes flanked by four small squares.

Although not unique to Talish – examples from Karabagh, Kazak and Gendje are known – the plain open field, *met-hane*, sometimes embellished with either one or two scattered elements, is the design most often associated with this area. However, many Talish rugs also have lattice or diagonal striped designs such as those we have encountered previously in rugs from Karabagh and Gendje. The almost invariable border design is interesting; it would seem to derive quite unequivocally from what Charles Grant Ellis called the 'frozen border' found on many central Persian 17th century 'vase' carpets, which may well have been woven in Kirman. This particular type of rosette, however, has been used on many different types of rugs from all over the Near East and is found being used as a carpet motif at least back to the 16th century and as a motif in architecture and metalwork considerably before that.

In his book on Caucasian carpets, Jean Lefevre remarked that "a number of known examples of Talish weaving have inscriptions in Farsi, pointing clearly to a Persian connection." However, only one inscribed and dated Talish open field rug is known to me, the extraordinary example sold by Lefevre himself in November 1976; this rug, which had a beautiful blue-green field with a marked *abrash*, had a square white-ground cartouche in the centre with a long Farsi inscription and the date 1267 A.H. (A.D. 1850). Such a rare occurrence cannot be taken as proof that Talish rugs were woven by peoples of Persian origin or that they somehow represent an isolated group within south/south-central Caucasian weaving. In Raymond Benardout's book, for instance, there is illustrated an obviously old Talish with a red lattice field which bears a long Armenian inscription. It should be remembered that there has been a large Armenian population in the Talish area for centuries — a cathedral was built there by Grigor Mamikonian between A.D. 662 and 685.

Roger Gardiner, in his Canadian collections catalogue, makes the interesting point that open field Talish rugs are generally more finely woven than examples with designs in the field and suggests that the *met-hane* composition was first introduced at the end of the 19th century, probably by Western merchants, to replace the indigenous weaving style of the more coarsely knotted pieces with field ornamentation. This contradicts the usually held view that the original rugs had plain fields, which were then decorated at the insistence of Western merchants. Gardiner's case is not altogether convincing; of the 50 Talish rugs for which I have structure notes,

173 Although typical in most respects, this piece has unusual features, one of which is the appearance of 'tuning fork' ornaments between the three groups of four small squares in the upper border. It also lacks an outer reciprocal border, although the selvedges of this rug have been replaced and it is possible that this outer border was once present. However, the piece has an unusual inner reciprocal border, slightly narrower than the outer red guard, which itself is quite wide. Since the colour and general appearance of this piece indicate a reasonable age, it may be slightly older than the main group of *met-hane* rugs, which would explain some of the idiosyncrasies of its design. Probably late 19th century.
183 x 93 cm

30% have knot counts of over 1,500 per sq. dm (98 per sq. in.); of that 30%, the ratio of plain field pieces to decorated field pieces is approximately 60:40. The presence of the date on the Lefevre piece suggests that the open field design is the older (and also refutes Gardiner's statement that Talish rugs are never dated).

However, the age of Talish rugs does represent something of a puzzle. If we compare 174 to 184, the stylistic features, leaving aside the presence or absence of field decoration, is remarkably similar. Although this may, of course, be a symptom of a highly insular tradition which changed little over the years, I am inclined in part to agree with Gardiner and say that the majority of the pieces illustrated represents a late 19th century commercial development. Certainly if we compare these pieces to the Lefevre dated rug, the latter seems to have an overall strength of composition and a more delicately constructed series of border ornaments than do any of the pieces from this probably later group. Something of this delicate quality can be seen on our 181 (which, however, is almost certainly not Talish), although 182-186 return to the more pedantic style. The appearance of more dated examples would give us a better idea of comparative chronology.

In structure, Talish rugs usually have a wool warp, although in quite a high proportion—probably between 40% and 50% — the weft may be either cotton or a mixture of cotton and wool. The warp is usually undyed wool Z2S and the weft is dyed red-brown wool or undyed ivory wool, Z2S; cotton wefts are usually undyed, Z2S. The edges are normally of overcast red or blue wool, around either 1 or 2 warps. The knotting is, for south Caucasian weaving, quite fine, counts rarely dropping below 900 per sq. dm (58 per sq. in.), averaging around 1,200 to 1,400 per sq. dm (77 to 90 per sq. in.), and sometimes going as high as 2,000 per sq. dm (129 per sq. in.). The pile is of medium length, and usually of glossy, almost silky, appearance. In length, most open field Talish rugs are between 8 and 9 feet (243-274 cm), although rugs up to 12 feet (365 cm) long are known. However, perhaps the most consistent feature is the ratio of width to length. Of some 100 pieces either examined or seen recorded in the literature, all fell into the bracket 1:1.9—1:2.5, with the majority between 1:2 and 1:2.2; it was interesting that when the ratio rose above 1:2.5, one was generally dealing with a rug, the attribution of which to Talish was, in any case, doubtful.

174 Here we have what is in every respect a typical Talish—even the width/height ratio of 1:2.15 is exactly what we would expect. Although well drawn and with a good spacing of the border design, this rug has a somewhat stereotyped appearance and a probable late date is reinforced by the orange shade used. However, rugs of this composition, whatever their age, are among the most powerful and impressive examples of 19th-20th century Caucasian village weaving. One of the symbolic interpretations of rug design put forward by Professor Schuyler Cammann and others seems to have a particularly forceful relevance to rugs of this type, the field itself resembling heaven, with the *medachyl* frame acting as a protective barrier between this world and the next. Probably late 19th century. 213 x 99cm

175

175 Another typical example, almost identical to 174; however, note the tiny irregular ivory centred red diamond in the field, with a few tiny specks of red elsewhere. It has been suggested that this is a typical weaving conceit to destroy the otherwise immaculate blue surface, which smacks of the perfection of work allowed only for Allah. Late 19th/early 20th century.
231 x 109 cm

176

176 This piece has the border rosettes repeated in the field, a most unusual compositional feature. However, once the field becomes ornamental, these rugs lose much of their individuality. This piece has an all-wool foundation and may contain a synthetic dye. Probably early 20th century.
245 x 108 cm

177 I am a little doubtful as to the attribution of this piece. The main border elements are unusually crude, the field is uncharacteristically narrow and the proportions (1:2.66) atypical. The combination of a Talish-type format with many non-Talish features is suggestive of a Gendje origin. It may, however, simply be rather poor work by an apprentice weaver. Difficult to date, but could be as late as the early 20th century.
275 x 103 cm

177

178 Another typical Talish, probable late, but with that hint of majesty which so distinguishes this group. The small animal at the bottom of the field may serve the function suggested for the diamond and red flecks on no. 175. Late 19th/early 20th century.
226 x 114 cm

178

156 TALISH

179 This and the following rug, which have a similar all-over field design of small stylised shrubs, lack the strength of the previous examples. This piece has an unusual dark blue on red minor border on the outside flank of the main border, with a floral meander close in style to Kurdish rugs (a design previously encountered on a number of pieces attributed to different regions). It has cotton wefts, and may be a piece in Talish style but woven elsewhere. Late 19th/early 20th century.
266 x 112cm

180 Although this rug, too, has an all-over field composition of tiny flowers, the borders are more typically Talish, both in design and colour. It is interesting to note, however, that very few of the non so-called *met-hane* rugs appear to have *medachyl* frames to the field. Unfortunately the poor quality of the colour reproduction does not give a clear picture of the piece. Probably late 19th/early 20th century.
262 x 105 cm

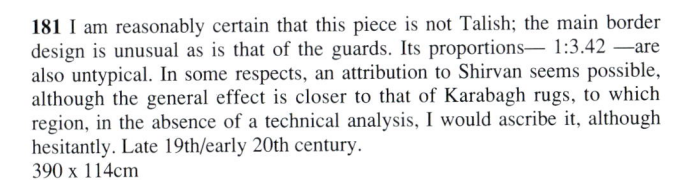

181 I am reasonably certain that this piece is not Talish; the main border design is unusual as is that of the guards. Its proportions— 1:3.42 —are also untypical. In some respects, an attribution to Shirvan seems possible, although the general effect is closer to that of Karabagh rugs, to which region, in the absence of a technical analysis, I would ascribe it, although hesitantly. Late 19th/early 20th century.
390 x 114cm

182 A typical piece with small stars, one of the most usual compositions when the field is ornamented. However, this is one of the few examples with decorated fields to have a *medachyl* frame. An attractive piece, with good clear colours. Probably late 19th century.
240 x 112 cm

158 TALISH
LATTICE RUGS

183

184

183 This and the following two pieces have lattice designs, this example with shrubs, the other two with stylised *boteh*. 'Talish' rugs with blue minor borders are rare, and the proportions are atypical for Talish and more characteristic of Gendje rugs. Late 19th/early 20th century.
311 x 110 cm

184 This piece has a most unusual red-ground main border and dark blue minor borders. Again, I am not convinced of its Talish origin. The yellow-ground lattice field pattern with its geometric, but well drawn, *boteh* seems more Gendje, or even Karabagh, in style. Probably late 19th century. Some examples have been seen probably dating from as late as the 20th century.
217 x 107 cm

185 This piece has the stepped cruciform motif in the main border which we have encountered on Gendje rugs and it also lacks the usual outer border. However, the style and the colour indicate that it is from the same area as the previous piece, and of the same date.
211 x 100 cm

Lenkoran

A distinctive group of Talish rugs are named after the south-east coastal town of Lenkoran. They are distinguished primarily by their design, which consists almost always of two or more large horned medallions on the vertical axis. These medallions are derived from dragon rugs and, indeed, it requires no great leap of the imagination to see the close connection between Lenkoran medallions and the pair of outward-facing dragons flanking palmettes, after which the group of Caucasian rugs made from the late 16th to the 18th centuries is named. On later rugs of the transitional or floral type, made probably in the 18th century, this dragon and palmette arrangement has been reduced to a single outward curving white bar surrounding an octagon, almost exactly the motif associated with Lenkorans and, of course, one which, in more stylised form, can be seen at either end of the so-called Kasim-Usag rugs previously described. The bars which are usually found between the medallions on Lenkoran rugs, and which end in a 'St. Andrew's cross' arrangement, are thus the highly stylised remains of the serrated-leaf lattice which once adorned the field of dragon rugs.

Not surprisingly, the structure of Lenkoran rugs is indistinguishable from the main body of Talish rugs previously described, although a smaller proportion seem to have been woven with cotton wefts. The knot count is usually around 1,000 to 1,200 per sq. dm (64 to 77 per sq. in.). The surface appearance of the pile is also similar, the wool of middle height and with a soft, silky feel. A few examples, however, seem to have a heavier, shaggier pile, although there seems to be no appreciable difference in age. To judge by the examples with large quantities of synthetic dyes, Lenkorans with almost unchanged designs seem to have been woven well into the 20th century.

186 A typical design, with three large medallions. The lightish colours, however, including a striking blue and mid-green, are unusual; the outer *medachyl* guard, although of typical design, is brightly coloured. Late 19th/early 20th century.
246 x 134 cm

187 Another typical rug, although the three medallions have four arms and thus cease to resemble the original dragon and palmette motif. However, a hexagon or octagon with four radiating leaves is a common motif on 18th century floral carpets and can be clearly seen on a large example in the Ulu Cami at Divrigi in Turkey (Yetkin, op. cit. vol. 1, pl. 43). Late 19th/early 20th century.
381 x 161 cm

188 Another typical Lenkoran with the more attractive dragon and palmette medallion. The drawing, however, is somewhat skimpy and crude. Late 19th/early 20th century.
262 x 114 cm

189

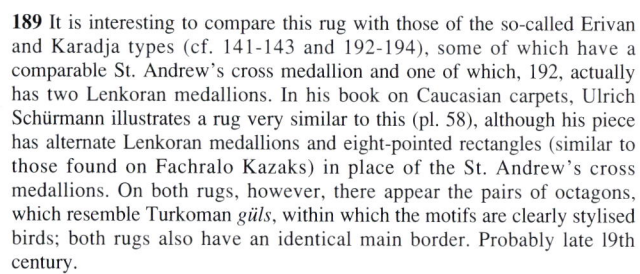

190

189 It is interesting to compare this rug with those of the so-called Erivan and Karadja types (cf. 141-143 and 192-194), some of which have a comparable St. Andrew's cross medallion and one of which, 192, actually has two Lenkoran medallions. In his book on Caucasian carpets, Ulrich Schürmann illustrates a rug very similar to this (pl. 58), although his piece has alternate Lenkoran medallions and eight-pointed rectangles (similar to those found on Fachralo Kazaks) in place of the St. Andrew's cross medallions. On both rugs, however, there appear the pairs of octagons, which resemble Turkoman *güls*, within which the motifs are clearly stylised birds; both rugs also have an identical main border. Probably late 19th century.
283 x 105 cm

190 (detail). Although this piece substitutes the Lenkoran motif for the St. Andrew's cross medallions of the previous rug, it has an identical border system, the same Turkoman minor *güls* and the same kilim-like cross motifs down each side of the field, motifs which are echoed in the main border. There can be little doubt that both pieces are from the same area and of roughly the same age.
298 x 107 cm

191 Although a bold and striking use has been made of the Lenkoran motif, this rug has a very different look to the previously illustrated pieces. Roger Gardiner, in *Oriental Rugs from Canadian Collections*, illustrates a piece of the same type (no. 38), although with a leaf-and-calyx main border and linked S guards; it also has diamond-like flower sprays in place of the *boteh* seen on our rug. Both, however, have the same shade of pinkish-red. In the Gardiner example this dye has bled and he suggests that this is due to inexpert mordanting (a phenomenon also associated with red-wefted Qashqa'i rugs from south-west Persia), although the use of a synthetic dye, either alone or in combination with madder, should not be discounted. As to their place of origin, Murray Eiland, in *Oriental Rugs* (no. 156), illustrates another related piece, but with typical Gendje octagon borders; there is little doubt in my mind that one should think in terms of the early 20th century for most examples of this type.
187 x 125 cm

Karadja

The carpet trade rejoices in imposing upon itself such a weird and wonderful assortment of names—real and imaginary—that confusion is bound to reign. In the present context, I can do no better than to quote the American author Murray Eiland: "Karadja rugs should not be confused with those labelled 'Karadje' or 'Karadj', although with some justification they may be called 'Karadagh', a term referring to the region just south of the Araxes, opposite Soviet Karabagh". In other words, Karadja rugs are, strictly speaking, Persian and not Caucasian. The oldest, or what appear to be the oldest, have an all-wool foundation and fine lustrous wool; it is thought by many people that those which are cotton wefted are late in date (cf., however, the note to 97) — they are certainly much more coarse in handle.

192 This piece and the following two are closely related in design and are probably part of the older Karadagh group which Eiland suggested may have been woven by nomads in the Caucasian/Persian border area, although the larger sizes of all these pieces indicate a more sedentary group. This rug has, at either end, a particular form of medallion associated principally with Lenkoran rugs from the most south-easterly of the Caucasian weaving areas, Talish. Probably late 19th century.
350 x 105 cm

193 On this piece the Lenkoran medallions have changed into a type reminiscent of that rather strange group of striped pieces (cf. in particular 120). There are also star medallions which are like distant echoes of the medallions found on the great star Ushak carpets from 16th and 17th century Turkey. Probably late 19th century.
357 x 100 cm

Far left and left: typical Karadja medallion and motif.

194 This piece has attractive white-ground minor borders containing floral meanders, which lend a dramatic contrast to the dark blue of the field and deep red of the border. It is the most pleasing of the Karadja rugs we illustrate and, although it is impossible to be accurate about the age of any of them, no. 194 is probably the oldest. Second half of the 19th century.
340 x 110cm

166 MOGHAN

Moghan

Moghan is a hilly district to the west of Talish just above the Persian border, although once, of course, part of Persia; it is one of the few areas in the Caucasus in which true nomadism was practised. The rugs associated with it come in a number of different styles, as can be seen from the following illustrations, although three are particularly well-known — the stylised version of the medallion and bar (199-200), the hooked octagon lattice (204-206) and the Chajli, with three or more large squarish octagons on the vertical axis (207-209). Field designs with variations on the hooked diamond are also encountered frequently (195, 196, 201, 202 and 203).

A frequent border design is the polychrome interlock which we have seen on a number of south Caucasian rugs but which is particularly associated with the northern Caucasus. In this context, and in others, the dated rug illustrated as 198, is a fascinating documentary piece of considerable importance in the discussion of Caucasian village weaving.

196 The stencil S border is not typical nor is the format. Late 19th/early 20th century.
155 x 129 cm

195

195 A number of rugs with a design of conjoined diamonds on the vertical axis are attributed to Moghan, although only an analysis of their structure can properly decide whether they should be given as Kazak, Gendje, Moghan or even Karabagh. This piece has the polychrome interlock border particularly associated with Moghan rugs, although it is not unknown on both Kazak and Gendje examples. Murray Eiland, in *Oriental Rugs* (fig. 150) reproduces an example with an almost identical field design, although the zig-zag portions of the red field are filled with flower-heads seen in the outer guard of our rug, the main border containing a different floral pattern, and the guards a highly simplified rendering of the leaf-and-calyx. Eiland attributes his rug to the Karabagh, a possibility we should not exclude. Late 19th/early 20th century.
221 x 114 cm

196

In structure, Moghan rugs differ from most other Caucasian weavings in that a fairly high percentage have cotton warps and wool wefts. When the foundation is all-wool, the wefts in apparently old pieces are dyed blue. They are also comparatively finely knotted—of all the examples for which I have records, and the attribution of which to Moghan is not in doubt, none fall below 960 per sq. dm (62 per sq. in.), the largest number have between 1,050 and 1,250 per sq. dm (67 and 81 per sq. in.) and a not inconsiderable number have knot counts as high as 2,000 per sq. dm (129 per sq. in.).

197 An atypical example. The medallions on the pale yellow field are obviously related to the palmettes on the so-called Kuba kilim (cf. 452) but are also found in almost identical versions on rugs attributed to Shirvan (cf. in particular 225). The pale colours of this piece—especially the beautiful and rarely encountered yellow field—are not typical of Moghan rugs and the same might be said both of the field design, the border drawing and the small square format—indeed, as far as I am concerned this is difficult to attribute to Moghan. An attribution to Kazak is possible, or to Gendje, or even to Shirvan itself. An examination of the structure would help in making a firmer attribution. Late 19th century.
146 x 119 cm

198 This is a very beautiful and important rug. It is inscribed and dated 1275 A.H. (A.D. 1858/9) and thus, like the apparently unique dated Talish mentioned in connection with the previous group, can give us some insight into the development of the style. The first thing to notice is the plethora of ornaments both in the field and borders — small *boteh*, flowers, shrubs, vines and meanders are everywhere with a few small animals thrown in for good measure. The design of the main border is perhaps the most interesting feature, however. In his discussion of this design on a Shirvan rug dated 1321 A.H. (A.D. 1903/4), Roger F. Gardiner (op. cit., p.58) writes: "The white main border displays a particularly dynamic pattern which carries the graphic idiom of eastern and north-eastern Caucasian rugs to its extreme. It appears to be composed of tiny triangles hung together on hooks, illustrating the degree to which a running vine pattern could be reduced through progressive geometric stages to a complex, abstract, linear design. This border is further complicated by the addition of tiny angular 'bird' silhouettes to the triangle (although they are upside down in relation to the rug) and the addition of 'horns' to the connecting hooks, suggesting that the weavers perceived these motifs as animal heads." The use of this particular border design is widespread throughout the Caucasus; among the rugs we illustrate it is encountered in one form or another on Gendjes (164, 165), Moghans (195, 198, 203) and Akstafas (217, 218, in the second of which the bird silhouette referred to by Gardiner can be clearly seen), as well as Shirvans (225, 240, 257, 263, 281, 282), Kubas (393, 402) and the so-called Lesghistan rugs (436). It is also related to the almost equally widespread S border — e.g. the Karachov no. 29 — to certain other interlocking designs and to the double T border — e.g. the Karachovs 34 and 35 — and to the umbrella border — e.g. the Karachov 36. For all these designs an ancient totemic origin of pairs of birds seems the most likely interpretation, certainly more likely than an original floral meander. Schuyler Cammann argued, perhaps less convincingly, for such a derivation for even so apparent a floral design as the misnamed Persian 'turtle' border and we know from the development of the dragon design into a floral pattern that, over the years, animal motifs have a habit of changing into apparently floral ones on Oriental carpets. In the present rug, one of the earliest dated examples attributed to Moghan known to me, and one of the earliest, if not the earliest dated example with this particular border design, the side borders are drawn quite unequivocally as pairs of addorsed birds of the same colour, even though the end borders slip into the abstraction we see on all the other examples mentioned above. It may be that this rug, which is probably at least 20 years earlier than the other examples we illustrate with this design, is a rare example of nomadic tradition continuing long past the time when, logically, we would expect it to be dead. It would certainly seem to leave the origin of this particular border pattern no longer in doubt. This piece has a cotton warp and wool weft (which contradicts the oft-made suggestion that the introduction of cotton into the structure is a late, commercial feature) and is finely woven. Related to 201 and probably from Shirvan.
264 x 124 cm

199 This and the following rug both show designs of large cruciform medallions with bar appendages. Such designs show strong Turkish as well as Persian influence. This piece has the hooked Memlinc gül associated with Moghan rugs in particular and is probably not of great age. Late 19th/early 20th century.
190 x 98 cm

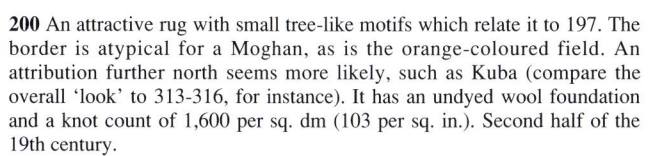

200 An attractive rug with small tree-like motifs which relate it to 197. The border is atypical for a Moghan, as is the orange-coloured field. An attribution further north seems more likely, such as Kuba (compare the overall 'look' to 313-316, for instance). It has an undyed wool foundation and a knot count of 1,600 per sq. dm (103 per sq. in.). Second half of the 19th century.
312 x 129 cm

201 A somewhat problematic rug which I would prefer to attribute to Shirvan. Note how the interlock border has been further reduced to a series of arches surmounted by hooks. The striped-meander minor borders are unusual features. Late 19th/early 20th century.
180 x 115 cm

202 A beautiful prayer rug with an ivory ground, a piece which, although not necessarily very old, would certainly cause a stir among collectors of Caucasian carpets. However, an attribution to Shirvan seems more appropriate. Probably late 19th century.
131 x 84 cm

203 A piece of the type more usually attributed to Lenkoran. This example has particularly beautiful colours. Second half of the 19th century.
268 x 108 cm

HOOKED DIAMONDS

MOGHAN 171

202

203

204 A rug with the hooked Memlinc *gül* in an octagonal lattice, the design most frequently attributed to Moghan, although many examples are more obviously of Kazak origin. Compare this and the two Kazaks 65 and 71. The somewhat subdued colour range, the long format and the drawing of the motifs within the hooked octagons suggest a Moghan rather than a Kazak origin for this piece. Late 19th/early 20th century.
372 x 135cm

205 A rug with a single vertical row of Memlinc *güls* and with a beautiful bright colour range; this latter feature, in the absence of structural evidence to the contrary, seems quite clearly to indicate that the piece is of Kazak origin. Second half of the 19th century.
215 x 130 cm

206 This is a beautiful example of the Memlinc *gül* lattice which, to judge by the asymmetry of the design, in the right-hand portion of the field, is either the work of a novice weaver or of a genuine nomadic tradition. The piece has particularly beautiful colours and is obviously of some age. Mid- to late 19th century.
252 x 137 cm

207 The first of the so-called Chajli rugs, with a design of four octagons instead of the more usual three. This example has a somewhat cluttered composition. Probably first quarter 20th century.
385 x 120 cm

208 The white and red ground colours for the octagons and a dark blue field are almost unchanging features of Chajli rugs. The motifs within the octagons are quite clearly anthropomorphic and hark back to a totemic origin. Late 19th/early 20th century.
228 x 116cm

Chajli

Although placed wiehin the Moghan section, many authorities, including Schürmann, prefer to place these carpets within the Shirvan orbit. Like the previously described group of Moghan rugs, they are often found with cotton warps or wefts. Chajli rugs seem to have been popular in Europe, as a number of examples can be found in paintings and photographs of interiors from the 1870s onwards. In the absence of early dated examples, however, I am not convinced that any of them are of great age, and the continuance of the design in an only slightly altered form is shown by examples with dates in the 1920s and 1930s.

209 Although only slightly larger than the previous rug, the spacing of the composition on this piece is far more accomplished and the drawing is clearer. Of the three Chajli design rugs we illustrate, this one is probably the most beautiful. Probably last quarter of the 19th century.

Akstafa

The name Akstafa has become entrenched in popular carpet literature to describe in particular rugs with a composition of large, fan-tailed birds, probably meant to represent peacocks, flanking a vertical series of large, squarish eight-pointed stars. On the basis of structure, colour and some strong similarities in compositional details, a small number of prayer rugs have been added to this group.

There is only one place in the Caucasus named Akstafa, a fairly large town in the Kazak weaving district near Lambalo and Shulaver. The majority of so-called Akstafa rugs, however, are structurally uncharacteristic of Kazak weaving but are strongly allied to those from the Shirvan district in the central east coast area; indeed, few, if any, writers have ever queried Shirvan as their place of origin. Quite how the name Akstafa came to be applied to rugs of this type is not clear. However, I have retained it, albeit reluctantly (no author likes to perpetuate myths unnecessarily) simply because it has become a convenient adjective which immediately conjures up a mental image even for those with only the most superficial knowledge of Caucasian rugs.

However, there are one or two slight problems. In his catalogue *Shirvan and Related Weavings from the North Caucasus*, published in 1978, the English dealer Richard Purdon remarked of a rug (no. 11) in his possession: "The design is often copied in other parts of the Caucasus." This would suggest that there are a number of rugs with the Akstafa design but with such marked structural differences as to make a common place of production unlikely. In fact, the majority of Akstafa rugs have undyed brown and white Z2S wool warps, natural white Z2S cotton wefts and sides of two cords of two warps with blue cotton wrapping. Knot counts range between approximately 1,150 and 1,950 per sq. dm (74 and 126 per sq. in.). A few examples are recorded with warps a mixture of undyed wool and white cotton and I know of two pieces which, apparently, have all-wool foundations.

continued on p. 179

210 In every respect a typical Akstafa. Apart from the large fan-tailed birds, there is a wide variety of animal and bird figures, including, above the bottom pair of large birds, what appear to be double-headed camels with riders. Note the presence of vivid light green and turquoise, colours often found in Akstafas, especially in the borders. However, the crowded composition and stiff drawing suggest a fairly late date, towards the end of the 19th century.
243 x 119 cm

AKSTAFA 177

211 Some Akstafa rugs, such as this example, have more realistically drawn birds, with well-defined legs, feet and beaks. This piece has two pairs, at top and bottom, which would appear to have their fan-tails closed. This rug may be older than the previous piece.
290 x 125 cm

212 Another typical example, although the presence of only two star medallions is a little unusual. Again a plethora of animal and bird figures can be seen, as well as two small human figures. Probably late 19th century.
220 x 103 cm

178 AKSTAFA

213

213 Although the pairs of bird-like creatures which appear on this rug seem to relate it to Akstafa rugs, its length and its border design are both atypical and the rug is probably from the Kazak region.
334 x 121 cm

214

214 Another atypical piece with a complete absence of any obvious animal or bird figures. The motifs seen between the two large medallions strongly resemble those found on pile-knotted rugs attributed to the Kuba region of the north-east Caucasus, particularly to the so-called 'Zejwa' type; but the resemblance is perhaps most strong to the motifs found on Shirvan pile rugs, for instance our 248, and kilims. Note the unusual leaf-and-calyx border. Probably from around the turn of the century.
300 x 143 cm

Akstafa continued

Although I do not place total reliance on the structure analysis of these two all-wool foundation pieces, both are of sufficient interest to merit further comment. The first was illustrated in Albert Achdjian's book *Le Tapis*, and was catalogued as 'Shirvan, 18th century'; compositionally, it was unremarkable except for a leaf-and-calyx border which, according to Roger F. Gardiner in his Canadian catalogue, who in turn was quoting Walter B. Denny, is not usually found on rugs of the Akstafa group. However, one exceptionally interesting feature of the Achdjian rug is that it is the only published example with a date, which can be read clearly as 1334 A.H. (A.D. 1917). This rug serves a useful yardstick with which to measure other pieces of the same type.

The introduction of cotton to many groups of traditionally all-wool Caucasian rugs is frequently taken as an indication of late date; as a general statement, however, this concept is probably unsupportable. Nevertheless, in that the majority of Akstafa rugs are cotton-wefted, the Achdjian rug, with its late date, might lead one to assume that all rugs of this type with wool warps and wefts are also late. It is for this reason that the second all-wool Akstafa known to me is so interesting. This piece is illustrated in Coen and Duncan's *The Oriental Rug* (plate 74). It has an unusually low knot count— 868 per sq. dm (56 per sq. in.) and, at 350cm (11ft. 4ins.) is also remarkably long. However, it is superbly drawn, has majestic spacing and beautiful colour; indeed, it has all the hallmarks of a very old rug of high quality. It has an unusual series of borders, the main ivory-ground one having a design of hexagons containing 'S' motifs, with small starred octagons between, a composition which would seem to be a more sophisticated rendering of a common Akstafa border design (cf. 210, 211, 212, 216, 219, 220 and 221).

Compositionally, there is no reason to suppose that either the Achdjian or Coen/Duncan rugs are not Akstafa but the presence of the leaf-and-calyx border on the former and the low knot count of the latter, coupled with the all-wool foundation of both, may possibly indicate a different weaving area from the main body of rugs with this design. They may have been woven in Gendje or even the village of Akstafa itself, since their structure is perfectly in accord with a Kazak origin. Nevertheless, it has to be said that these are hypotheses, the resolution of which requires further research.

We illustrate also three prayer rugs attributed to the Akstafa group, two of which—219 and 220—have the lattice design endemic to Shirvan prayer rugs in general. The majority of examples attributed to Akstafa have a large lattice with serrated edges, which are obviously highly stylised leaf forms and may, once again, be distant relatives of the large serrated-leaf lattice of 'dragon' rugs. The ground colour of these Akstafa rugs is invariably dark blue.

215 The large birds on this unusual white-ground piece are reduced to serrate-edged figures which seem to have a closer resemblance to stylised caterpillars or even dragons. The zig-zag border is more common as a minor border design in Caucasian rugs. These points might suggest a relatively late date, but on the other hand the colours are good. One would like to see the piece before being too dogmatic about its age.
212 x 91 cm

180 AKSTAFA

216 Another typical Akstafa. A minority of examples have one pair of birds, usually the top pair, woven upside-down in relation to the rest of the field. There seems to be no obvious reason for this and it spoils the symmetry of the composition. Probably late 19th century.
315 x 117 cm

217 This and the following piece have the same small, squarish format, similarly drawn birds and large quartered diamonds in the medallions. They also have the 'interlock' borders, which are not usually found on Akstafa rugs. Late 19th/early 20th century.
180 x 111 cm

218 This piece has considerable charm. The pair of realistically drawn camels with riders in the centre diamond is a particularly attractive feature. Probably late 19th century.
182 x 124cm

182 AKSTAFA PRAYER RUGS

219

220

219 The first of three Akstafa prayer rugs we illustrate is a lattice design, related closely to Shirvan and Daghestan prayer rugs. The borders are typical.
185 x 97 cm

220 Another handsome prayer rug. The motifs with red and white diamond appendages which appear in the top row of the lattice are found on many tribal and village pieces throughout the Caucasus, Turkey and Iran. Probably made around the turn of the century.
180 x 95 cm

221 An attractive rug. Like the two previous examples, it lacks the large birds typical of Akstafa rugs. It is worth noting that a prayer rug with birds and a leaf-and-calyx border is illustrated in Spuhler, König and Volkmann's *Alte Orientteppiche* (no. 62). Second half of the 19th century.
157 x 80 cm

221

Shirvan

Shirvan is one of the principal weaving areas of the Caucasus, stretching from the central east coast some three or four hundred kilometres inland. Located within it are several towns which, according to Kerimov and Schürmann, have become associated with particular designs; these include Bidjov, Marasali, Khila, Surahani, Baku and Saliani. Many authors also include Chajli and Akstafa rugs, although we have included the former with Gendje pieces and the latter have been treated as a separate sub-group. There are, of course, many rugs which, both structurally and stylistically, can be assigned with some degree of confidence to Shirvan but not to any particular place within it (although many authors and dealers would maintain that it is possible to differentiate, again on structural evidence, between rugs from the north and south of the region).

The main problem is to separate Shirvan rugs from those made in the more northerly Kuba and Daghestan districts. Since the designs of many of the latter are very closely allied, it has been possible to make distinctions only by a close comparison of weaving methods. The principal differences which have been found between the groups are these: the backs of Shirvan rugs tend to be flat and those of Kuba and Daghestan to be ribbed, due to uneven warp tensions; secondly, the edges of Shirvan rugs are usually overcast in white cotton and those of Kuba and Daghestan in blue cotton (wool is sometimes used in both cases). The incidence of cotton wefting, which is certainly greater in eastern than western Caucasia, is not much of a taxonomic tool; it is sometimes held that there are more

222 Typical Shirvan field design of a tight floral lattice. The main border is, of course, ubiquitous. Probably from the Kuba area in the second half of the 19th century.
290 x 137 cm

cotton-wefted Shirvan than Kuba rugs but, although this may be true as a very general statement, there are many cotton-wefted rugs from Kuba and very many wool-wefted ones from Shirvan. Rugs with brocaded ends are often considered to be of southern origin but there are many examples with such work which, in all other respects, would seem to have originated in the north, so this feature also should not be regarded as decisive.

However, having given some indication of the differences which are sometimes said to exist between north- and south-east Caucasian weaving, it has to be said that there would appear to be as many exceptions as there are adherents. Any number of north-east rugs will be found with white cotton overcasting as there will Shirvan rugs with blue (almost all Akstafa rugs, it should be noted, have their sides overcast in blue). In other words, all that it is possible to say is that a flat-backed, whitesided rug is probably from the south and a rib-backed, bluesided rug is probably from the north, but they may not be. Only experience and a certain acquired instinct can make one reasonably certain about groups, but there are many examples —especially, it would seem, among prayer rugs—about which there is seldom any unanimity of opinion.

One should also note that, although many writers suggest that silk is often found in the foundation of east Caucasian rugs, its use is, in fact, exceptionally rare; moreover, from the examples I have seen, its use is not confined, as is sometimes said, to very old pieces but can be seen on rugs which, in every other respect, seem quite late.

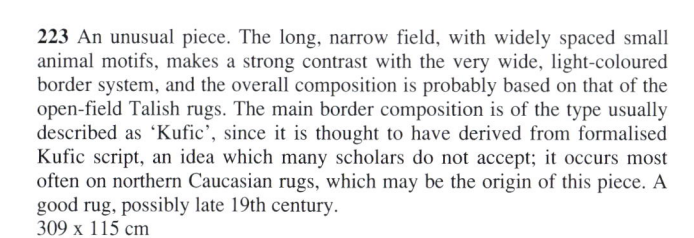

223 An unusual piece. The long, narrow field, with widely spaced small animal motifs, makes a strong contrast with the very wide, light-coloured border system, and the overall composition is probably based on that of the open-field Talish rugs. The main border composition is of the type usually described as 'Kufic', since it is thought to have derived from formalised Kufic script, an idea which many scholars do not accept; it occurs most often on northern Caucasian rugs, which may be the origin of this piece. A good rug, possibly late 19th century.
309 x 115 cm

186 SHIRVAN　　　　　　　　　　　　　　　　　　　　　　　　　　WHITE GROUND PRAYER RUGS

224

225

WHITE GROUND PRAYER RUGS

224 This white-ground prayer rug has a system of large stylised shrubs within a serrate-edged lattice, the latter probably derived from leaf forms. Ascending shrub designs are often found on Safavid Persian rugs but more often on 17th and 18th century pieces from India and East Turkestan. This very attractive example has several small animals in the field. Second half of the 19th century.
163 x 76 cm

225 On this piece, the palmettes have been so highly stylised that they resemble huge insects. The 'interlock' border is not often found on prayer rugs of this type. Not perhaps the best drawn example. Late 19th/early 20th century.
190 x 91cm

226 Very similar in design to 224. The serrate-edged lattice, which may be connected to the huge serrate-edged leaf lattice of 17th and 18th century 'dragon' carpets, is found in very similar form on many Persian tribal rugs, principally those of the Baluch. The large, geometric floral motifs seem related to the equally stylised lotus palmettes of 18th century Caucasian 'shield' carpets, which may be from Shirvan. Second half of the 19th century.
154 x 83 cm

227

228

227 A rug with a cramped composition, compared with the previous example. The field motif, a hooked diamond, is often called the 'tarantula' in popular literature, a piece of romantic nonsense. Note the two hands in the spandrels. Probably late 19th century.
183 x 107 cm

228 A very attractive hexagonal lattice containing flowering shrubs, the whole strongly reminiscent of Mogul Indian design. Late 19th century.
166 x 96 cm

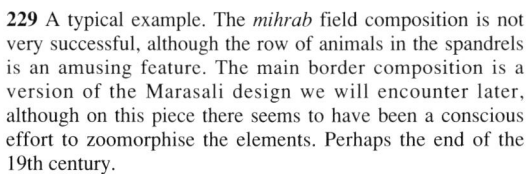

229 A typical example. The *mihrab* field composition is not very successful, although the row of animals in the spandrels is an amusing feature. The main border composition is a version of the Marasali design we will encounter later, although on this piece there seems to have been a conscious effort to zoomorphise the elements. Perhaps the end of the 19th century.
164 x 99 cm

230 Another typical east Caucasian prayer rug, which in many books is as often called Daghestan as Shirvan and which only advanced technical expertise, coupled with considerable experience, can differentiate, and even then more subjectively than objectively. Most examples have either an ivory or yellow field. The border design, which probably represents the final, highly stylised degeneration of a once flowing floral meander, is typical. Most rugs of this type are fairly finely woven, with between 1,300 and 2,200 knots per sq. dm (84 to 142 per sq. in.). This rug has *boteh* similar to those found on so-called Marasali rugs. It probably dates from the second half of the 19th century.
170 x 89 cm

Marasali

A specific group of rugs, most usually prayer rugs, is attributed to Marasali, a village some fifty kilometres south of Shemakha. A wide variety of dates is found on published examples, ranging from the last decade of the 18th century to the second decade of the 20th. As we have encountered previously on other groups of Caucasian village rugs, what evidence as there is to be gained from a study of dated pieces suggests that so-called Marasalis maintained a fairly consistent standard of quality well into the 20th century. There seems to be very little structural difference between examples with early 19th century dates and those dated a hundred years later. Murray Eiland has suggested that only the later examples have cotton wefts, although this is countered by the example in the Straka collection dated 1233 A.H. (A.D. 1818), which has white cotton wefts.

Among the earliest dated examples are those in the Metropolitan Museum (ex Ballard collection), dated 1223 A.H. (A.D. 1808/9), and the Straka piece mentioned above. We illustrate an example apparently dated 1211 A.H. (A.D. 1796/7), although I doubt this — the date seems to be indecipherable. The same is true of the example (no. 236) described by one authority as being dated 1216 A.H. (A.D. 1801/2). The date on no. 239, interpreted as 1225 A.H. (A.D. 1810/11), does seem to be in the 1220s (A.D. 1805-1814), although the last digit is open to doubt, and this piece has a weft which is a mixture of wool and cotton.

continued on p. 192

231 This tight and overcrowded piece has the typical colour range of the so-called 'black' Marasalis, the majority of which are prayer rugs, although a small number of secular examples are known. The equine-like motifs in the main border, resembling knights on a chessboard, facing alternately left and right, are characteristic features of this group and their presence on a white ground constitutes what has become known in the trade as the 'Marasali' border. The origin of the motif may be a realistic floral meander but the resemblance to birds, which is stronger on some rugs, especially the triangular-shaped heads, suggests that this may be a highly stylised rendering of an heraldic bird motif, possibly an eagle (indeed, dealers of an older generation sometimes refer to this composition as the 'parrot' border). Probably mid-19th century.
143 x 114 cm

232 Another characteristic piece, which is dated 1304 A.H. (A.D. 1886/7), which there is no reason to doubt. It certainly looks considerably later than 231.
130 x 110 cm

233 This is the 'classic' type of 'black' Marasali prayer rug, the large **boteh** with their multifarious polychrome interiors and zig-zag frames standing out like flashing lights on the deep midnight blue of the field. These pieces are usually finely woven in a soft velvety wool. The date on this rug has been interpreted as 1211 A.H. (A.D. 1796/7), which would make it the oldest documented example of its type. However, although the rug, both in the *mihrab* arch and in the upper borders, shows an inscription, I do not believe that any date can be read accurately. There is some evidence to suggest that this piece is not as old as either the Straka or Metropolitan Museum examples; the floral elements of the Metropolitan's minor guard borders, which have become slightly stylised on the Straka rug, have here become reduced to simple crosses between upside-down 'ticks'. It should be noted that the *boteh* on 'black' Marasali rugs are invariably free-standing; pieces with other ground colours — ivory, yellow, red — almost always having a diamond lattice within which the *boteh* are usually arranged in chromatic patterns.
140 x 99 cm

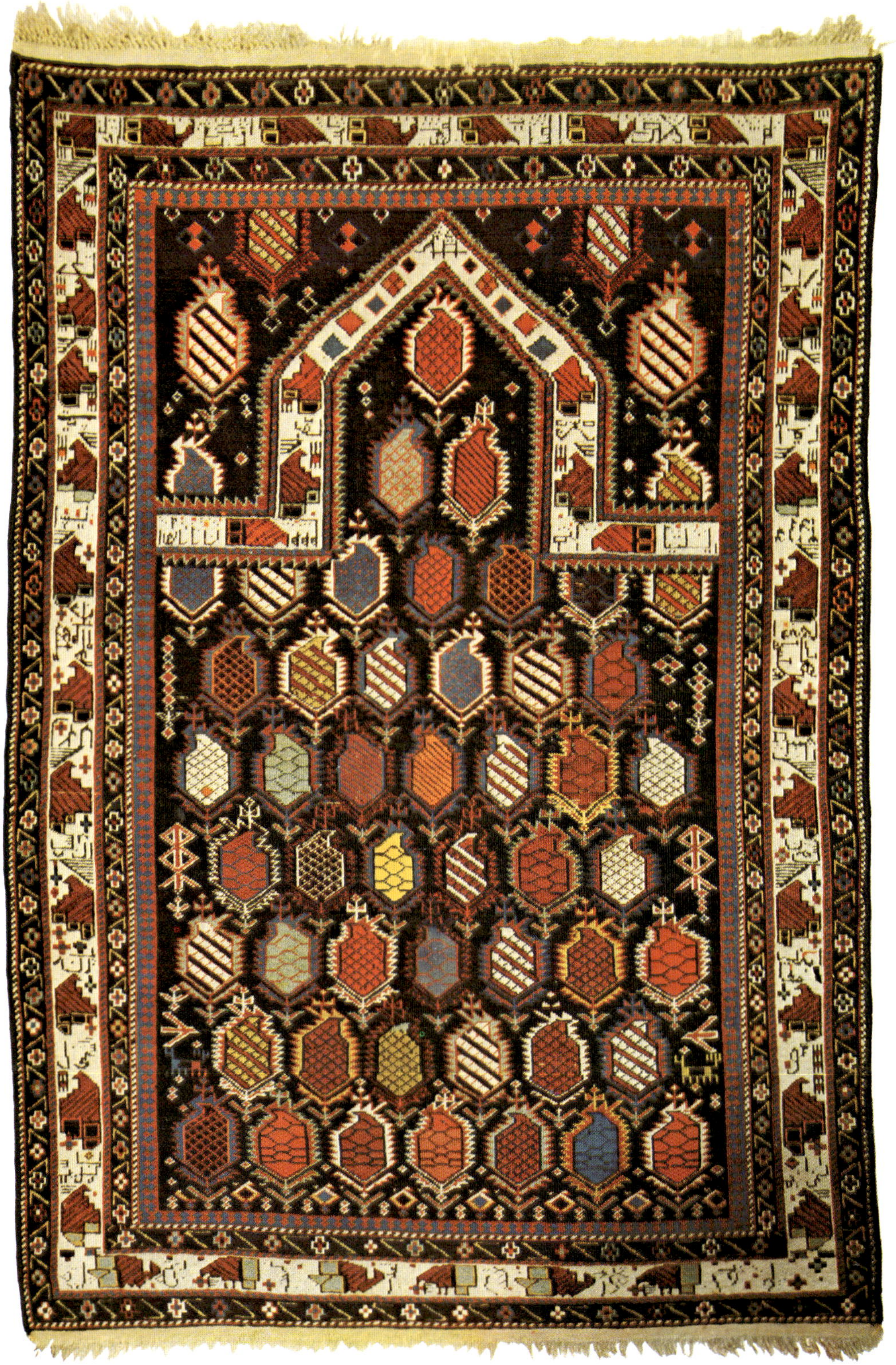

233

Marasali continued

Interested readers are invited to compare these apparently very old pieces with the white-ground rug sold by Sotheby's in London (12th October, 1978, lot 129), dated 1307 A.H. (A.D. 1889/90), the 'black' Marasali sold by the same auctioneers (24th March, 1978, lot 48), dated 1325 A.H. (A.D. 1907/8), the odd 'black' Marasali illustrated by Arthur Gregorian in *Oriental Rugs and the Stories they Tell,* which has a man on horseback either chasing a deer or being accompanied by a dog, which is dated 1310 A.H. (A.D. 1892/3), the example illustrated in Peter Bausback's 1973 catalogue (p.115), which has a peculiar 'Chinese' border and is dated 1332 A.H. (A.D. 1913/14), or, finally, the very fine example illustrated by Raymond Benardout in his book *Caucasian Rugs,* which is dated 1320 A.H. (A.D. 1902/3). A close comparison between the 'early' and 'late' pieces will confirm what I have said about the surprising continuity of quality over a comparatively long period and makes one consider the authenticity of dates in the late 18th or early 19th century with some suspicion.

The majority of Marasali rugs, like the majority of Shirvan rugs, have cotton in the foundation, usually in the wefts, and have a comparatively high knot count, another characteristic of Shirvan weavings in general. From published statistics, there would appear to be a surprising range of knot counts; one of the most finely woven is the 'black' prayer rug in the Straka

continued on p.194

234

234 Was it not for the Marasali border elements in the arch of the *mihrab*, it is probable that this piece would have been described as Daghestan. The main border, with its composition of conjoined diamonds each containing a double latch-hook, is typical of yellow-ground prayer rugs; two other examples will be found in the Straka catalogue, nos. 103, dated 1233 A.H. (A.D. 1817/8) and 104. The latter piece has large diamond-shaped flowers and not the angular *boteh* of the present rug and Straka no. 103. However, like the present rug, Straka no. 104 has an unusually placed animal at the top left-hand corner of the main border; on our rug, the animals appear in single *boteh* in the spandrels. Straka no. 103 has no animals. Straka no. 103, with its early date, has wool warps, cotton wefts and a knot count of 1,705 per sq. dm (110 per sq. in.); no. 104 has an all-wool foundation and a knot count of 1,535 per sq. dm (99 per sq. in.). Stylistically, the present piece is closer to Straka no. 103, and is certainly of good quality and age.
134 x 109 cm

235 This very beautiful piece has wool warps, white cotton wefts and the sides are two bundles of two warps overcast in white cotton, the usual finish for a Marasali (although wool overcasting is sometimes found). It has a high knot count. The layout of the flowers on the field of this piece is almost identical to that of Straka no. 104. Both have a block of red and white flowers within the arch, below which the ornaments are arranged both stylistically and chromatically in a chevron pattern pointing downwards. The present rug has the 'Marasali' border more commonly associated with 'black' pieces, whereas the Straka rug has the linked diamond border. The outer guard of the present piece, with its composition of angular linked 'S' motifs is more satisfactory than the somewhat skimpy flowers which appear on the Straka rug; it is interesting to note that the latter has wool wefts and the present piece has cotton and, despite the argument put forward by some writers that cotton-wefted pieces are later, the fine quality and drawing of our rug strongly suggest that it is at least as old, if not older, than the Straka piece. Probably mid-19th century or earlier.
168 x 122 cm

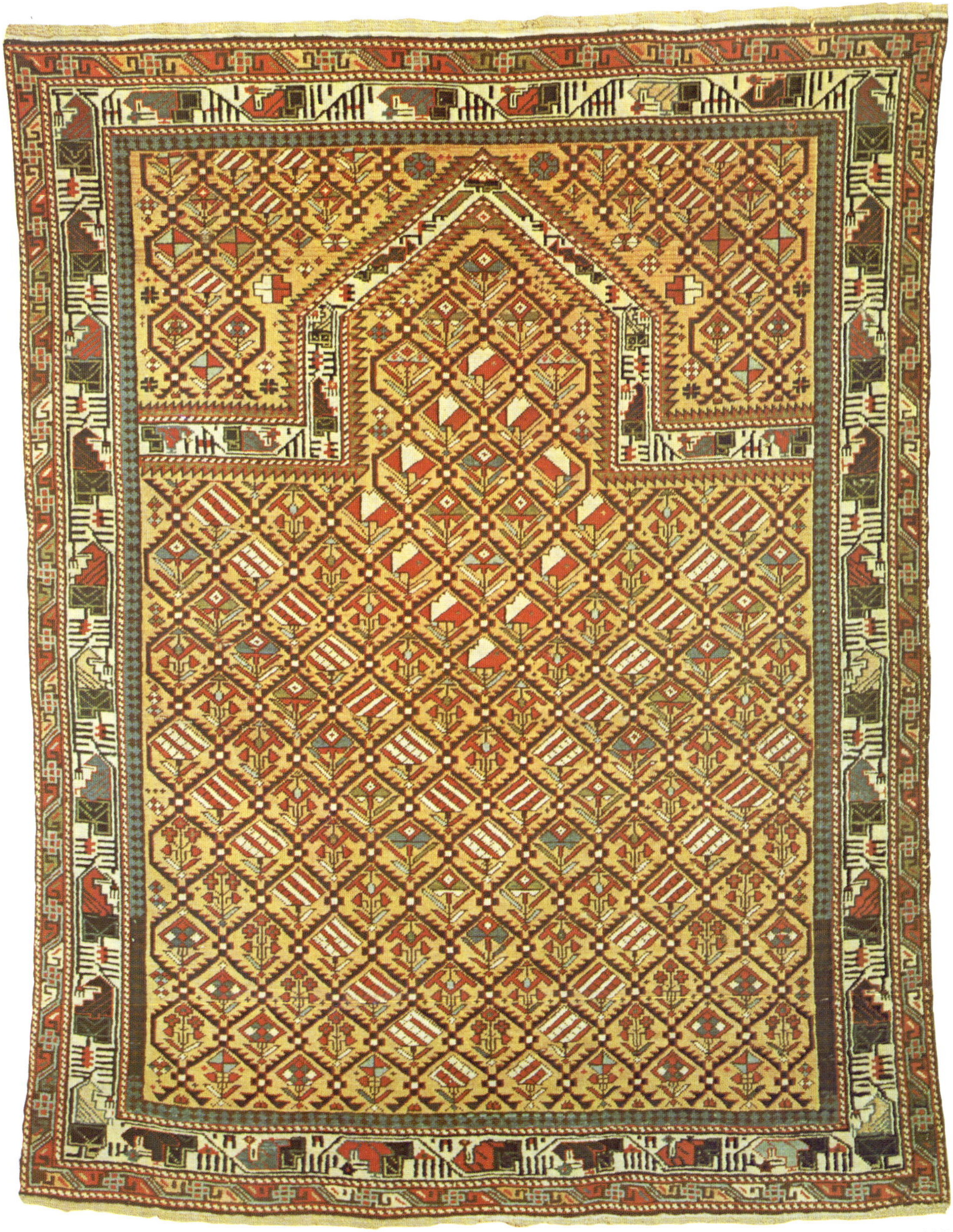

235

236 *(facing page and detail below)* This is an exceptionally beautiful piece, apparently dated 1216 A.H. (A.D. 1801/2), a very early date which, it seems to me, is impossible to decipher clearly from the inscription which appears on the rug. I might add that one or two of the colours, notably the orange which appears inside some of the flowers, look a little suspicious. However, the combination of a rich red field (and Marasali prayer rugs with red fields are very rare), brilliant white border and the two dark blue guards framing the *mihrab* arch, create a most striking yet harmonious effect, as does the diamond pattern created by the flowers in the field. The piece has exceptionally well-drawn 'Marasali' borders and the extraordinary bright blue line of flowers in the spandrel creates a remarkable sense of restraint and tension. Altogether a fine and most interesting piece.
124 x 100 cm

Marasali continued
collection, which has an all-wool foundation and a knot count of 4,456 per sq. dm (287.5 per sq. in.). This should be compared to the Metropolitan Museum 'black' Marasali dated 1223 A.H. (A.D. 1808/9) which also has an all-wool foundation and 3,255 knots per sq. dm (210 per sq. in.); an undated 'black' Marasali illustrated by Peter Bausback in his 1978 catalogue, which has wool warps and cotton wefts, is apparently woven with 4,000 knots per sq. dm (258 per sq. in.).

These pieces represent the highest grade for fineness of weave. At the other end of the scale, there is the 'black' Marasali illustrated by Roger Gardiner in his catalogue *Oriental Rugs in Canadian Collections* (no. 29), which has 1,302 knots per sq. dm (84 per sq. in.) or the yellow-ground, cotton-wefted example in the Straka collection dated 1233 A.H. (A.D. 1817/18) which has a knot count of 1,705 per sq. dm (110 per sq. in.); this latter piece, if the date is to be believed, indicates that neither fineness of weave nor an all-wool foundation are necessarily characteristic of early weavings from Shirvan.

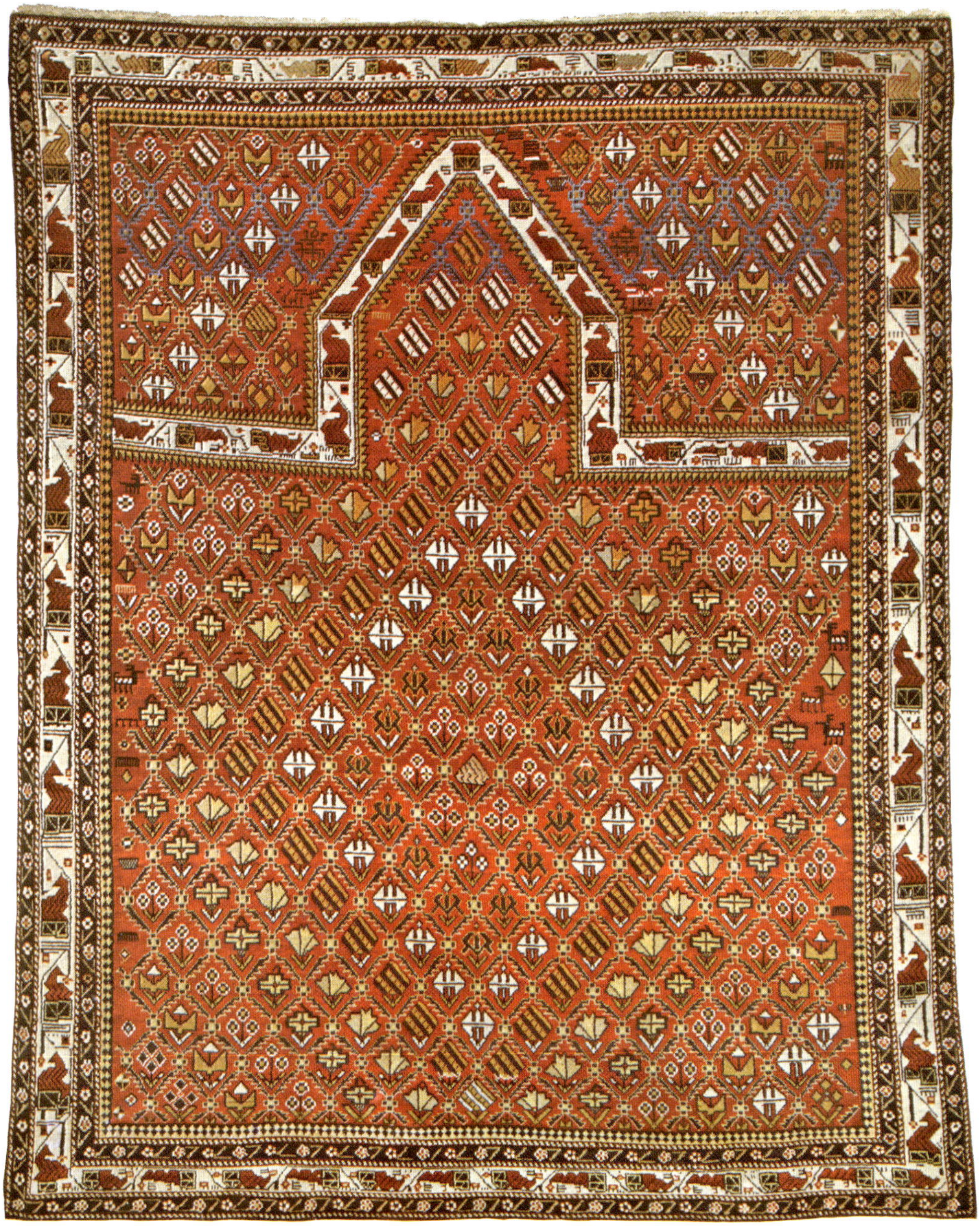

236

196 SHIRVAN — MARASALI

237

238

237 This piece makes an interesting contrast with the previously described prayer rug. It has an ivory coloured ground, with red main border and *mihrab* arch; the inner *medachyl* guard has an extraordinarily vivid shade of blue, present also in some of the flowers, and there are a few other rather weird colours, including what would appear to be a washed-out mauve in the right-hand border. In its compositional elements, the piece is rather a disappointment; the 'Marasali' border design, which appears in the *mihrab* arch, is poorly drawn and seems only half understood, the composition of the main border and flanking guards are weak, and the arrangement of the flowers on the field into two alternating diagonal lines is undynamic. The piece is cotton wefted. Late 19th/early 20th century.
190 x 150cm

238 Another late piece, attractive—as are all Marasali rugs—but of no outstanding merit. The starred octagon borders are unusual, and the handling of the 'Marasali' border motif in the arch is a little perfunctory. Late 19th/early 20th century.
182 x 117cm

239 Another white-ground prayer rug. Although it has the 'Marasali' border, it has a flat-topped *mihrab,* a most unusual feature for rugs of this type. It has wool warps, mixed cotton and wool wefts. The borders aside, the piece is atypical of Marasali rugs in general, the three large medallions—one in each spandrel and the other within the *mihrab*— being features the like of which are rarely encountered on Marasali prayer rugs; the random arrangement of flowers within the field lattice is also uncharacteristically clumsy. The piece is apparently dated either 1225 A.H. (A.D. 1810/11) or 1220 A.H. (A.D. 1805/6).
165 x 117 cm

239

240

241

240 The only secular rug of the group. The *boteh* are somewhat squashed and the interlock border is not very often found on rugs attributed to Marasali. The piece is cotton wefted and, although probably of Shirvan origin, may not be Marasali. Note the tiny animals, birds and a solitary human figure in the field. Late 19th/early 20th century.
177 x 110 cm

241 A secular rug similar in feel to the previous piece. The chromatic double zig-zag in the field lattice heightens the dramatic impact of what would otherwise be a somewhat boring design. Apparently dated 1305 A.H. (A.D. 1887/8), which seems acceptable.
130 x 92 cm

242 The field has rows of shrub-like flowers arranged without a lattice on an attractive yellow ground. The main border composition and that of its flanking guards are sometimes found on Shirvan rugs which, from other indications, would appear to be late in date. A rug with an identical border system is illustrated in the catalogue of *The George Walter Vincent and Belle Townsley Smith Collection of Islamic Rugs* (pl. 40). Around the end of the 19th century.
151 x 96 cm

242

200 SHIRVAN

243

244

243 The 'lotus' palmettes of this piece, with their arrow head tops, are not only found on many Caucasian rugs but also on several groups of Persian tribal weavings (they are called 'bouquets' by the Baluch). From the geometric arrangement of flower forms seen on this and closely related pieces, it is possible to assume that what is being attempted is a stylised rendering of several different varieties of flower—Kerimov, for instance, illustrates several closely related designs which he calls variously 'cotton ball', 'Pomegranate flower', 'Starwort', *et al*. However, such names may represent the weaver's ignorance of the original motif and were probably mere fanciful suppositions on her part. This piece retains the guard borders of the previous piece but the main border composition is a somewhat botched version of the standard Caucasian floral border. Towards the end of the 19th century.
150 x 96 cm

244 This would seem to be the stylised palmette which Kerimov calls 'Pomegranate flower'. The linked and stepped medallions of the border are sometimes seen as separate motifs arranged in the field in place of floral motifs. This rug probably dates from about the turn of the century.
126 x 97 cm

245 This rug, with its polychrome palmettes well spaced on a white ground, has great subtlety of colour. However, the dark blue-ground main border and its flanking guards are heavy, clumsy and crudely drawn, spoiling the visual impact of the piece. Probably late 19th century.
141 x 102 cm

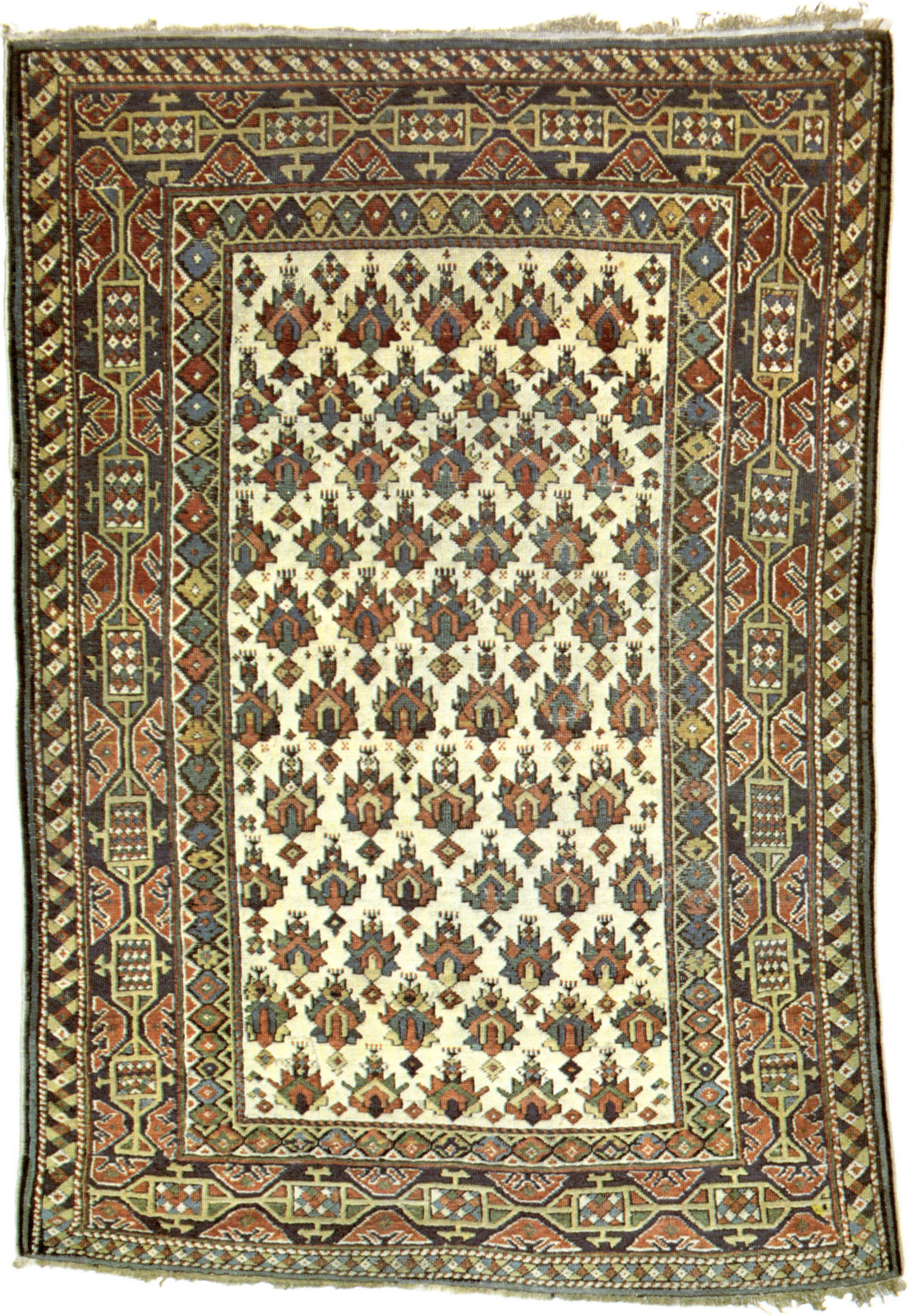

245

202 SHIRVAN

246

247

246 Something of an odd-ball. The stiff, abstracted, design suggests that this is a late piece. Late l9th/early 20th century.
205 x 110 cm

247 An unusual rug, which is close in composition to certain Turkish village products. Not particularly attractive. Note the lack of an outer guard, which is how the piece was woven; Schürmann illustrates a somewhat similar piece (pl. 135) which he attributes to Derbend in the Kuba area. Probably towards the end of the 19th century.
147 x 85 cm

248 An attractive and unusual piece in which one of the most famous of kilim designs is transferred to the pile-knotted medium. The flat-woven rugs of this design are normally attributed to Kuba, although Jenny Housego, in her book *Tribal Rugs,* illustrates an example (pl. 20) which, she suggests, has several design features more reminiscent of Azerbaijan weaving. There are a number of extant photographs of kilim of this design being used as covers for open ox carts in Georgia, as well as photographs of them being sold by rug dealers in the same area, such pictures dating from around the turn of the century; these photographs suggest a more northerly origin than Azerbaijan and a more westerly one than Kuba. Another pile-knotted rug with this field design is illustrated in the catalogue *Oriental Rugs from Canadian Collections* (pl. 22); this latter piece has the same guard border composition as our 242, 243 and 247, but has a wide main border with the Kufic composition, in contrast to the more kilim-like composition found in the main border of our piece. The Canadian rug is attributed to Daghestan or Kuba, an attribution which is, perhaps, more acceptable for the present piece. It has attractive colour, although is somewhat spoiled by the overall pinkish tone in the lower half. Compare the border composition with that on the kilim 446 and the field composition with no. 453. It is difficult to be definite about dating without examining this rug. I have seen some similar examples which were as recent as late 19th century.
163 x 118 cm

248

Detail of 248

204 SHIRVAN

249

250

249 A somewhat crude prayer rug. The inscription and date within the cartouche are almost illegible, although the date would appear to be 1305 A.H. (A.D. 1903).
140 x 90 cm

250 A very attractive small mat, very similar in design to 252. The bold floral composition of the main border is not only attractive but very interesting; it appears in almost identical form on many Baluch rugs, usually of good quality and attributed to the Mashed area of Iran. It can be seen on a Marasali prayer rug illustrated in *Oriental Rugs from Canadian Collections* (pl. 29). Probably late 19th century.
143 x 122 cm

SHIRVAN 205

251

252

251 A very attractive but otherwise undistinguished rug with a linked diamond lattice. Late 19th/early 20th century.
270 x 160cm

252 A very similar rug to 250. Late 19th/early 20th century.
146 x 126 cm

206 SHIRVAN — FLOWER SHIRVAN

253

254

FLOWER SHIRVAN

253 This and the following two rugs forms part of a well-known and popular group of 'flower Shirvans' which have large star-like polychrome flowers free-standing on a dark blue ground. This piece, with its Kufic borders, is very similar to an example in the Metropolitan Museum (Dimand, fig. 235); this latter piece is wool wefted, however, while the present piece has cotton wefts. As is usual, the flowers are arranged chromatically in diagonal rows. Dated 1875.
267 x 122 cm

254 A less inspired example than the previous piece, with small tight flowers and a leaf-and-calyx border. The missing outer minor border unbalances the composition. Probably late 19th century.
395 x 103 cm

255 This handsome piece has an all-wool foundation and a finely knotted pile. The attractive main border composition is unusual and, like the Kufic type, is reminiscent more of rugs of a north-east Caucasian origin. Very beautiful colouring. Many of the 'flower Shirvans' are very long, this piece being an example. Mid-to late 19th century.
426 x 117 cm

256 This and the following five rugs represent a well-known type of Shirvan carpet composition which has rows of stepped-edged and conjoined hexagonal motifs arranged in a single vertical row, with a flattened, saw-edged medallion at either end of the row; the latter motif has been related by some authors to ancient Egyptian and Persian Royal insignia. On some examples, such as that illustrated in Raymond Benardout's *Caucasian Rugs* (p.51), large saw-edged medallions are found in a single vertical row, with small hexagons at their centres. In general, these rugs, like the previously described 'flower Shirvans', are long and narrow. Usually they have all-wool foundations and are slightly ribbed at the back, suggesting a provenance to the northern part of the Shirvan area, an idea borne out by their resemblance to so-called 'Zejwa' rugs from the area south of Kuba (compare 402-404). As with all generalisations about Caucasian weavings, however, there are numerous exceptions—for instance the cotton-wefted piece with white cotton overcast sides illustrated in Murray Eiland's *Oriental Rugs* (no. 159), the two examples with similar structure in Richard Purdon's *Shirvan and related Weavings from the North Caucasus* (nos. 2 and 3), and the cotton-wefted rug with blue cotton overcasting illustrated in Peter Bausback's 1976 catalogue (p.89). These rugs almost all have dark blue fields with myriad filler ornaments including animals, birds and human figures; a yellow-ground border with linked 'S' motifs is commonly found—a border which, both in colour and design, is also found on north Persian tribal and village rugs (cf. Jenny Housego, *Tribal Rugs*, pl. 82). I know of two published dated examples. The first is illustrated in the Australian Society for Antique Rugs' 1974 catalogue, *Antique Rugs from the Caucasus* (no. 13), with the date read as 1902, although I prefer the reading 1304 A.H. (A.D. 1886/7). The second dated example of this type came to light recently in a provincial auction in England (Elliott and Green, Lymington, 28 June, 1979, lot 363); this had the typical field and 'interlock' border composition, also similar to our 261, was dated 1333 A.H. (A.D. 1914), and was of very good quality apart from the albeit sparing use of synthetic orange and pink. The present rug is very similar to examples in the Metropolitan Museum (Dimand, no. 174) and in Schürmann's book (no. 66). A very good piece, probably late 19th century.
252 x 118 cm

HEXAGON COLUMNS
SHIRVAN 209

Various *gubpa* ornaments

257 The colour reproduction may be misleading; the piece seems to have dark and muddy colours, with a distinctly suspicious orange in the central hexagon (seen also in the borders). Despite this, however, the design is well drawn and with splendid compositional spacing. Late 19th/early 20th century.
210 x 120 cm

257

258 An unusually dark and gloomy example with a western Caucasian floral main border composition. A number of obviously synthetic reds, pinks and oranges can be seen. Probably no earlier than about 1900.
209 x 140 cm

259 A very attractive rug with the leaf-and-calyx border; another comparable example is illustrated in *Oriental Rugs from Canadian Collections* (no. 27). This latter piece has selvedges wrapped in blue cotton and a distinctly ribbed back, features which suggest a more northerly origin; it also has large birds like those found on Akstafa rugs, which also have slightly ribbed backs and blue cotton overcasting on the selvedges (although they usually have white cotton wefts). Probably mid- to late 19th century.
264 x 115 cm

260 This and the following example have 'interlock' borders; on this rug, however, the motif appears in an unusual form on a yellow ground. The myriad animals and birds add an attractive note. Probably late 19th century. 180 x 120 cm

261 This piece has a somewhat more formalised design, with the usual plethora of in-fill ornaments replaced by two flanking rows of flowers of the type found on 'flower Shirvans', with a few scattered floral motifs. Like most examples of this type, it has an all-wool foundation. The typical colours include the vivid light blue which is a particular feature of Shirvan weavings. A very attractive rug. Probably second half of the 19th century. 220 x 116 cm

212 SHIRVAN

262

263

262 Rugs with this large, basically hexagonal medallion containing an elongated octagon with a floral lattice and appendages at either end, are called 'bird Shirvans' in the German carpet trade; yet another meaningless term with which to confuse the lay-person! The motifs within the lattice may be highly stylised birds, but are more likely to be stylisations of the floral motifs seen on many east Caucasian rugs. Each of these ornaments has two tiny bird figures at the top. This example has curious bow-like motifs in the minor borders. It would appear to have good clear colours and, before I realised it was dated, I had assumed it to be early 20th century, the design and drawing being stiff and the overall appearance somewhat mechanical. However, it bears the surprisingly late date of 1343 A.H. (A.D. 1924/5).
205 x 123 cm

SHIRVAN

263 Another example with an almost identical design to 262. Probably late 19th/early 20th century.
212 x 116 cm

264 This piece is unusual in that the floral motifs in the lattice face each other and do not all point downwards. Probably late 19th century.
180 x 107 cm

265 An example with good colours and the inner running dog motif, not usually found used in this way on Caucasian rugs. The white ground main leaf-and-calyx border is almost identical to that on 262. As in other examples, the bird and animal figures in and around the main hexagon are all one way up, thus making the overall composition directional. This piece, like the majority of examples of its type, is cotton wefted and finely knotted. Probably late 19th century.
237 x 131 cm

266 This is a typical example but with a 'Baku' border composition of flowerheads and birds. It is an exceptionally well drawn and designed piece, with a beautiful rendering of the ascending Bidjov design even though, as in other pieces of its type, the colours do not indicate great age. An alternative border is the white and blue Seichur border (e.g. 268) with an outward pointing red 'arrow'. This latter motif is often found on those types of Kuba rugs called 'Alpan' (e.g. our 400, one of the 'Alpan-Kuba' rugs with an ascending 'vase' composition), the group which in many respects seems most closely related to the Bidjovs. It is also seen on 391, an unusual piece which is relatable to 'Bidjov' rugs as well as Baku. The Baku connection is reinforced by the presence on 266 — otherwise a typical 'Bidjov' — of a distinctive border design traditionally taken to be a fairly firm indication of a Baku origin! (Cf. nos. 288, 289, 290 and 305 for 'bird and rosette' Baku borders.) Late 19th/early 20th century.
240 x 124 cm

266

267

267 This piece is badly worn and has lost its bottom border; however, the design is well-spaced. Probably second half of the 19th century.
135 x 89 cm

Bidjov

A particular group of Shirvan rugs is attributed to an area surrounding the town of Bidjov, a few miles north of Marasali. In colour, these pieces may either be fairly sombre or can have a variety of bright colours, somewhat reminiscent of the typical Karabagh palette, on a very deep blue ground. The warps and wefts are normally of wool and the side overcast in either blue, or less often white, wool. The knotting is slightly less fine than for other groups, under 1,550 per sq. dm (97 per sq. in.) and although, as with most Shirvans, the wool is of high quality and clipped short, the handle is firm and sturdy. However, there is considerable variation not only in the delineation of the complex composition but also in knot density, wefting, wool quality, etc. in rugs of apparently similar age; this suggests not one, but many widely scattered places of manufacture.

As with many place names, the attribution to Bidjov is by no means certain; this group as a whole seems closer to north-eastern Caucasian weaving, the backs usually being slightly ribbed and cotton being rarely found in either the foundation or the sides. Indeed, in the literature, any number of rugs will be found attributed to Kuba, Seichur and Derbend which seem part of the same group, and it is probable that the composition was produced throughout the eastern Caucasus.

The design consists of an ascending series of palmettes flanked by large serrated leaves and smaller palmettes. In many respects, it can be linked quite closely with the 'dragon' and 'floral' rugs of the seventeenth and eighteenth centuries, and through them to Persian floral carpets. Indeed, on one extraordinary example illustrated in the catalogue of *The George Walter Vincent and Belle Townsley Smith Collection of Islamic Rugs* (no. 32), connection with the lattice 'vase' carpets of Safavid Persia is clearly stated, the palmettes being transferred into two huge double-ended vases, from each mouth of which grow floral bouquets, all surrounded by an elaborate criss-cross lattice with flowers and palmettes. Three very similar examples are shown by us (391-393) one of which is dated 1312 A.H. (A.D. 1894/5). Only two dated examples are known to me, the first of which is illustrated in Ulrich Schürmann's *Caucasian Rugs* (plate 79); according to the author, the date is 1274 A.H. (A.D. 1857), although the first two digits seem to me to be 13 and the second two are illegible. This would date the piece at the earliest A.D. 1887, which seems more acceptable. The second is our no. 392. Examples are found not only with some of the more usual Caucasian border compositions but also with several less usual varieties, the same being true of 'Bidjovs'. It should be noted that there is one group of rugs attributed to Kuba which seem particularly close in style to rugs of the Bidjov type. This is discussed in the caption for no. 266.

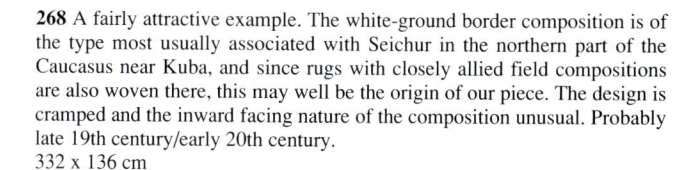

268 A fairly attractive example. The white-ground border composition is of the type most usually associated with Seichur in the northern part of the Caucasus near Kuba, and since rugs with closely allied field compositions are also woven there, this may well be the origin of our piece. The design is cramped and the inward facing nature of the composition unusual. Probably late 19th century/early 20th century.
332 x 136 cm

269

269 There are several Shirvan rugs which seem to have designs based upon *saphs*—multiple-niche prayer rugs. They are obviously too small to have been used as such and it is possible that the proper usage of the design was not appreciated by Caucasian village weavers (many of whom were either Christian or only very peripherally Moslem). Whatever the explanation of their design, these are somewhat quirky pieces. Probably from between the two World Wars.
177 x 128 cm

270

270 Another *saph* Shirvan with many of the same motifs as the previous piece. The chain-like motifs with four 'legs' seen on all rugs of this design have been interpreted by some authors as thrones.
193 x 107 cm

271 Here the reliance on the *saph* design *is* clear, although it would be impossible for six people to pray together on a rug measuring only about 4½ft. by 4ft! Note the row of strange, humanoid, motifs at the top and bottom of the field. The colour, if not the composition and drawing, suggests a slightly earlier date than the previous pieces.
134 x 118cm

271

Baku

Although part of the Shirvan weaving area, the rugs woven in the coastal district around the hook-shaped Apsheron Peninsula are grouped together under the generic heading Baku, after the largest town. The three principal types are Baku, Khila (the most inland village) and Surahani, a village slightly to the north-east of Baku. Ulrich Schürmann also gives a fourth type, which he calls Saliani, after a village seventy miles or so to the south of Baku on the border of the Talish area. So-called Saliani rugs usually have *boteh* as the field decoration, and a piece such as our 181, which we call Talish, might well be described as Saliani by some authors.

As I have emphasised before, however, the names of small Caucasian villages applied to specific designs or groups of designs should not necessarily be considered correct. 'Baku' rugs may well

272 A particular version of the Surahani design which can be related to the composition of Fachralo Kazaks. The leaf-and-calyx border is frequently encountered on rugs of this type. This rug has particularly pleasing colour, heightened by the widespread use of white. Note the colour change from red to blue in the outer 'ribbon' guard at the bottom. Dated 1305 A.H. (A.D. 1887/8).
260 x 105 cm

273 This rug is close to the well-known Surahani type although the octagonal outlines are not present, giving the central medallion a stiff and uninteresting appearance. The main border design is also unsatisfactory. Late 19th/early 20th century.
163 x 118 cm

Baku continued

have been woven in the Apsheron Peninsula area but structurally they are indistinguishable from the main group of east Caucasian rugs attributed to Shirvan (unless it be in their apparently consistent use of an all-wool foundation) and to treat them as a separate entity, although convenient, may be gratuitous.

To Surahani is attributed a particular group of rugs which have a single large vertical medallion with an alternate octagon and rectangular outline (cf. 276, 277, 278, 279, 282 and 283). This design is considered to be a highly stylised rendering of the Safavid garden composition, which is also found on later Persian village and tribal rugs. This would mean that the white 'channels' which frame the large centre medallion and which contain a series

continued on p. 220

274 Very similar in design to 272, although the somewhat fussy nature of the field composition and the cramped border suggest a later date.
300 x 113 cm

275 Another example of the Fachralo type; it has very well drawn animals but is more mechanical and dull in colour than 272. About 1900-1920.
274 x 112 cm

Baku continued

of fin-like motifs (seen, perhaps, most clearly on 277) represent the water channels containing fishes and ducks surrounding islands with trees and flowers, which is the typical lay-out of Safavid gardens.

Why this single group should be singled out to represent a Caucasian version of the Persian garden composition, in preference to several other groups of rugs which have geometric motifs decorated with animals and flowers, it is difficult to understand, especially since the resemblance of these Surahani rugs to Persian garden carpets is, to say the least, superficial. Nevertheless, as a skilful and imaginative interpretation of what would otherwise be an attractive but purely abstract and decorative composition, it is worth recording.

It should also be noted that the attribution of all rugs of this design to the eastern Caucasus is by no means certain, several authors preferring a Kazak origin. Certainly the resemblance of many of them, in particular pieces such as our 276, to the Sewan Kazak group, make the preference for a more westerly origin understandable. Raymond Benardout illustrated a particularly fine example in his *Caucasian Rugs* (p.93), which is dated 1856 of the Christian calendar, something which the author suggests is added evidence of a more westerly, probably Armenian, origin. Rugs of this design, following Kerimov, are also known as 'Ordutch-Konagkend' and are supposed to have been made in Kuba (cf. 333-339).

276 An attractive small piece, with the main medallion surrounded by tree-like elements. The ground of the main medallion is covered with myriad floral motifs of star form, which on some examples are even more realistically rendered. Compare the overall handling of the composition to the Sewan Kazak. The composition of the main border is unusual. Probably late 19th century.
140 x 109 cm

277 A well-defined example of the Surahani 'garden' design. The large rosettes in the guard borders suggest an affinity with Talish designs but in describing a particularly good example sold at auction in England in 1979 (Lawrence of Crewkerne, 22.5.79, lot 423), the cataloguer made the interesting observation that in structure the piece revealed "a strong affinity" with weavings from Shulaver in the Kazak district. Another very similar piece will be found illustrated in the catalogue of *The George Walter Vincent and Belle Townsley Smith Collection of Islamic Rugs* (no. 33), immediately preceding an example similar in format to 276 but with the colour and overall appearance strongly reminiscent of Kazak weaving. Probably late 19th century.
193 x 118 cm

278 Surahani 'garden' designs are often found on carpets of considerable length, of which the present piece, over 13ft., is an example. Again, probably not much more than eighty years old.
396 x 104 cm

279 The first of the Surahani compositions proper. The totemic skeletal figures found within the octagons in the medallions are typical and have a strong Chinese flavour. The dark tonality and fussy composition are of its period. Dated 1312 A.H. (A.D. 1894).
270 x 114 cm

222 SHIRVAN-BAKU

280

281

282

SHIRVAN-BAKU

280 According to Schürmann, strong geometricity of design is a feature of rugs from the Baku district. The present example, on structural grounds, can be assigned to the eastern Caucasus but may be attributed to Shirvan as well as to Baku.
145 x 129 cm

281 A number of Shirvan rugs have features which suggest a more westerly origin and the rule with these, as with other indeterminate Caucasian rugs, seems to be to attribute them to Gendje. In fact, this piece is closer in style to some of the rugs we have attributed to Moghan but one can go on playing guessing games like this for ever. 'East central Caucasus' is probably the best solution, albeit a non-committal one.
220 x 123 cm

282 The design of this rug is a Surahani garden but the colour and structural elements suggest a more south-westerly origin. Since, however, Surahani itself is only one hundred miles away from the Moghan and Talish districts, it is probable that the design itself was not confined to one small village but was woven over a fairly wide area.
208 x 124 cm

283 A bold and handsome example of the Surahani garden design, with a similar colour range and overall primitive quality to the example illustrated in the Smith catalogue (no. 34). Probably late 19th century.
195 x 108 cm

284

286

285

284 An attractive small rug of the type usually attributed to Khila in the Baku area. Late 19th/early 20th century.
257 x 150 cm

285 A design of three conjoined hexagons and a rather peculiar rendering of the 'crab' composition in the main border. An example of a particular group of white Baku rugs which often have a triple conjoined medallion composition and restrict themselves mainly to variations on two colours — blue and orange. The central hexagonal medallion, however, is the one which is typical of this particular group. Late 19th/early 20th century.
189 x 126 cm

286 An example of a fairly well-known type of medallion rug attributed to Khila. The large rosettes are of the type found on the 'Afshan' pattern long rugs assumed to have been woven in the Khila area (cf. no. 308-9). Like all the rugs of this group, the large central medallion and the area around it is filled with many animals. A virtually identical piece in the Victoria and Albert Museum, entered that institution in 1925, although, unfortunately, it has suffered a chemical wash (T.207.1925). Like the present piece, it is probably late 19th century, and is related to the early 19th century medallion carpets illustrated by Serare Yetkin in *Early Caucasian Carpets in Turkey* (plates 101-103), although the latter does not have the white cotton sides and ends of the later pieces.
117 x 112 cm

Khila

Baku is a town on the hook-like protuberance of land between Kuba and Shirvan. Not far from Baku is the town of Khila to which are ascribed specific groups of carpets, the most important of which are the large examples with *boteh* such as 290, and the 'Afshan' pattern rugs such as 308-9. There are also some later medallion carpets with rosettes attributed to Khila on the basis of a) the rosettes themselves and b) the characteristic white cotton selvedged end. Examples illustrated as nos. 284-287.

287 An elongated version of the previous piece. Early 20th century. 305 x 186 cm

288 This is not the usual type of *boteh*-Khila rug, the typical composition of which can be seen on 290. However, like 289 and 305, two other atypical pieces, it is linked to the classic *boteh*-Khila composition, not so much through the *boteh* which appear on its field — such a composition is found on many different Caucasian and Persian rugs, but through its extraordinary border of 'perching' birds between rosettes, a composition particularly associated with rugs of this group. This is an attractive piece, probably late 19th century.
291 x 134 cm

289 Many of the same comments apply to this piece as to 288. The composition of vertical bands containing single rows of motifs, while extremely common on Turkish and some Persian village products, is not often encountered on Caucasian carpets, although the majority of examples I have seen — the bands containing a variety of designs — have been from Shirvan. Made about 1900.
140 x 94cm

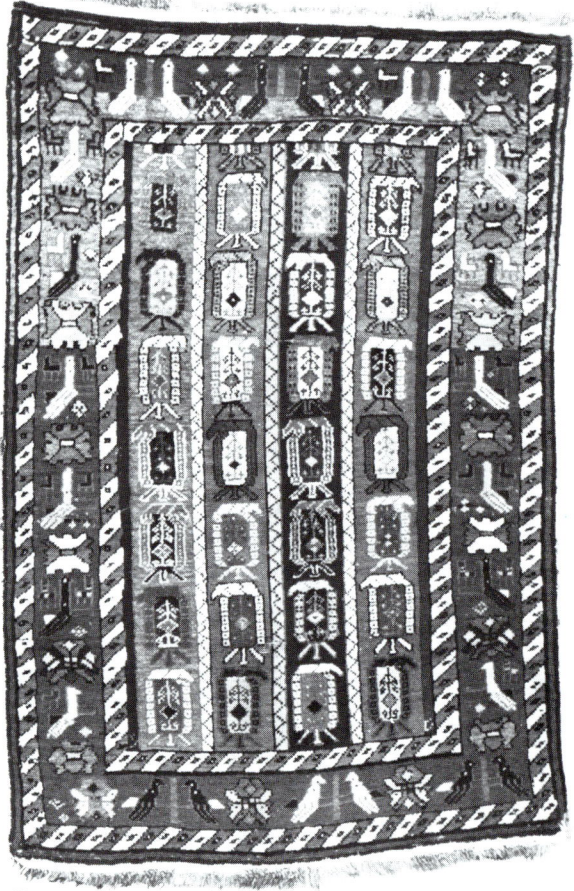

290 In design, this is a classic example of the type of rug which, in the carpet trade, is known as a *boteh*-Khila. Good old examples, which often reach considerable sizes, are seldom encountered, especially in good condition, and are among the most sought-after and highly valued of Caucasian carpets. The present piece, although handsome and well drawn, does not appear well in the illustration. Early 20th century.
350 x 150 cm

291

292

291 To the village of Khila is attributed a group of rugs with *boteh* as the predominant motif. The present rug is somewhat similar to the one illustrated by Kendrlck and Tattersall in *Hand-woven Carpets,* attributed to Baku. Probably late 19th century.
150 x 101 cm

292 A multiple medallion carpet of the same group as 285 but with the outline of the medallion very similar to the last piece and lacking the *boteh* usually associated with this group. Probably late 19th century.
177 x 120 cm

293 A smaller version of 290, with the typical *boteh*-Khila palette of, predominantly, yellow, red and blue. Many rugs of this type have a somewhat coarse appearance and their use of colour suggests that they may have been woven with Western markets in mind. Examples of this size are not common and the present piece is in good condition. Although not to everyone's taste, a rug such as this would create considerable competition at auction.
136 x 98 cm

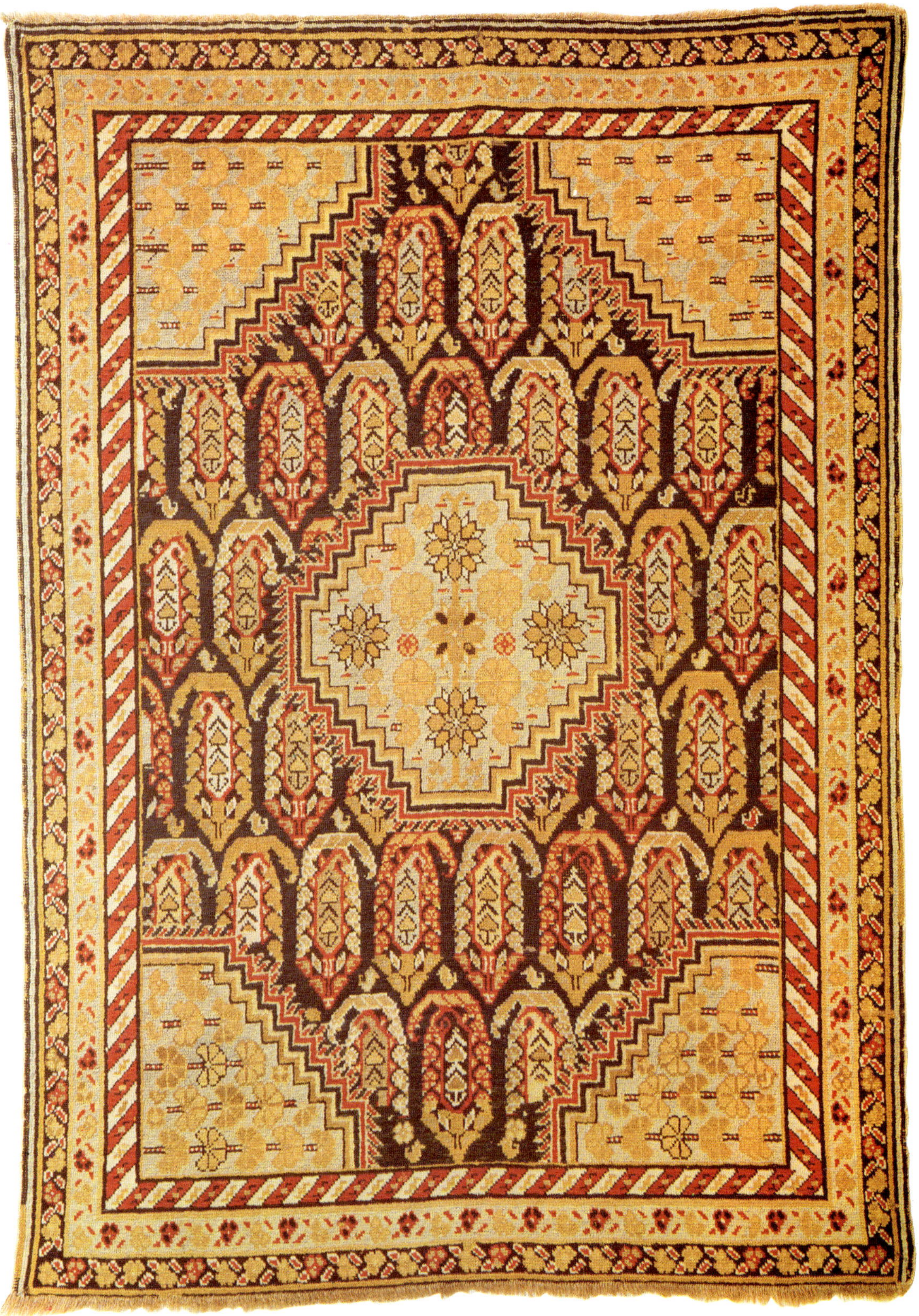

293

230 SHIRVAN-BAKU

294

294 The pale tonality is typical of rugs from this area, although this piece has what would appear to be faded synthetic colours. Late 19th/early 20th century.
265 x 123 cm

295 A distinctly odd-looking rug with its strange inner field and variety of geometric ornamentation, which lacks overall compositional strength. Probably late 19th century.
147 x 118cm

SHIRVAN-BAKU 231

295

232 SHIRVAN-BAKU

296 Another rug attributed to Baku with cross-like medallions, this time contained within a square trellis. Probably late 19th century.
175 x 115 cm

297 Like the previous piece, this rug has affinities with Surahani garden carpets and is probably of the same group. The main border contains a series of serrate-edged motifs found also on the Surahani garden rug in the Smith catalogue (no. 34), which the authors posit are similar to motifs encountered on Yomut Turkoman weavings. An attractive rug, probably late 19th century.
156 x 117 cm

298 This Baku rug has cross-like medallions, similar to those seen on the previous piece, as well as octagons with interior motifs very similar to those we encountered on the Surahani garden rugs. Probably late 19th century.
145 x 113 cm

299 The field composition of this attractive rug suggests a more northerly origin than Baku, as does the colour; Schürmann illustrates a comparable piece, which he catalogues as Daghestan (no. 127), and we should note also the similarity of the cross-shaped motifs to those found on the Kuba rug 311. The 'double S' motifs in the main border are, admittedly, found on a number of Shirvan and Baku rugs, although not, of course, exclusively so; nevertheless, in the absence of a structure analysis, I would prefer an attribution to Kuba. The colour of the piece appears to be particularly rich and harmonious. Probably late 19th century.
345 x 118 cm

300 This piece also has a more northerly look about it. Murray Eiland, in his *Oriental Rugs,* illustrates a closely related piece (no. 169), which he attributes to Konagend. Probably late 19th century.
155 x 115 cm

301 Much the same comment applies to this rug as to the previous example. It has a number of somewhat faded colours, has an all-wool foundation and is finely knotted. Probably late 19th century.
142 x 127 cm

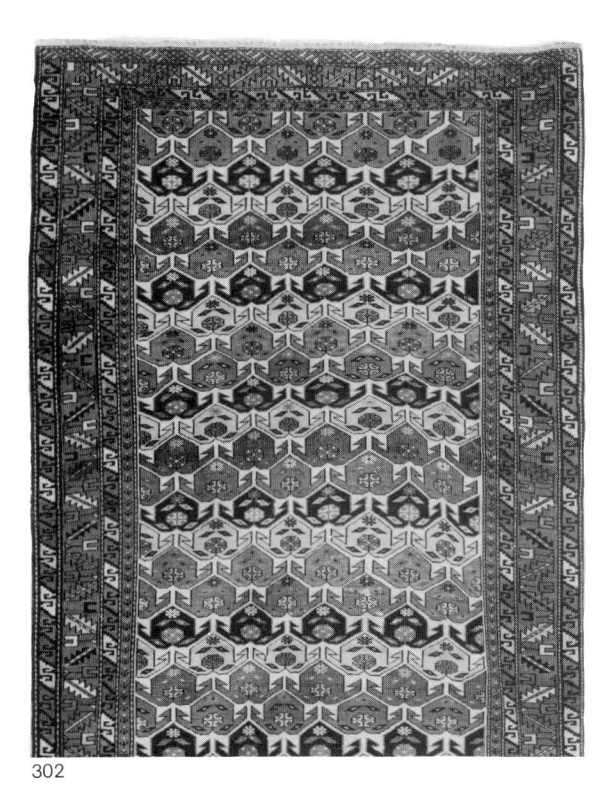

302 This rug and 304 have designs which may have been derived from brocades; we should note, for instance, the two flat-stitch silk embroideries illustrated by Schürmann (pls. 140 and 142), which are attributed to Khila and Surahani respectively, and the rug attributed to Surahani (pl. 89), which Schürmann himself compares to "a fine old tapestry of Flemish origin." The tight repeat design of our rug obviously relates to the floral lattice of east Caucasian rugs but may also be a highly stylised and degenerate form of the repeat 'shield' motif of the eponymously named group of rugs attributed to Shirvan. Probably late 19th century.
180 x 118 cm

303 A distinctly over-crowded and stiffly composed piece with little of obvious merit in the design. It has the overall appearance of a 20th century piece.
176 x 122 cm

304 A rug with a somewhat similar lattice design illustrated in *Caucasian Carpets* (pl. 88) is attributed by Schürmann to Surahani; the author remarks that the use of beige, blue and aquamarine is typical of rugs from the Baku area, which seldom use more than five colours. The 'Kufic' border is associated with rugs from the north-east.
136 x 108cm

305 A repeat pattern of highly stylised floral palmettes makes up the field composition of this large piece; it should probably be attributed to Khila and we note once again the 'perching' birds and rosettes in the border. Late 19th/early 20th century.
414 x 109 cm

Kuba

Kuba is the principal town in an area between Shirvan to the south and Daghestan to the north. To it were attributed many of the older groups of Caucasian carpets, including the 'dragon' rugs; this traditional view is now coming under increasing attack, primarily on historical grounds — the town of Kuba itself having been founded only in the mid-18th century. The Kuba area is, in reality, part of north Shirvan and an attribution to southern Shirvan for many of the earliest extant Caucasian carpets is, at least, a reasonable hypothesis.

The rugs of Kuba are divided into several well-known groups based on either a putative place of origin, or, in the case of the Harshang and Afshan rugs, on specific designs. As with other closely defined groups, however, the accuracy of such descriptions is questionable. Each group will be discussed in detail in the following pages.

In structure, much play is made of the displacement of the warps and the blue overcasting of the sides and the blue soumak-stitch ends. It may be that these features constitute real evidence of a north-east Caucasian origin but I tend to doubt it. Wefts seem to be wool slightly more often than they are cotton.

306 We start with a splendidly archaic-looking and beautifully coloured Kuba rug. The relationship of the overall composition of this piece, with its huge octagonal medallions and generously spaced Kufic borders, to the so-called Large Pattern Holbein rugs of 15th/16th century Turkey is obvious. Among more recent Caucasian weaving, however, it is an unusual design to find on pile-woven carpets, being closer to certain soumaks, with their bold geometric medallions. Among the latter we illustrate, 473 has a clearly relatable central 'star' motif within each octagon, which in turn is contained within a huge star. We might also compare the design of the fine soumak illustrated by Joseph V. McMullan in *Islamic Carpets* (plate 51). The author comments on the motifs within each medallion, similar to those seen here: "These . . . large, effulgent stars, which appear in the Spanish rugs of the 15th century, using a design transmitted from Western Asia through Egypt into Spain by the Muslims. The design disappeared from Spain by the 16th century, but was still occasionally used in the Caucasus . . . " The maroon and pink floral inner border of our rug, so beautifully drawn and well-spaced, is also worthy of special note. A very fine piece and, although earlier examples are known, one cannot help feeling that this might prove to be early 19th century.
202 x 107 cm

307 Despite having been slightly trimmed at top and bottom, this is a most unusual and attractive rug. It is obviously close in concept to the large floral carpets of the late 17th and 18th centuries, a number of which have huge stylised floral medallions (although the yellow and light blue medallions seen lower left and upper right of the present rug are very close to the large palmette medallions of heraldic type seen on so-called Yomut 'Ogurjali' carpets). The main border composition, on its vivid red ground, is also most unusual. The only comparable example known to me is the piece illustrated in McMullan's *Islamic Carpets* (pl. 65); this has an exceptionally wide white-ground arabesque meander with a wide outer red-ground guard containing a row of highly stylised floral motifs with a single continuous indented 'bracket' line. The main border of the present rug closely resembles the outer guard of the McMullan rug, although the latter has a somewhat mean and narrow lattice composition in the field. There is also a highly fragmented rug with a related floral field composition and a white-ground flower-and-bracket border in the Turk ve Islam Museum, Istanbul which Serare Yetkin illustrates (*Early Caucasian Carpets in Turkey,* vol. I, pl. 58) and describes as 18th century. This has what could be interpreted as an earlier, less stylised, version of the border seen on the present piece, a border which might ultimately have derived from a 16th century Ottoman court carpet design. Probably mid-19th century
163 x 106 cm

308 This is the first of four carpets with versions of a very famous Caucasian design, called the Afshan pattern by Lyatif Kerimov, a description followed by most subsequent authors. The pattern consists of a series of vertical vine stems with two pairs of split-palmettes bracketed back-to-back. Large rounded florettes are arranged on a diagonal system between rows of flame-like and starlike flowers, with smaller flower heads arranged on the stems. On some examples, such as 308, the rows are repeated exactly, while on others, such as 309, there is considerable chromatic variation. As Charles Grant Ellis points out in his monograph *Early Caucasian Carpets*, a freer version of the design, with more realistic plants, can be seen on a fragment of an Indian carpet in the Textile Museum, Washington, attributed to the 17th century. This, in turn, was probably derived from the all-over repeat pattern of north-east Persian carpets from Khorasan, as well as from 16th and 17th century 'vase' carpets, probably from Kerman in central Persia. The clear and generous drawing of the flowers and the soft, muted, colours all suggest that this is, indeed, one of the many comparatively early Caucasian examples to have survived, probably dating from the mid-18th century. It is, of course, only a fragment of a once much larger carpet (the measurement given is of this fragment).
144 x 108 cm

309 This boldly coloured example of the Afshan pattern is to my eye of an earlier date than the previous piece. On examination I would not be surprised to find it of 19th century date. The majority of obviously early examples have either floral or *medachyl* borders and it is doubtful whether the wide Kufic border began to appear on such pieces before the 19th century. The Metropolitan Museum has a large Kuba carpet with a floral field more closely allied to the Harshang pattern but an identical border system to the present piece; Dimand (*Oriental Rugs in the Metropolitan Museum of Art*, fig. 234) describes this rug as a "Shirvan, early XIXth century", although an attribution to mid-19th century Kuba would probably.be more widely acceptable. A rug which could almost be the pair to the present example entered the Victoria and Albert Museum London in 1892 (cf. Michael Franses and Robert Pinner, *Hali*, vol. 3, no. 2, p. 102). Serare Yetkin in *Early Caucasian Carpets in Turkey*, Vol. II, fig. 190, attributes this type as 'Khila-Afshan' and remarks that many examples are cotton-wefted and suggests that the Kufic border design was introduced from Anatolia in the 19th century. Most of these pieces are almost identical and were probably made in a workshop. A simplified version on the London market in 1980 (illustrated in Nicholas Fokker, *Caucasian Rugs of Yesterday*, p. 88) is dated 1878. Probably early 19th century.
370 x 158 cm

310 A long, narrow, carpet made for the side seating platforms in a Caucasian house and used in the west as a corridor runner. The colours are dark and the split-palmette motifs have here become translated into heavy angular saw-edged motifs with distinctly zoomorphic characteristics. This motif is clearly related to that which appears in certain of the so-called Shield group carpets attributed to Shirvan, specifically those in the Musée des Arts Décoratifs, the Brooklyn Museum and the Gulbenkian Foundation, Lisbon (Robert Pinner and Michael Franses, *Hali*, vol. 1, no. 1, pp.19-20, figs. 23, 24, 25). Probably late 19th century. 428 x 107 cm

311 The latest and most degenerate of the Afshan pattern, in which the beautiful upward sweep of the composition has been reduced to a series of geometricised motifs. On some examples, however, the small 'shrub' motifs seen between the cruciform medallions have become even more stylised; however, both varieties have the small 'bird-like' leaves identical to those which appear in the Tekke main carpet *göl*, as well as having scattered 'double E' motifs, these being identical to those used on Tekke weavings, especially in the borders of *ensi*, and called, in its Turkoman manifestation, the 'Sainak' ornament. Probably late 19th/early 20th century. 151 x 113 cm

312 The same type as the previous rug but considerably more attractive. Like the cross-shaped flowers of 311, the flattened star-shaped flowers on this rug are found on very many tribal rugs, notably those of the Baluch. The particularly beautiful colouring of the white-ground squared 'crab' border is worth noticing, this making a dramatic contrast to the dark blue of the field. Although the attribution to Kuba cannot be challenged without careful examination of the rug, it is difficult to believe that it could have been woven in the same area as the previous piece, and even harder to believe that if both *are* from the same place, they are also contemporaries. Probably late 19th century.
126 x 97 cm

244 KUBA

313 This is a frequently encountered type of Caucasian carpet, with a single vertical row of 'open' shield-like palmettes on a pale blue ground. We illustrate a group of pieces attributed to Gendje (note in particular 161) which can be compared closely with the present rug. An example, very similar in colour, shape and field composition (with a mixture of wool and cotton in the wefts), is illustrated in Schürmann's *Caucasian Rugs* (pl. 99); a smaller example with a light green field (and an all-wool foundation) is illustrated by Peter Bausback in his 1977 catalogue (p.70); a third, ex-Ballard collection, is in the Metropolitan Museum of Art, New York (with a dark blue field and an all-wool foundation) of which Dimand (*Oriental Rugs in the Metropolitan Museum*, no. 167) says: "Probably Shirvan, first half of the XIXth century"; and a fourth, which like the Metropolitan piece, has a white ground 'crab' border, is illustrated in Jean Lefevre's *Caucasian Carpets* (no. 30). This last piece, which has a mid-blue field and two small human figures included in the main composition, is certainly the best of these rugs I have seen; it has a long Farsi inscription, giving the name of the maker and indicating the piece was a wedding gift; it is dated 1271 A.H. (A.D. 1854/5). The present piece can certainly be no older. Second half 19th century.
292 x 84 cm

314 An attractive side carpet with an all-over floral lattice and a predominant pale gold colouring. Probably late 19th century.
366 x 102 cm

315 This piece is dated 1136 A.H. (A.D. 1723/4), and is, therefore, another example of the oft-encountered phenomenon — a rug with an impossibly early date; it is a phenomenon, moreover, which is probably found with greater frequency among Caucasian rugs than among those of any other eastern country, city, town, village or tribe. One explanation sometimes advanced is that treasured family rugs would be replaced by exact copies when they were too worn to be of further use and that these copies would, naturally, incorporate any woven dates and inscriptions, these being considered integral to the original rug's composition. Such an explanation may well be true in certain instances, especially in those cases of rugs which, despite being obviously late (e.g. they incorporate 'wrong' materials or have synthetic dyes), nevertheless have very fine, or recognisably archaic, versions of well-known designs. It seems more likely, however, that in the majority of such cases (and especially in those in which the rug's design does not seem to be particularly old or fine as in the present instance), such dates represent attempts to deceive buyers in the West, during a period when very few people had any serious knowledge of Oriental weaving. Second half 19th century. 360 x 122 cm

316 This attractive white-ground long rug has design elements which link it both to Shirvan and Chichi weavings. Second half 19th century. 243 x 82 cm

317 This is an example of the 'Harshang' design; the principal motifs are the slanting palmettes from which 'grow' usually four, but sometimes two, split-palmettes, and the flame-like palmettes which on this piece are in white and blue. The composition is linked not only with the previously described Afshan pattern but also with the composition found on Karagashli rugs, which also have slanting palmettes and split-palmettes (cf. 324 and 325). Once again, we look to Safavid prototypes for this design, which in older literature is called either the 'Shah Abbas' or 'Joshagan' pattern. This rug, although finely drawn, has a slightly crowded composition and Kufic borders. It may date, however, from the first half of the 19th century.
300 x 141 cm

318 The first of two rugs which form part of a group of pieces with this distinctive composition. Three large vertical medallions, each with four 'arms' and a claw-like top, are flanked by four motifs which are clearly more stylised versions of the 'split-palmettes' seen on the previous piece in more realistic form (although the peculiar cross-like appendages are present on both rugs). There is also a variety of small floral ornamentation and tiny, more realistically delineated, animals in typical Caucasian style. The majority of examples have white or ivory grounds and usually measure approximately 175 x 130 cm. All have a Kufic main border flanked by guards containing small star-like floral motifs. The central large medallion is usually dark blue, the outer ones red. Apart from the two we illustrate, two others have been published in recent literature, one in Jean Lefevre's *Caucasian Carpets* (no. 37) and the other, which is unusually long and narrow, in Schürmann's *Caucasian Rugs* (plate 98). Most examples are cotton wefted and the majority of writers prefer to call them Shirvan. However, their resemblance to certain white-ground Perepedil rugs is striking (cf., for instance, 373), not only in overall appearance but also in the resemblance of the main motifs to those found within the octagons of Perepedil rugs. Nevertheless, the strongest connecting link between these rugs and those of any other rug is the stylised split-palmette motif with its cross-like appendage. This motif is so striking and so 'eccentric' that its presence also on rugs of the so-called 'Karagashli' group (cf. our 324 and 325), of which this is one of the three chief design characteristics, makes

318 continued
the connection between nos. 317-319 and the Karagashli pieces incontrovertible. Like the latter, nos. 318 and 319 are variant derivatives of the earlier so-called 'Harshang' pattern rugs, some of which probably date from the early 19th century but which continued to be made in the 'realistic' style seen on no. 317 well into the century. However, it is interesting to note how on this rug in particular (and this is a unique feature among all the pieces with the stylised 'split-palmette' motif we illustrate) the weaver seemed to have been unaware of the derivation of the motif, as from the way she composed it, she appears to have laboured under the misapprehension that it was a motif of zoomorphic origin. Probably second half of the 19th century.
174 x 130cm

319 Except for the comments about the composition of the 'split-palmette' motif, the description of the last rug could as well apply to this one, although the more generous spacing of the field composition on the present rug is preferable. Note the abundance of small animal and bird figures scattered throughout the field (two of which have perched in the top left-hand corner of the border), including at top left a horse with six legs and two heads supporting a standing human rider! It is interesting to note that the white motifs in each medallion formed by the sharp indentations in the medallions' outlines are less 'swan-like' on this rug than on 318, perhaps a further indication of 318's weaver being concerned with the possible zoomorphic origins of some of the motifs which she did not understand. This lack of knowledge may also indicate that 318 is further removed from 'source' than 319 and I am inclined to think that the present rug is slightly older, perhaps mid-19th century.
180 x 128 cm

320

321

322

320 This and the three following rugs form an interesting group. With the exception of 322, which has a dark blue field, they have white grounds with four different medallions — a flattened serrate-edged hexagon, two types of open-ended octagon with wide flanges and a starred rectangle (decahedron). On 323, there is a fifth medallion, a star-like form, which appears only in the top and bottom rows, and two variants on the other motifs, which appear in the centre row. The serrate-edged motif can be compared to that found on certain 'shield' group carpets, as well as on Turkoman weavings of the Tekke, Salor and Saryk, while the borders of 323 are reminiscent of Yomud Turkoman motifs. The variant open-ended octagon with two 'heads' and 'feet', seen particularly clearly in the centre row of 320, has strong zoomorphic characteristics, and the overall appearance of these rugs links them to the two previous pieces and to Perepedils. This example probably dates from the late 19th century.
177 x 128cm

321 A slightly more crowded and stiffly drawn example but with the more usual border system. Probably late 19th century.
162 x 111 cm

322 The design has become more regular on this unusual blue-ground example. Late/early 20th century.
167 x 119 cm

323 An example with good colour and spacing, well drawn and with an interesting variety of motifs. This may well be the oldest of the four. Second half 19th century.
170 x 124 cm

250 KUBA

KARAGASHLI

Detail of 325 showing the arrangement of slanting palmettes, and split-palmettes flanked by white snow flake flowers and stylised tree motifs. The present of myriad tiny animals on rugs of this group is also typical.

324 This is not a particularly attractive, but nevertheless common, example of the type, with two rows of palmettes. Stiffly drawn and unadventurous in colour, it is almost certainly of the 20th century.
150 x 90 cm

Karagashli

Following Kerimov, a group of rugs with large red slanting palmettes on a blue ground have been dubbed Karagashli, after a small town just north of Perepedil. Their relationship to earlier floral carpets is apparent, the slanting palmette having been used on Safavid 'vase' carpets and later derivatives. In structure, the majority of pieces would seem to have an all-wool foundation, although certain examples, especially those such as 324 which appear to be late, may have white cotton wefts. As for their date, there is a tendency on the part of many authors to describe them as being comparatively early, either first half of the 19th century, or even 18th century. This may be due in part to a consistently high knot count — between 1,750 and 2,000 per sq. dm (113 to 130 per sq. in.) being recorded in many instances. A high knot count, however, is certainly no indication of age and what evidence as there is actually seems to indicate that most so-called Karagashli rugs are fairly late in date. In this context, there are not only the dated rugs mentioned in connection with 325, but also a small group of very beautiful long rugs which can be dated to the late 18th/early 19th century and which seem to be the obvious antecedents of both the Karagashli and Harshang pattern rugs. Of two well-known examples, one appears in Schürmann's *Caucasian Rugs* (pl. 109) and has a most unusual white-ground border with large 'S' motifs, mixed wool and cotton wefts and a knot count of 1,260 per sq. dm (81 per sq. in.), and the other, even more splendid piece, in Spuhler, König and Volkmann's *Alte Orientteppiche* (pl. 67), which has a white-ground border containing an angular floral meander, an all-wool foundation and a knot count of 986 per sq. dm (65 per sq. in.). Both examples have a single row of motifs, the Schürmann example having the slanting palmettes and split-palmettes alternating with a circular rosette and the second piece the usual Karagashli motif alternating with a medallion resembling that seen on 318 and 319.

325 This piece represents the Karagashli design at its most typical — a vertical system of three slanting palmettes, with slightly geometric split-palmettes, flanked by two rows of alternate white star-like flowers and stylised tree motifs. The border system is also typical, with a yellow-ground leaf-and-calyx border appearing almost invariably. As for the date of this piece, many writers would persist in calling it 18th or early 19th century. However, a similar example, with much brighter colouring and unusual 'interlock' borders, illustrated in Peter Bausbeck's catalogue, is apparently dated 129(1) A.H. (A.D. 1874/5), and a second, which appears to have no 'wrong' colours (and lacks the tree motifs) is illustrated in Inge Lise Jensen's *Kaukasiske Taepper en dansk Privatsamling* (no. 13); this is dated as late as 1331 A.H. (A.D. 1912/13). This piece has an all-wool foundation and is finely knotted. Second half of the 19th century.
135 x 92 cm

326 Differentiating between Kuba, Daghestan and Shirvan prayer rugs is rather like a game of blind man's buff. One can make educated guesses but in most cases, there will be more disagreements than agreements. Certainly structure can help but the majority of prayer rugs one sees described as Kuba or Daghestan could as well be Shirvan and vice versa. If anything, prayer rugs attributed to Kuba rather than Shirvan or Daghestan, have a somewhat bolder, rough-hewn, look, without the delicacy and almost feminine grace of the other two groups. The present rug has a dark blue field on which is an hexagonal lattice with large curlicue shrubs, the latter possibly highly stylised renderings of the ancient totemic image of the tree-of-life flanked by two animals or birds. The strange device within the *mihrab* arch itself also has strong totemic overtones, with what would appear to be two clearly recognisable bird figures within it. The field of the *mihrab* is filled with a hexagonal lattice, each unit of which contains what at first glance could be interpreted as a 'lotus palmette' reduced almost to a series of interlocking geometric shapes. However, closer examination reveals a central 'stem' ending, at its top, with a pair of inward-curving hooked brackets. This is surmounted by a free-standing diamond with a central diamond 'dot' and is flanked at the base by a pair of outward-curving brackets. This motif, apparently a simplified version of that which appears in the lattice of the following piece, immediately strikes a chord. The clue lies in the resemblance of this motif to that seen at the base of the more complex trees seen on the eponymous group of Kazak rugs (cf. nos. 63, 64, 159 and 160). The Kazak trees, which, coincidentally, also have diamonds which are used to embellish their trunks, can, in turn, be related to the not dissimilar 'animal and tree' motifs found on a very rare group of Baluch rugs, a point made when discussing the examples of 'tree' Kazaks illustrated in this book. Of course, the image of the 'Sacred Tree' flanked by animals at its base is one of the most powerful and ubiquitous of the ancient totemic symbols. In an extensive essay on the subject, "The Animal Tree and the Great Bird" *(Turkoman Studies,* vol. 1, 1980), Robert Pinner traces its origins back to the 4th millennium in western Asia and to the 12th/13th century B.C. on Chinese bronzes; and in terms of comparatively recent textiles, Pinner not only illustrates an example of that most famous of tribal renditions, found within the stylised leaf lattice on a very rare group of Tekke *asmalyk* (and in identical form in the *elem* panel on a slightly less rare group of Tekke *ensi,* but also related examples of the motif

326 continued
found on 'dragon' rugs and later Caucasian weavings such as those of the Akstafa and Perepedil groups. Although the motif as it is found here and on no. 327 has been changed into what would appear to be a highly stylised floral spray, the particular form it takes on this piece gives a strong clue as to its proper antecedents. Late 19th century.
137 x 91 cm

327 This white-ground prayer rug is visually a very splendid piece. The hexagonal lattice contains angular 'lotus' palmettes in a variety of subtle shades which relate very closely to old 'dragon' and floral carpets (although note our description of the previous piece for further thoughts on this motif). Schürmann, in *Caucasian Rugs*, illustrates two very similar prayer rugs (pls. 122 and 125) which he describes as Daghestan and the first of which, an exceptionally beautiful old piece with a most unusual border similar to the bird-and-pole borders of Yomut Turkoman *asmalyk*, is apparently a specific sub-group called by Kerimov 'Mahatshkala'. A third related rug is illustrated in the catalogue of *The George Walter Vincent and Belle Townsley Smith Collection of Islamic Rugs* (plate 36); this has a most unusual dark blue border containing a version of the 'crab' design close in style to that found on Baluch carpets attributed to the Adraskand Valley. Joseph V. McMullan, in his description of the Smith piece, also remarked on the strong similarity between its palmettes and those of earlier 'classical' Caucasian carpets. Note the animals in the spandrels above the *mihrab*, a further rebuttal to the oft-repeated myth that animals are never found on Oriental prayer rugs; these animals, moreover, facing inward towards each other, only emphasise the 'animal-tree' motif implicit in the palmette within each unit of the hexagonal lattice. If, by the way, our interpretation of this motif is accurate, it is ironic that it should be found surviving on an aid to Islamic worship, the prayer rug! The delicate colouring of this piece and the beauty of its drawing suggest a Daghestan origin. Late 19th century.
172 x 113 cm

328 This and the following rug share a very distinctive border design, which on this piece is somewhat simplified but is clearly recognisable, none the less, as a highly stylised floral arabesque. Its presence is associated principally with two distinctive field designs, one of which is an apparently directional pattern of stylised, angular, flowering shrubs, as seen on this piece, and the other a floral lattice, of which that seen on 329 is, as we shall discuss, an unusual variant. In general, the first consists usually of long side rugs with yellow fields. Their attribution to either Shirvan or Kuba is controversial, most authors favouring the former. A particularly fine example, in small rug size, appears in Richard Purdon's catalogue *Shirvan and Related Weavings from the North Caucasus* (plate 5) and again, but in colour in Eberhart Herrmann's *Von Lotto bis Tekke* (no. 37) (this is cotton wefted). The field design is not, however, confined only to pieces with this border; two examples, with blue grounds and diamond pole borders, are illustrated in Ian Bennett's *Book of Oriental Carpets and Rugs*, (p. 107) as Shirvan, and Murray Eiland's *Oriental Rugs* (no. 176) as Derbend. Although the stylised floral nature of the composition is obvious, it is interesting to note that on some rugs, the tall, spindly, shrub has a 'W-shaped' base, perhaps another distant echo of the 'animal-tree'. Related rugs with less complex designs are illustrated in the Frankfurt catalogue, *Kaukasische Teppiche,* nos. 54 and 55; these two examples are related to no. 313 in this book, and also nos. 161, 162 and 164. Inevitably, one also sees a number of more realistically drawn tree and shrub carpets of the late Safavid period from Kurdish north-west Persia, a particularly handsome example of which is illustrated as plate 124 in Erdmann's *Oriental Carpets* (1976). Such palmettes can also be found on the Kuba Chi-Chi rugs, those on our no. 364, for instance, being much the same. The best old examples are usually described as 18th century and, although I tend to doubt this, a date in the first half of the 19th century is not impossible.
462 x 102 cm

329 This prayer rug is a very unusual variant of a rare and well-known group of rugs attributed either to Shirvan or Kuba. Perhaps the most famous example is that illustrated by Schürmann in *Caucasian Rugs* (pl. 97). Another, and possibly even finer example, was in the British art trade in 1979 and is illustrated in *Hali* (vol. 2, no. 1, p. 77). The majority of extant examples in this group are prayer rugs, with an all-over floral lattice and either a tall, pointed, *mihrab*, as in the Schürmann example, or a more rounded and shallow arch, as in the piece illustrated in *Hali*. Again, the majority of examples share two distinctive flowers — a red, tulip-like flower with three conjoined blooms, and a somewhat angular shrub with a diamond-shaped head, leaves growing upwards from only one side of the stem and with two bell-like appendages on the other side. Neither type of flower is present on this rug, however, which also has the other most unusual feature of a row of octagons at the top end of the field. All three rugs of this group mentioned here have identical main borders and in the same three colours — blue-black, mid-blue and red. The date of the group is, as usual, problematical. Perhaps the finest example of all. which is not a prayer rug, is illustrated by Schürmann in *Caucasian Rugs* (plate 64); this has an all-oval floral lattice and the two distinctive flower forms are present, although drawn in a much more realistic way. The border is a more elaborate and splendidly drawn version of the one which appears on our 328, and in the same colours; many of the flowers on the Schürmann piece are piled in silk. If this latter example is 18th century, as Schürmann supposes — and its brilliant quality suggests that it might be — then it is probable that both the second Schürmann and *Hali* rugs date from the first half of the 19th century. Our rug, which has far less satisfactory drawing and paler colouring, is probably from the second half of the 19th century. It is worth adding that no. 329 has some of the tiny 'shrubs' or 'trees', which appear in the serrate-edged lattice, particularly in the fourth complete row from the bottom (e.g. immediately above, and to the left of, the pale blue hexagon appearing in the third lattice unit to the left in the third row from the bottom) have a double outward-curving 'bracket' form which relates to certain of the shrubs on the previous rug and which, of course, seem quite obviously to be distant and faint echoes of the once realistically depicted 'animal-tree' image.
174 x 135 cm

328

329

Konagkend

There are three principal designs for rugs attributed to Konagkend. The first has a large cruciform medallion, the second, called by Kerimov and Schürmann 'Ordutch-Konagkend', has a series of large octagons and the third, and probably best known, has a stiff, angular lattice based on hexagonal forms.

Each type has a quite different aesthetic appeal and in each case, the design is reminiscent of other rugs. The cruciform medallion type usually has a bright, light palette and in both colour and design is reminiscent of Kurdish weavings and certain Turkish village rugs. The 'Ordutch-Konagkend' pieces have strong affinities with Baku and other north Shirvan rugs, and the lattice type is the closest to the concept of design most normally associated with Kuba as well as having links with earlier groups of, principally Turkish, carpets.

Among the rugs we illustrate, however, are some groups whose origins are a little controversial. These include 333-339. Examples 333 and 336, although catalogued as 'Ordutch-Konagkend', are of the same type as those illustrated in the Shirvan section, 276-283, which are

continued on p.258

330 A fairly spectacular example of this particular design. The overall composition is quite closely related to a group of soumak rugs with large medallions, which are usually attributed to Kuba, many of which have the odd bell-like motif seen each side of the field below the central octagon and also at the centre of the field's base line (cf. 468). Circa 1900.
173 x 143 cm

331 A stiffly and unimaginatively drawn rug, less interesting than the previous example, which possibly post dates it. The design within the corner octagons relates to the lattice 'Konagkend' design. Probably 1920s.
199 x 130cm

332 A dark and slightly gloomy piece but the condition is excellent and there are some beautifully drawn birds. It seems, compositionally, to fall between the last two, so logically it should date from around 1910.
180 x 134 cm

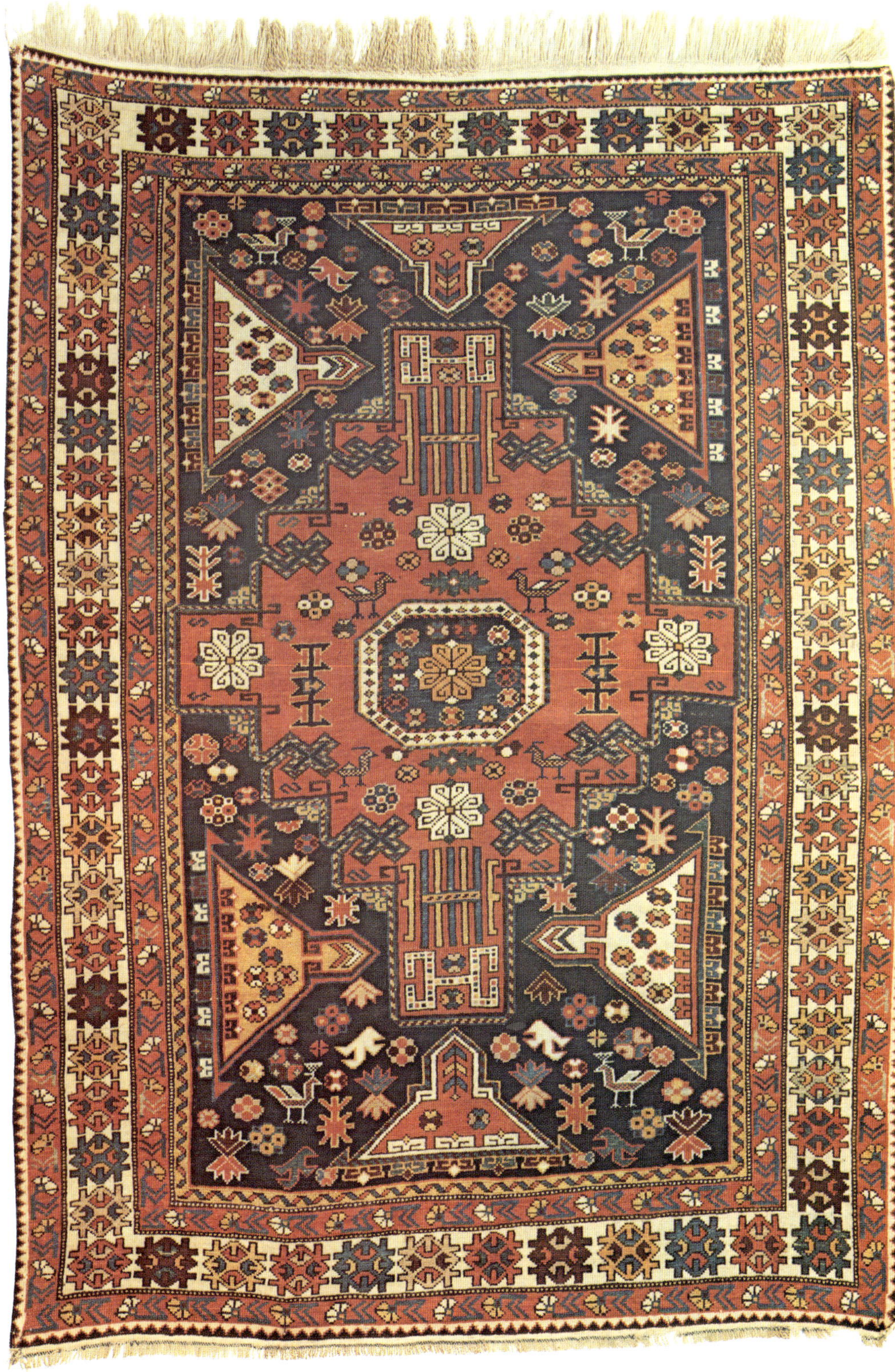

332

333

334

Konagkend continued
presumed to be a stylised garden design and are often called 'Surahani'. It is difficult for the expert, let alone the layman, to distinguish between the two types, if, indeed, there is any real reason for *making* such a distinction. According to Schürmann, the *gül*-like medallion characterises the 'Ordutch-Konagkend' rugs; however, the octagonal *gül* as it appears on 333-339 can also be seen on the Shirvan rugs mentioned above as well as on innumerable Baku rugs (e.g. our 297 and 298); indeed, in terms of design at least, our 298 and 337 are so similar that there seems no logical reason why they should be attributed to two different places.

The confusion that is obviously present here is symptomatic of the dangers inherent in making definitive attributions based upon design. It would seem as if there is still considerable confusion about what design should be called by which name; it should be accepted, perhaps, that many of the same designs were woven in very different areas and although structural analysis can often help us to sort out which, this is neither an infallible nor always positive tool. It is also obvious that the term 'Ordutch-Konagkend' is a very dubious one.

333 The first of the rugs with the 'garden' design discussed in connection with the Surahani rugs in the Shirvan section. This piece is of a very similar design, size and construction to 283 and I see no reason why it should be considered to emanate from a different area. At least until more information is available, it is logical to follow Kerimov's lead and discuss certain rugs under more generalised headings and refer to this group as 'Kuba-Shirvan'. Late 19th century.
188 x 116 cm

334 The composition of this piece has lost the clarity of that on the previous rug and the border is somewhat mean. It is similar in appearance to 273 and 282 and, again, is best attributable to Kuba-Shirvan. Early 20th century.
151 x 99 cm

KONAGKEND KUBA

335 Another rug which, like 282 and 334, has squared rather than octagonal sides to the large central medallion. The piece has an overall blue-beige tonality characteristic of Baku rugs, from which area it probably comes (cf. nos. 337 and 338). Late 19th/early 20th century.
164 x 110 cm

336 One of the most attractive of the garden rugs we illustrate. The latch-hook diamonds within the outer octagons are attractive features not previously encountered on rugs of this type and the overall composition is beautifully spaced, with excellent drawing and fine colour. The flower heads in the minor borders plus the white selvedges and plaited ends (visible at the top of the rug) are the clearest indications we have yet encountered of a Shirvan rather than a Kuba origin. Second half of the 19th century.
210 x 112 cm

260 KUBA

337

337 This rug is very similar to the piece illustrated in Schürmann (pl. 105) which, following Kerimov, is called 'Ordutch-Konagkend'. In overall tonality, it is very similar to 407, with which it also shares many minor motifs. The octagons and the motifs they contain also link it with north Shirvan rugs, as does the leaf-and-calyx border. However, despite its clear compositional links with the other rugs illustrated hereabouts, and the distinctly Shirvanlike appearance of the two flower-head guards (compare them to those on the previous piece), the attribution of this rug is not so straightforward. Examining its design carefully, one is immediately struck by a sense of *déjà-vu*, a feeling quickly explained if we glance back at no. 298 (and further satisfied by a comparison between nos. 338 and 297). There can be little doubt that all four rugs form part of a definable group, a group which may not necessarily include *all* the pieces illustrated here (for instance, no. 336 is possibly of a different type) but which seems also to embrace nos. 335 and 338). The attribution of rugs similar to no. 298 to Baku may evince structural features inconsistent with a Baku attribution; one must, in the absence of evidence to the contrary, suggest that it, too, is from the Baku region. An attractive piece, probably dating from the late 19th century.
148 x 129 cm

KONAGKEND

338 A less attractive version of the previous rug, probably slightly later in date. It is very close in style to no. 335, although it lacks that piece's indented rectangular frame; both pieces can also be related to no. 297. Probably attributable to Baku. Late 19th/early 20th century.
149 x 108 cm

338

339 This beautifully coloured rug is, stylistically, something of an anachronism. It has a coarse look, the main border is characteristic of a certain sub-group of rugs attributed to Chichi and the main field composition is related to rugs usually attributed to north Shirvan. An origin in north Shirvan seems most likely, but there would, no doubt, be many people who would support a Kuba attribution or even an 'Ordutch-Konagkend' one. One would certainly hesitate to suggest that it and no. 337 are part of a group, despite some superficial similarities and a few shared motifs. Late 19th century.
144 x 113 cm

339

340

341

340 This and the following rugs represent perhaps the best defined group of Konagkend rugs, with an overall angular arabesque lattice based on hexagonal forms. The majority have a predominantly dark blue tonality, the borders and the main field colours usually matching. Invariably they have a Kufic main border composition. The lattice design itself would seem to be a highly stylised floral arabesque, although on certain examples there appear to be included equally highly stylised bird figures. However, in his notes to no. 35 in the catalogue of *The George Walter Vincent and Belle Townsley Smith Collection of Islamic Rugs,* Joseph V. McMullan pointed out that the eminent scholar Rudolf M. Riefstahl, an authority on Turkish rugs, had suggested that the composition was derived from the 16th century Anatolian Lotto pattern. The present piece is a typical example, datable probably to the second half of the 19th century.
160 x 104cm

341 This rug, which is in generally poor condition, is dated 1282 A.H. (A.D. 1865-6). It has a greater spaciousness in the composition than any of the other examples we illustrate, although the field is unusually narrow in relation to the borders. The simple border system, and the loss of part of its outer minor border, gives the rug an unusually austere appearance. The Kufic borders are very beautifully composed, an especially noticeable feature being the rounded floral motifs between the 'brackets', which in later examples tend to be more angular. It is interesting to compare this rug to no. 33 in the Smith catalogue which, according to McMullan, has a cloth label which "indicates Mr. Smith purchased this rug in Florence, probably about 1880". Although an excellent example, the Smith rug does not appear to be as old as the present piece. Second half of the 19th century.
158 x 70 cm

342 This rug is very similar to the Smith rug mentioned in connection with the previous piece and also with examples in the Metropolitan Museum (ex-Ballard collection) catalogued by Maurice Dimand as Shirvan, with another in Albert Achdjian's *Le Tapis* (p. 75), also catalogued as Shirvan and with a fourth illustrated in Schürmann's *Caucasian Rugs* (pl . 104). The
continued on p.264

342

343

344

345

342 continued
Metropolitan Museum piece has *medachyl* guards, as opposed to the 'ribbon' guards of the present piece or the beautifully drawn linked-S guards of the Smith piece. All five examples, including the present one, have the characteristic colour combination of a deep blue-black field and dark green main border. Purely on stylistic grounds, I am inclined to think this rug, the Metropolitan Museum example and the one illustrated by Achdjian are slightly younger than the Smith and Schürmann pieces. However, some confusion is caused by various dated examples. In Werner Grote-Hasenbalg's *Der Orientteppich* (vol. 11, pl. 34) there is illustrated an example dated 1247 A.H. (A.D. 1831/2). This piece is very similar to the present rug, and on this evidence it would be tempting to assume that all the examples mentioned in connection with our piece actually date from the first half of the 19th century, with 341 probably *post*-dating them. This, however, I find difficult to believe, although there is no real evidence to suggest that the date on the Grote-Hasenbalg rug is not to be believed. Nevertheless, an excellent example known to me with a date in the second half of the 19th century is illustrated in Richard Purdon's *Shirvan and Related Weavings from the North Caucasus* (no. 12). This is the only one of the examples mentioned here which does not have a Kufic main border but one of the sloping double-S type (cf. our 430 *et al* for the same main border composition). The field design of the Purdon rug is excellently drawn and the colour beautiful. On an all-wool foundation, this piece is dated 1304 A.H. (A.D. 1886-7) and I see no reason why it should be considered to post-date any of the undated rugs mentioned here.
157 x 124cm

343 An unusual piece in that it has a main 'crab' border. The design in the field at the top end is more free and widely spaced than in the rest, and hence more attractive; there does not seem to be a logical explanation why the weaver should have changed in this way; the answer may be that the composition is the work of *two* weavers or that the rug is a sort of sampler allowing prospective purchasers to choose from two variants. Circa 1900.
165 x 120 cm

344 The angular 'S' guard motif is not usually found on these rugs (although it is frequently encountered on a wide variety of Caucasian weavings). There is a group of lattice Konagkend rugs in which the overall composition is extremely simple and regular; this piece and 346 are examples. Probably late 19th century.
145 x 104 cm

345 This piece would seem to be almost identical to 342 and is probably of the same age. One interesting difference is the drawing of the brackets in the Kufic border, which on 342 have small S-shaped motifs at each extremity. The rug illustrated by Schürmann (pl. 104) has borders in which the brackets are of the same type as those on the present piece but has one pair of brackets with S-motifs in the lower left hand corner. The border florettes of our rug have become cruciform, something which, I suspect, is characteristic of later pieces. Second half 19th century.
148 x 115 cm

346 This rug has a beautifully drawn field composition and is an extremely good example of its type. It has very short pile and wool of extremely high quality. It is also very finely knotted. Like the majority of Konagkend rugs, it has an all-wool foundation (a small number of them have either cotton or mixed wool and cotton wefts). Second half of the 19th century.
165 x 120 cm

346

347 This is the first of two Chichi prayer rugs. This example is unusually long and narrow, and has atypical borders for rugs of this group; the field pattern, however, is characteristic. Late 19th century.
148 x 71 cm

348 This second Chichi prayer rug has a field design called 'Khirdagyd-Chichi' by Kerimov, a name discussed in our section on Chichi rugs. Although the field design is typical, this example, like the secular rug 363, has a border design not usually associated with weavings from this area. Late 19th century.
139 x 110cm

349 The field design of this Konagkend prayer rug is typical, although the main border is uncharacteristic, having something in common with certain Turkoman weavings, particularly those of the Beshir/Ersari. Nevertheless, an attractive example with a number of small animals in the lattice. Late 19th/early 20th century.
161 x 126 cm

Chichi

A group of finely woven rugs, the field composition consisting of a tight overall series of geometric and floral motifs, is attributed to the village of Chichi, about thirty kilometres south-east of Kuba. This village is presumed to be, or have been, inhabited by descendants of the Chechens, a tribe which once inhabited much of the north-east Caucasus but which was, apparently, forcibly moved to central Asia by the Soviet authorities in 1943.

Perhaps the most distinctive feature of Chichi rugs is the border, which often consists of a continuous diagonal and rosette pattern, which can be seen on all the examples we illustrate with the exception of those rugs which Kerimov, followed by Schürmann, called 'Khirdagyd-Chichi'. This does not mean, of course, that all rugs with this border design are necessarily Chichi; indeed, many authorities prefer a less defined attribution and describe them simply as north-east Caucasian. Others find little to distinguish them from the main body of Daghestan prayer rugs.

To confuse the issue further, Schürmann, in his book on Caucasian rugs, reproduces a rug (pl. 110) which, he says, is of a type called by Kerimov 'Khirdagyd-Chichi'. The field design of this piece contains rows of various small spiky floral motifs, almost identical to those on our 362 and 363, alternating with rows of open octagons containing florettes. Schürmann contrasts this rug with another (pl. 111) which, he says, has the typical Chichi design. This latter design consists of diagonal rows of latch-hook sided octagons of the type seen on our 355. Although Schürmann illustrates no other examples, a number of different rugs have been described as 'Khirdagyd-Chichi' by other authors for no immediately obvious reason.

Dated Chichi rugs do not give us much help in placing other examples into an ordered chronology. Two almost identical prayer rugs illustrated in recent literature, one in Jean Lefevre's *Caucasian Carpets* (no. 49) and the other in the Textile Museum's catalogue *Prayer Rugs* (no. XXXII) bear dates of 1268 A.H. (A.D. 1851-2) and 1297 A.H. (A.D. 1879-80) respectively. There is no reason to suspect either date and there is no discernible quality difference between these two

continued on p.270

350

350 A piece which displays many of the characteristic features of Chichi rugs, including the dark blue field slightly tinged with green, the diagonal and flower border, and the wealth of compositional details. Chichi rugs are renowned for the extraordinary, jewel-like, quality of their compositions which, on the best examples, give the surface great movement. This piece has somewhat dull colours. Late 19th century.
210 x 152cm

351 This is a particularly pleasing example. The colours are more vivid than on the previous rug and, although there is no diminution of the lively, kaleidoscopic effect of the busy design, the compositional elements are more generously spaced. Note the way one bar goes the 'wrong' way two-thirds of the distance down each long border. The faded area at the right edge of the rug near the bottom is a re-weave. Second half of the 19th century.
155 x 113 cm

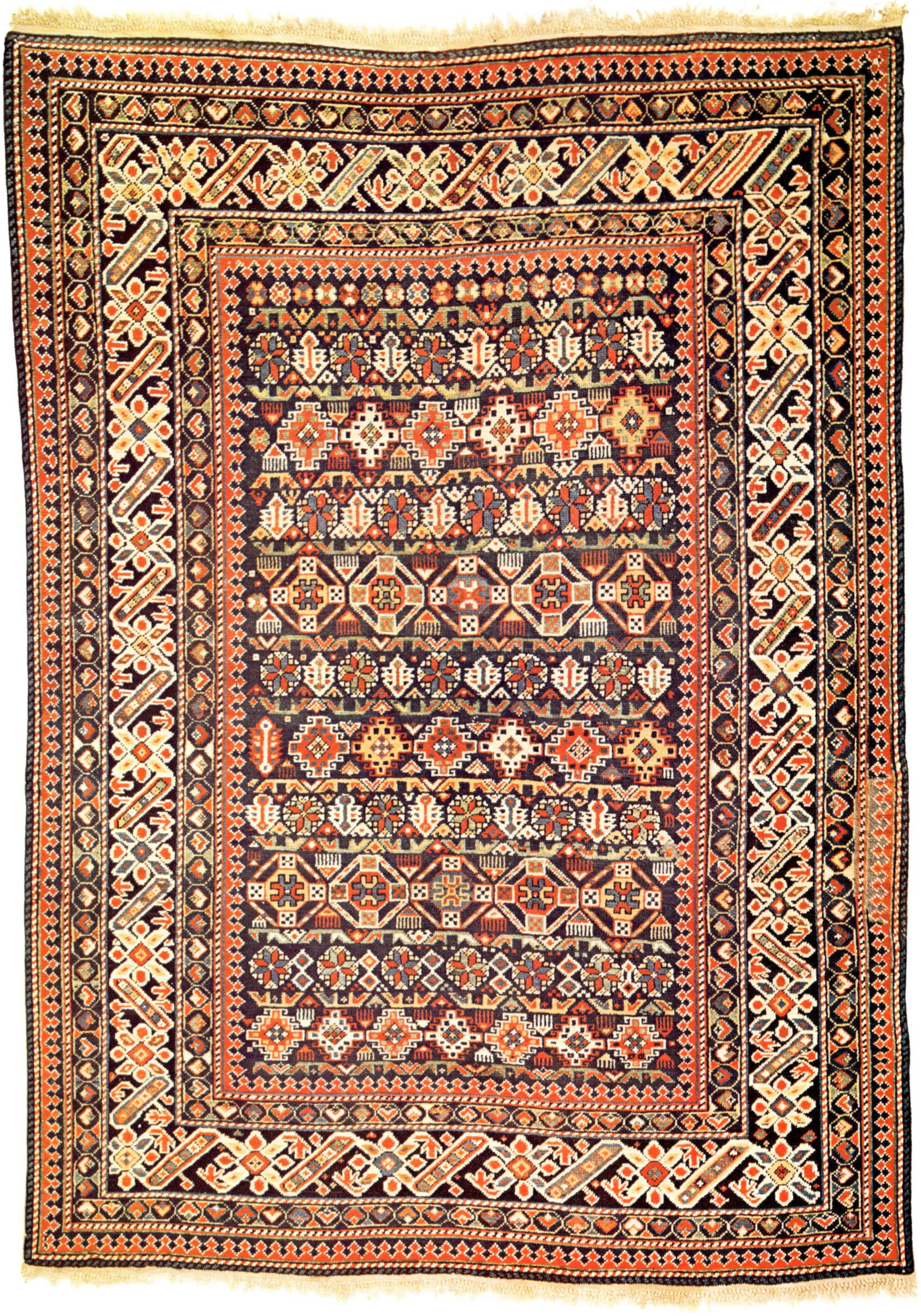

351

352 A rug with compositional elements similar to those seen on the previous piece. The lightish blue tonality is unusual. Later in date than 351, with what may be some synthetic dyes. Circa 1900.
190 x 129 cm

Chichi continued

pieces woven thirty years apart. Another example, with Kufic borders, is illustrated in *Hali* (vol. 2, no. 1, p. 97) and is dated 1295 A.H. (A.D. 1878). These three examples, all bearing dates in the second *chichi* half of the 19th century, suggest that the quality of weaving did not deteriorate to any great extent probably until the early 20th century.

Chichi rugs are usually of fine weave, with knot counts of more than 1,500 per sq. dm (97 per sq. in.). Schürmann, however, illustrates an example (pl. 111), which has the unusually low knot count of 672 per sq. dm (43 per sq. in.). The majority are cotton wefted but a not insignificant number have wool wefts; most have a ribbed back indicative of a northern origin. In colour, the majority have a dark blue field, although both red and yellow ground pieces are known. Most authorities agree that, along with compositional and structural features, a particularly pleasing dark green colour is also indicative of a Chichi origin.

In conclusion, it has to be said that the provenance of these pieces to a single village is not proven and it seems likely that many 'Chichi' rugs were, in fact, woven over a wide area of the north-east Caucasus.

CHICHI

354

353 Not a very pleasing example, with an unusually long and narrow field. Once again, rows of hooked octagons and plain-sided octagons alternate. Late 19th/early 20th century.
230 x 136cm

354 A distinctly better drawn example than the previous piece. Probably late 19th century.
160 x 116cm

Characteristic Chichi border

KUBA

355

355 This is the design which Schürmann considers to be 'typical' of Chichi rugs. The inner white ground guard, with its polychrome floral stars, is a very pleasing feature of this piece. Note the greenish tonality of the guards flanking the main border. Altogether a delightful rug, although the handling of the main borders at the bottom end is a little crude — normally a somewhat more fluid turn is achieved. Second half of the 19th century.
205 x 113 cm

356 This unusual white-ground rug is, in my opinion, dated 1282 A.H. (A.D. 1865-6), about the same period as the other dated Chichi rugs mentioned in the introduction to this section, and not as has been mentioned by some authorities 1212 A.H. (A.D. 1798). The alternating rows of octagons and spiky stylised flowers are typical of a group called Khirdagyd-Chichi. In fact, the closeness of this and nos. 357, 358 and 360 to certain Daghestan rugs (cf., for instance, our 410) suggests that an attribution to Chichi could be challenged. The border designs of this and the following two rugs are atypical.
143 x 97 cm

356

357

357 This piece has a dark yellow ground. The design is, once again, of the type which, following Kerimov and Schürmann, has become known as 'Khirdagyd-Chichi'. Note the two small animals on the left edge of the field, fairly unusual motifs on rugs of this group. Probably late 19th century.
130 x 107 cm

358 Here, the composition of the alternate open octagon and palmette rows is more diffused, and even the palmettes, which have been defined as highly stylised bird figures by some authors, are different. The piece has a border system perhaps more typical of Shirvan rugs, an all-wool foundation and blue overcast sides. An attribution to Chichi is doubtful and Peter Bausback, in his 1975 catalogue, illustrated a piece (p. 145) with a very similar field design but a leaf-and-calyx border and cotton wefts, which he catalogued as Shirvan; certain structural features of the present piece, notably the blue sides and ribbed back, are traditionally held to indicate a northern origin, but in appearance, an attribution to Shirvan makes slightly more sense. Possibly first half 19th century.
153 x 94 cm

358

359 This piece has the typical Chichi main border composition and the hooked octagon motifs in the field; the dark blue main borders also have a slightly greenish tinge. The overall effect is of a tight, well-organised, composition although stiff and with little individual flair. Probably late 19th century, although examples of similar quality, colour and appearance were woven well into the 20th century.
204 x 129 cm

360 An interesting piece, having an orange field with yellow *abrash* at the lower end. The field design is very similar to our 356, and this piece also is of the type called 'Khirdagyd-Chichi'. It is noticeable that rugs of this group have a wide variety of border compositions; a prayer rug, also with Kufic borders, was on the United States art market in 1979 and is illustrated in *Hali* (vol. 2, no. 1, p. 77). This latter rug has a blue-green *abrashed* field and light blue-green borders; it is dated 1295 A.H. (A.D. 1878). Like the present rug, it was quite finely woven and with a displaced warp. Second half 19th century.
184 x 135 cm

360

361 (*overleaf*) This rug is something of an oddity. Both in structure and composition, it seems to be a piece based on a Chichi but woven elsewhere. The serrate-edged lattice is a most unusual feature for a Chichi and the handling of the motifs within it relate the rug closely to certain Shirvans (cf. our 262-265) but also to other Kuba and Daghestan rugs. However, the handling of the main and minor borders is almost identical to that on 351. Late 19th century.
144 x 93 cm

362 (*overleaf*) Following on from our discussion of the previous piece, this rug, with 351, has a very similarly drawn main border and flanking minor borders, although it has attractive ribbon pattern inner and outer minor borders and a marked greenish tonality. It may be that these three pieces represent a specific group, although they are at present called 'Khirdagyd-Chichi'. This rug has wool warps, cotton wefts and is rather coarser in weave than most Chichis. Probably late 19th century.
170 x 115 cm

361

362

363 This rug is, again, something of an oddity, being the only example of a rug called 'Khirdagyd-Chichi' that I have seen with a 'crab' border (and a white-ground one at that). A closely related prayer rug, illustrated in *Oriental Rugs from Canadian Collections* (no. 30), is catalogued by Gardiner as Baku, presumably on the basis of its lightish palette, although it has the same light brown, blues, yellows and white border seen on our rug. A third example with a white-ground crab border was sold at auction in London by Lefevre's on 11 February 1977 (lot 31) and catalogued as Kuba. The inner white-ground border of our rug, with its beautifully drawn polychrome floral meander, is also a most unusual feature. This would appear to be an exceptional rug of great quality, although its attribution to Chichi is open to question. Second half 19th century. 178 x 110 cm

364 I would place this rug in the same group as 351, 361 and 362; its squarish format is unusual and the carnation motifs of its minor borders, although found on many other groups of east Caucasian rugs, are fairly rarely encountered on pieces ascribed to Chichi. The field motifs are also atypical and were it not for the main border, this writer would prefer a Kuba to a Chichi attribution. Compare the field motifs seen here to those in the field of our 328, a rug of undoubted Kazak origin. Late 19th century. 154 x 127 cm

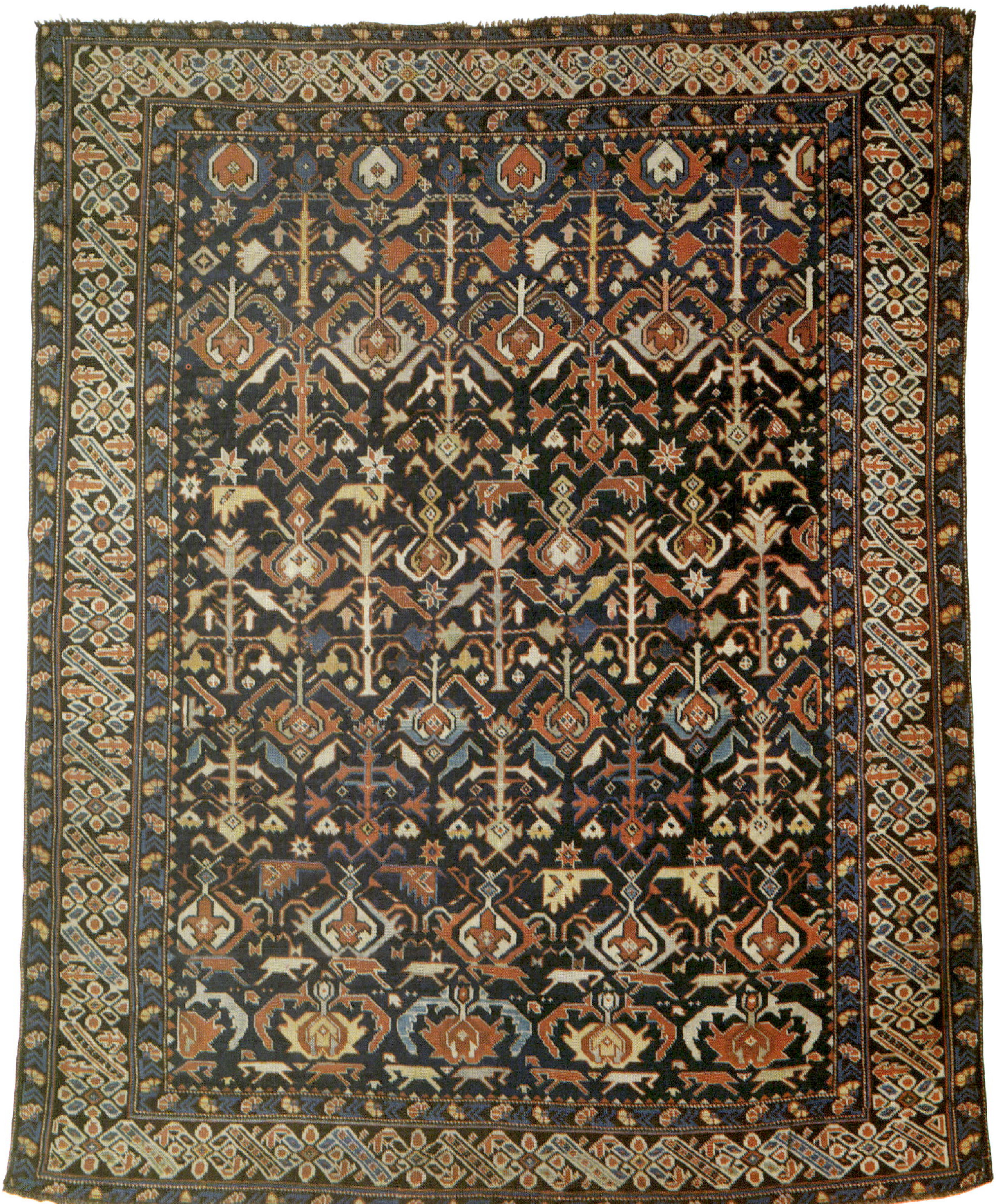

364

Perepedil

Sometimes spelled 'Perpedil', this is one of the most distinctive groups of Caucasian rugs, and is named after a village some thirty kilometres north of the town of Kuba itself. The majority of examples have a main border design of the so-called Kufic type—all the pieces we illustrate do so—and the field composition usually consists of series of ram's horn motifs in the centre of the field and pointing inward from each of the long sides. The vertical system of ram's horns is counterpointed either by octagons or large flowers of the type previously encountered on floral Shirvan rugs. Between these principal motifs is a variety of geometric ornaments and highly stylised floral motifs. Between each of the central ram's horns, there will be found a repeated series of geometric motifs with flanking birds. As we have said, almost all examples have a Kufic border. A very unusual rug with a leaf-and-calyx border will be found illustrated in *Oriental Rugs from Canadian Collections* (no. 18). Another unusual border can be seen on a white-ground piece in Peter Bausback's 1975 catalogue (p. 155). This has a series of cone-like motifs in orange and white alternately, between a light blue Greek key meander on a dark blue ground. Interestingly, an identical border is found on a very rare white-ground Perepedil prayer rug illustrated in Lefevre's *Caucasian Carpets* (no. 35); this piece is of added interest because, despite its beautifully drawn and well-spaced composition, its fine colour, closeness of weave and considerable rarity, it is dated 1308 A.H. (A.D. 1890/1). On this evidence, it is difficult to imagine many examples of the group being much older; however, to confuse

365 A typical example, with a fairly generous field composition. Late 19th/early 20th century.
110 x 84cm

366 A fussy and overcrowded piece which has lost its outer minor borders at top and bottom. Late 19th/early 20th century.
119 x 89cm

the issue somewhat, two almost identical prayer rugs were sold by Lefeve's on 26 May 1978 and 27 April 1979 and were dated 1284 (A.D. 1867/8) and 1281 A.H. (A.D. 1864/5). Three other rugs with this particular border design known to me are the white-ground Seichur, at one time with the firm of Mark Keshishian & Son in the United States (cf. *Hali*, vol. 1, no. 3, p. 32), our 381, also catalogued as Seichur, and the piece illustrated in Jack Franses' *European and Oriental Rugs for Pleasure* (fig. 19), which is perhaps the most interesting, since this border is found in combination with a 'Seichur' border.

The majority of Perepedil rugs have a dark blue ground, but both red and white ground pieces are not uncommon; probably the rarest ground colour is yellow. Most rugs of this group are finely woven, the backs ribbed and the sides overcast in white cotton or wool. The pile is cut short and is smooth and velvety. Few examples have the appearance of great age and very many seem stereotyped 20th century products made, presumably, for the western market. A well-spaced, comparatively uncluttered composition is usually encountered on examples which, for structural reasons, one might describe as reasonably old. The majority of pieces have wool warps and cotton wefts but wool-wefted examples are certainly not unusual.

The motifs found on Perepedil rugs have been the source of endless discussions. The figures which I have called birds (since they seem to represent birds quite clearly) have often, and somewhat fancifully, been described as camels in the carpet trade; this, however, seems no more unlikely than Roger Gardiner's suggestion, in his *Oriental Rugs from Canadian Collections*, that they represent complex and highly stylised floral motifs. It is interesting that almost identical figures appear in the spandrels of some late 18th and early 19th century Turkish prayer rugs of the so-called 'Van Dyck' Ladik type.

The principal compositional element, the ram's horn (*vurma*) motif, is also a complex one. The totemic significance of the horned ram's head, which has its place as much in western as eastern mythology, is one of protection and power; whole heads were often placed above the entrance

continued on p.282

367 Although crowded, this rug has a handsome appearance and a particularly pleasing palette. There is an unusual light blue-green colour in the field ornamentation and we note how the motifs within the central white-ground octagon can be related to the hooked motifs of Kazak rugs. The shell-like motifs in the mirror borders are unusual. Late 19th/early 20th Century.
170 x 107 cm

Perepedil continued

to nomadic tents. That the bifurcated arabesque of Perepedil rugs does actually represent a highly stylised rendering of horns is not, however, absolutely certain. Kerimov pointed out that the motif had become known as 'maternal flowers' (and within the series of motifs placed under that general heading, was known specifically as 'scissors') by the weavers in the Caucasus he encountered, although he remarked that the motif probably did originally represent animal horns (the changing of animal motifs into floral ones is, of course, a well-known phenomenon in Oriental weaving). However, the similarity of this motif and the highly stylised, ribbon-like animals found in ancient Chinese art suggests strongly that, once again, we are dealing with a totally degenerate motif which once represented pairs of opposing animals, probably dragons.

There is one very odd group of rugs often attributed to Perepedil which should be mentioned here. Examples are comparatively rare and have a field composition based quite clearly on 16th and 17th century Safavid rugs of the so-called Herati type; the composition found in the wide border is the so-called 'Kufic' pattern, most frequently encountered on Heriz carpets and other fine weavings from north-west Persia. An example is illustrated by Schürmann in *Caucasian Rugs* (100-107) with a rose-pink field and a dark blue border and a decidedly more dramatic example, with a deep red field and dark blue border, was offered for auction by Sotheby's in New York (31st October, 1980; *Hali*, vol. 3, no. 2, p.22). Two mysteries surround this very peculiar type — why an obviously Caucasian group of weavers should have produced a hybrid Persian design and why these rugs should be attributed to Perepedil. (The Sotheby piece, for instance, had white selvedges and white cotton plaited ends, all indications of a Shirvan origin rather than one in Kuba. The Schürmann piece lacks its original selvedge but it, too, has white ends, a mixture of cotton and wool). Schürmann gives no explanation and it could be of value to see a detailed study of such pieces attempting to explain the apparent peculiarities of this group.

368 A late and undistinguished piece. It is interesting to compare it with the dated piece, 370, as the similarities are obvious. Late 19th/early 20th century.
200 x 134 cm

369 Undistinguished, although the degree of stylisation apparent in the bird figures is worth noting. It has a mellower look than the previous example. Probably late 19th century.
173 x 122 cm

370 Apparently dated 1333 A.H. (A.D. 1914/5) and exactly what we would expect. It is interesting to see how, on this piece, the birds have become the dominant motifs and all stand the same way up. Not a rug which raises any enthusiasm.
214 x 162 cm

371 An attractive rug and possibly the oldest example of this group encountered so far. Four of the white squares contain a 'St. Andrew's cross' motif. The piece has particularly good drawing and despite the cluttered field, is an outstanding example. Second half 19th century.
183 x 127 cm

372

372 Not surprisingly, white-ground Perepedil rugs are keenly collected. This piece has some unusual, lightish, colours in the field and the border scheme is very similar to the previous example. Late 19th century.
165 x 142 cm

373 In overall design, this piece is preferable to the previous example. The field motifs are more clearly drawn and less crowded, and the main border, more generous. Of interest are the four octagons, each containing an abstract motif in white. These are obviously related to the similar compositions on the so-called Ordutch Konagkend rugs and to the related Shirvan and Baku pieces. There is also an echo of the Kazak 'triple medallion' type (e.g. our 105), to certain Gendjes (e.g. our 151 and 152), to the motifs within the central hexagon of certain Lenkoran rugs (e.g. our 186), to the free-standing motifs on our Moghan 197, to the motifs within the large octagon of Chajli rugs, to the three vertically arranged large motifs in the centre of the Kuba-Shirvan rugs 318 and 319, and to the white serrated-edged motifs seen in the field of the Chichi 362. Its origin is not easy to establish, but that it is a highly stylised animal or bird seems certain. The composition of octagon and central motif arranged in a single vertical row is quite commonly encountered on Perepedil rugs — cf. our 367 and 374. A very fine piece, although it has suffered some damage. Second half 19th century.
156 x 127 cm

373

374 The first of two red-ground pieces; fairly well drawn but cramped. Judging by the present-day carpet market, this design must have been extremely popular in the late 19th/early 20th century. Vast numbers have survived, often in excellent condition; the majority are very similar in colour, size and design and would appear to be the product of a well-orchestrated industry geared to export.
158 x 117 cm

375 An overcrowded and late piece, although as a 'furnishing' carpet, it has a high commercial value. Late 19th/early 20th century.
231 x 165 cm

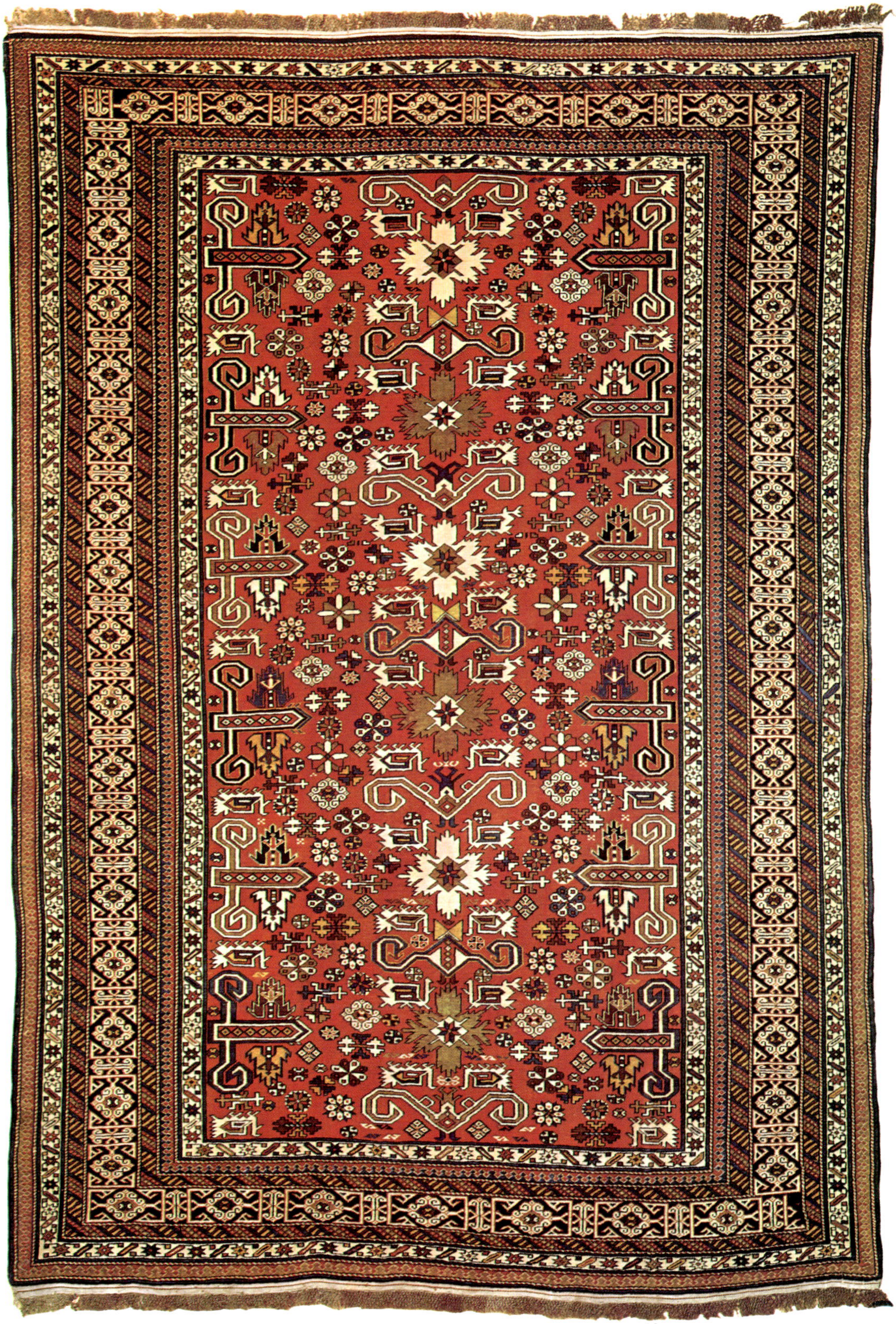

375

Seichur

This group is named after the most northerly town of the Kuba region, about thirty kilometres south of Daghestan. Like Chichi rugs, this group is characterised by the use of a particular border, usually in a predominantly duochromatic palette of blue and white. Although often described as a variant of the 'running dog', the principal motifs of this border seem to be an amalgam of 'wings' and 'torsos'; for example, on the blue reciprocal section of 378, the depiction of a bird's head seems particularly clear. It is also called the 'Georgian' border.

The most common type of Seichur rug is fairly long — eight to ten feet — and narrow, with a composition consisting of a series of large 'St. Andrew's' cross motifs with surrounding systems of stylised flowers, a design which, according to Kerimov, is called *Ispigyulchichi* or 'white flower'. The arrangement of the composition is usually in the form of a single vertical row of large crosses, although examples are known with a diagonal arrangement (cf. *Hali*, vol. 1, no. 4, p. 38 where this pattern reads vertically 1:2:1:2:1:2:1). Ground colours are usually dark blue or white.

However, Seichur rugs with all-over floral compositions are frequently encountered and there is a well-known group with western-style floral decoration similar to the Karabagh rugs previously discussed. In some instances, the 'western' flowers appear only in the main border, the 'Seichur' border appearing as an outer minor border.

The few dated examples of Seichur rugs give us little help, probably because most of them are atypical. A rug with Lesghi stars and Seichur border in the Fisher Collection (Virginia Museum of Fine Arts, illustrated in *Hali*, vol. 1, no. 2) is inscribed in Farsi: 'Hagia Ibshat' (probably the name of the recipient) and dated 1350 A.H. (A.D. 1931/2); the piece is of a quality which, were it not dated, would certainly have caused it to have been placed at least thirty years earlier. Another undated example of this type, with a double Seichur border, was sold by Lefevre in London on 2 November 1977 (lot 28); however, the attribution of rugs with Lesghi stars (e.g. our 433-441) poses considerable problems. This motif is found in conjunction with a wide variety of border designs, including those associated with specific groups — our 440, for instance, has Chichi borders.

The Seichur rugs which appear to have been dated the most often are those which, for convenience, I call the 'Bidjov' type; we illustrate one such example, 387, which is dated 1299 A.H. (A.D. 1881/2), and two others, sold by Lefevre in London (26 November 1976, lot 31 and 14 July 1978, lot 26) are dated 1290 A.H. (A.D. 1873/4) and 1267 A.H. (A.D. 1850/1) respectively. The latter is a rug of exceptional quality; however, the differences in quality and draughtsmanship between it and the Fisher rug woven eighty years later are hardly significant.

Structurally, the majority of rugs attributed to Seichur have a fairly high knot count — 1,500 to 1,800 per sq. dm (97 to 116 per sq. in.), wool warps, cotton wefts, dark blue overcasting at the sides and a ribbed back. In feel they are stiff and a little harsh.

376

376 A typical example of the most famous type of Seichur rug. The cross motifs and scattered flowers give these pieces a very majestic appearance and they have always been popular in the West. On the present piece, note the two equestrian figures at either side of the field just under two-thirds of the way down; these same features appear in a Bidjov type Seichur illustrated in *Oriental Rugs from Canadian Collections* (no. 15), and are also sometimes found on east Caucasian prayer rugs from Shirvan and Daghestan. This piece has a somewhat overcrowded design. Probably early 20th century.
308 x 94 cm

377 The spacing of the composition on this piece is considerably more pleasing than on the previous example and the lightish blue field is also most attractive (and unusual). On many Seichur rugs, there are two principal borders of almost equal importance, although the Seichur border here is usually the outer of the two and often narrower. An attractive rug, probably second half of the 19th century.
305 x 118 cm

378 The first of the white-ground Seichur rugs and a particularly good and handsome example. Many of these 'St. Andrew's' cross rugs have a tapestry-like appearance which may be due to western influence. I do not know of any example bearing an early date. Probably dates from the second half of the 19th century.
255 x 98cm

379 This piece has dull colours although the main field composition is well executed. There is no main border but a series of narrow borders containing the carnation motif. Late 19th century.
300 x 152cm

380 A most unusual piece. The 'St. Andrew's' cross has here been made into a lattice; the Seichur border is also used as an inner border, a feature seldom encountered. The pink would appear to be a synthetic dye. Early 20th century.
211 x 136cm

381

382

381 The use of this border on white-ground Perepedil prayer rugs is discussed in the introduction to the section on those rugs. As stated there, three white-ground Seichur examples have been published in recent literature, although one, illustrated in Jack Franses' book, has it in combination with the normal Seichur border. Our example is almost identical to the Keshishian rug, and both probably date from the late 19th century. The Franses rug is a more attractive example and may be slightly earlier.
214 x 123 cm

382 Perhaps the most attractive Seichur of this type illustrated here. The inner border, an angular flower and vine in pink on red, is a distinguishing feature of Seichur weavings but is certainly not exclusive to them. It appears in the same colours but in slightly different form (closer, in fact, to the style of borders found on some Bidjar rugs from north-west Persia) on an extraordinary white-ground rug with a directional design of shrubs illustrated by Schürmann in *Caucasian Rugs* (pl. 114); this piece, in the Bernheimer Collection, Munich, has been associated with Seichur by a number of authors and is almost certainly 18th century. The present piece is superbly drawn, not crowded and has splendid colours. Second half 19th century.
179 x 111 cm

383 Were it not for the borders, one would hesitate to give this rug a Seichur attribution (although it is difficult to think how else one would attribute it); the main points of interest are the blue diagonal lines which slope from right to left on the mid-blue field. Late 19th/early 20th century.
304 x 123 cm

384 The first of the rugs with westernised floral designs, the flowers themselves being arranged in diagonal rows on a dark blue-green field. Late 19th century.
180 x 112cm

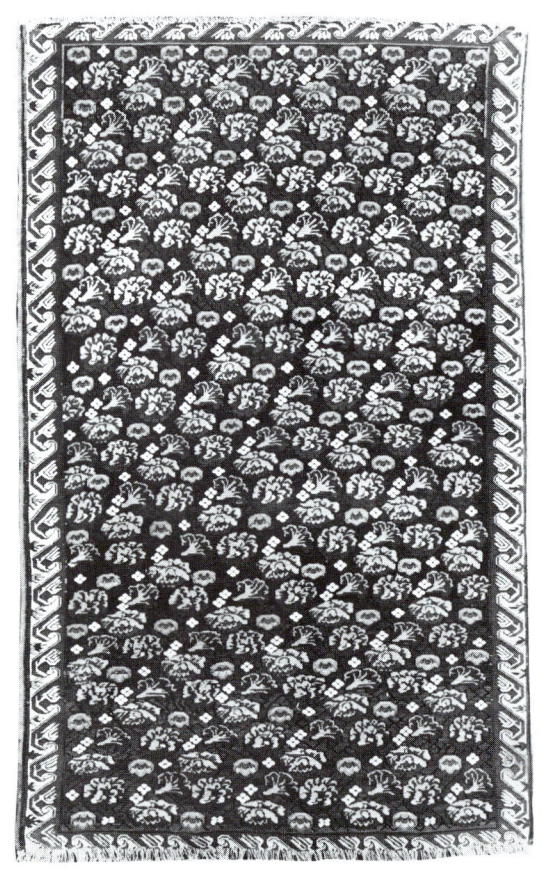

SEICHUR WITH WESTERN FLOWERS

385 This piece has only carnation heads facing in alternative directions, from row to row. Like 384 and 386, The field is dark blue with a light blue zig-zag trellis. Late 19th century.
127 x 93 cm

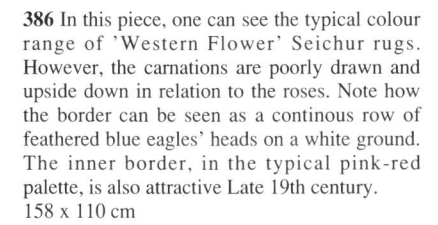

386 In this piece, one can see the typical colour range of 'Western Flower' Seichur rugs. However, the carnations are poorly drawn and upside down in relation to the roses. Note how the border can be seen as a continous row of feathered blue eagles' heads on a white ground. The inner border, in the typical pink-red palette, is also attractive Late 19th century.
158 x 110 cm

387 An interesting rug, the field composition of which relates it closely to the Bidjov rugs of Shirvan (cf. our 266-268) and to certain of the so-called 'Alpan-Kuba' rugs (e.g. our 399-401), a number of the latter actually having Seichur borders (e.g. our 391). As pointed out in the introduction to the present group, a few dated examples of this type are known, including one as early as 1267 A.H. (A.D. 1850/1). Our rug is dated 1299 A.H. (A.D. 1881/2); its field composition, with its carnations and broad, curling leaves, gives it a close affinity with the preceding group of western flower Seichur rugs. Woven on an all-wool foundation, it demonstrates clearly the fine quality of late 19th century Caucasian weaving.
143 x 133 cm

387

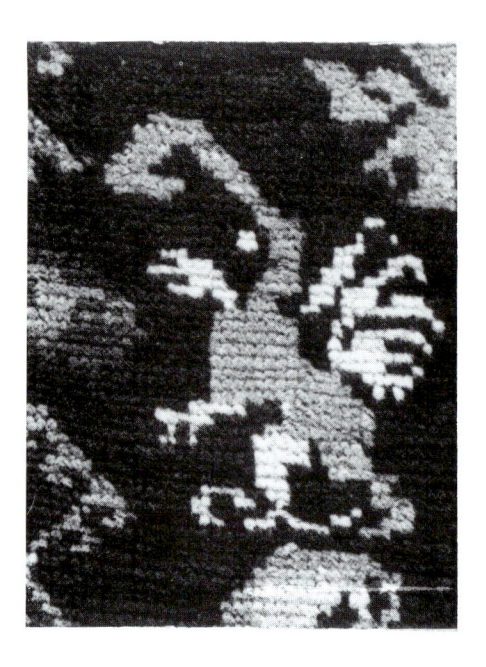

Detail of a dragon on a Seichur rug.

388 This is one of the most beautiful examples of Caucasian village weaving I have seen. The piece has outstanding colours including the use of red and blue in the Seichur border, the darkness of which makes a splendid contrast with the light blues and greens of the palmettes in the white-ground field. The overall composition of directional shrubs arranged in a directional diagonal lattice seems clearly derived from pieces such as the old Bernheimer rug discussed in the note to 382 and also the red-ground fragmented piece illustrated by Schürmann in *Caucasian Rugs* (pl. 128); this latter rug is dated, somewhat optimistically, to the 17th/18th century, and surprisingly, is attributed by Schürmann to the Lesghi. First half or mid-19th century.
159 x 113 cm

388

389 A number of long rugs are known with field compositions consisting of diamonds flanked by four palmettes. The present rug has a deep blue field with a light blue *abrash* and, like the other rugs of this type, the ornamentation is woven in vivid polychromy. Schürmann, in *Caucasian Rugs*, illustrates a smaller example (pl. 102) which has three large diamonds, with four leaf-like appendages and four diamond poles at the principal compass points. He attributes the rug to Kuba, but suggests that it shows the strong influence of rugs from Daghestan and Lesghistan. Perhaps a closer parallel, in terms of field composition, is the soumak rug in the catalogue of *The George Walter Vincent and Belle Townsley Smith Collection of Islamic Rugs* (pl. 50), which has two vertical rows of the diamond constellation almost identical in form to those which appear on the present rug. The four flanking motifs have been construed as highly stylised birds and on the Smith soumak, which, interestingly, has Seichur borders, each motif is accompanied by a tiny, clearly recognisable, bird, almost as if the weaver wishes to make it clear that she knew what she was doing; it will also be noticed that the motif is very similar to the highly stylised birds which appear on Perepedil rugs, the connection of which to earlier Anatolian weaving has already been mentioned. Second half 19th century.
350 x 132 cm

390 This piece is a distinct oddity, although a very interesting one. So often in the study of 19th century tribal and village weaving one reads that such-and-such a motif is a highly stylised and degenerate rendering of a bird or animal figure, the totemic significance of which was once clearly understood by the weaver, who would obviously draw it with great clarity so that it would more effectively perform its intended mystical function. As centuries went by and peoples were subjugated, dispersed or forcibly converted, the old totemic images slowly became diffused and misunderstood, thus beginning the gradual process of simplification and stylisation, so that, eventually, little of the original motif remained. In the discussion of 389, we remarked that the figures at the corners of the diamonds almost certainly represented highly degenerate bird figures. We then look at 390 which seems no older but has a far more archaic design — we can see four clearly recognisable birds surrounding diamond-like medallions; each system is contained within a vertical row of alternate pseudo-diamonds and rectangles. Many other bird and animal figures are scattered throughout the field, some of which are distinctly bizarre — there are two white figures two-thirds of the way down which look like crosses between an elephant and a duck, each having what would appear to be a headless rider standing on its back ! How such an anachronism of a rug came to be woven at the end of the 19th century it is difficult to explain. It may possibly be a copy of a very old Caucasian or even Persian rug, dating possibly to the 16th century (it has some affinities with Safavid garden carpets), or it may be the product of interpretative prompting on the part of some outsider. The large medallions are in dark blue and red on a mid-blue ground. Second half 19th century.
283 x 93 cm

391 Another archaic version of the so-called bird Kuba rugs, this one with extraordinarily vivid colours and a design which must be linked to the 17th century dragon rugs. The presence of the Seichur border is interesting but an attribution to a specific place within the Kuba region is impossible. Probably mid-19th century.
203 x 119 cm

389

'BIRD' KUBA

KUBA 297

390

391

392 This piece should probably be included within the Seichur group; its palette resembles that of our 379 and it has the combination of western flowers and Seichur borders often seen on Seichur pieces. Each hexagon has eight attachments which should be identified with the stylised bird ornaments of 389 and 391, and one cannot help feeling that the large striped *boteh*, with their vivid yellow detailing, end in heads of a distinctly dragon-like cast. Probably late 19th century.
275 x 129 cm

393 Another version of the bird Kuba type, although here there is an even greater degree of stylisation. The ground colour is dark blue. Late 19th/early 20th century.
146 x 118cm

394 A very similar field composition to the previous piece, a composition which some authors have interpreted as a tree-of-life flanked by birds. The interlock border is not usually found on Kuba rugs. Probably late 19th century.
188 x 114 cm

395 A flat-woven rug, again with the so-called tree-of-life motif; it has an unusual combination of a main red-ground crab border and an outer blue and white Seichur border. It is woven in the soumak technique. Late 19th/early 20th century.
251 x 107 cm

396 An attractive example with a profusion of colours, including a particularly bright yellow. The minor borders contain an attractive, very Japanese looking, floral composition, and both the Seichur border and the predominant dark blue-green (field) and rose-red colours enforce a Seichur attribution. However, the piece has an all-wool foundation, the sides being overcast in blue and green wool. Probably late 19th century.
183 x 122 cm

397 A not very exciting rug with an extremely stiff composition; the series of borders are equally uninspired. Although it has the red-pink and green dyes associated with Seichur, it has many of the hallmarks of a late example. It should be noted, however, that a specific group of rugs was produced around Derbend, a coastal town situated between Kuba and Daghestan. Rugs were made here in a wide variety of designs, but are recognisable by their coarse weave. Pieces in the Alpan-Kuba design are known, some of which have Seichur borders. The present piece may well have been woven there. The label Derbend is considered somewhat derogatory in the carpet trade and one gets the impression that often unscrupulous dealers will avoid calling any rug by this name if possible. Probably early 20th century.
142 x 97 cm

Alpan-Kuba

This is another of the groups which Kerimov claimed to have isolated and which was accepted by Schürmann; again, it should be treated with considerable circumspection. Schürmann illustrated only one example (pl. 113) in *Caucasian Rugs*, which has a basic field composition of a row of vertical irregular diamonds flanked by four hexagons, each with four claw-like appendages (often called 'lobsters' in the carpet trade). The design can be read as a series of 'St. Andrew's' crosses made up of four hexagons emanating from a central diamond, with large irregular diamonds between each cross. Facing inward from each side of the field are large lotus palmettes and arrowhead motifs, with various small geometric ornaments scattered throughout the field. The border system has two principal green-ground minor borders containing carnations, flanking a main border with an odd repeat design of what would seem to be pairs of highly stylised birds. The ground colour of the field is a dark green, matching the minor borders, that of the main border and the hexagons being red.

Schürmann suggests that the overall tonality of his piece posits a Seichur origin; certainly the two groups are structurally indistinguishable, the St. Andrew's cross is a major compositional link and many examples are known with Seichur borders, including the fine old example sold by Lefevre's in London on 26 November 1976, one of the most beautiful examples of this type I have ever seen. Another superb old example is illustrated in Spuhler, König and Volkmann's *Alte Orientteppiche* (no. 21). Both Jean Lefevre and the German authors shunned the 'Alpan-Kuba' designation, calling their pieces Seichur. A third apparently old example is illustrated in Peter Bausback's *Antike Orientteppiche (p.* 272-273). All three examples would appear to be older and of finer quality than the examples we illustrate, and might be from the first half of the 19th century. Two examples with Seichur borders, 396 and 400, are illustrated here.

The composition itself is an extremely interesting one, which would seem to be

continued on p.303

398 A very attractive rug, although one which appears to contain a number of synthetic dyes. Worthy of particular admiration is the boldly drawn crab border with a splendid polychromy to heighten the effect; it reminds me, in both its drawing and colour, of the Baluch version of the crab border seen on the famous Hartley Clark Adraskand carpet. It has cotton wefts, sides overcast in natural light brown cotton and a knot count of 1,200 per sq. dm (77 per sq. in.). Could be as late as 1900-10.
200 x 130 cm

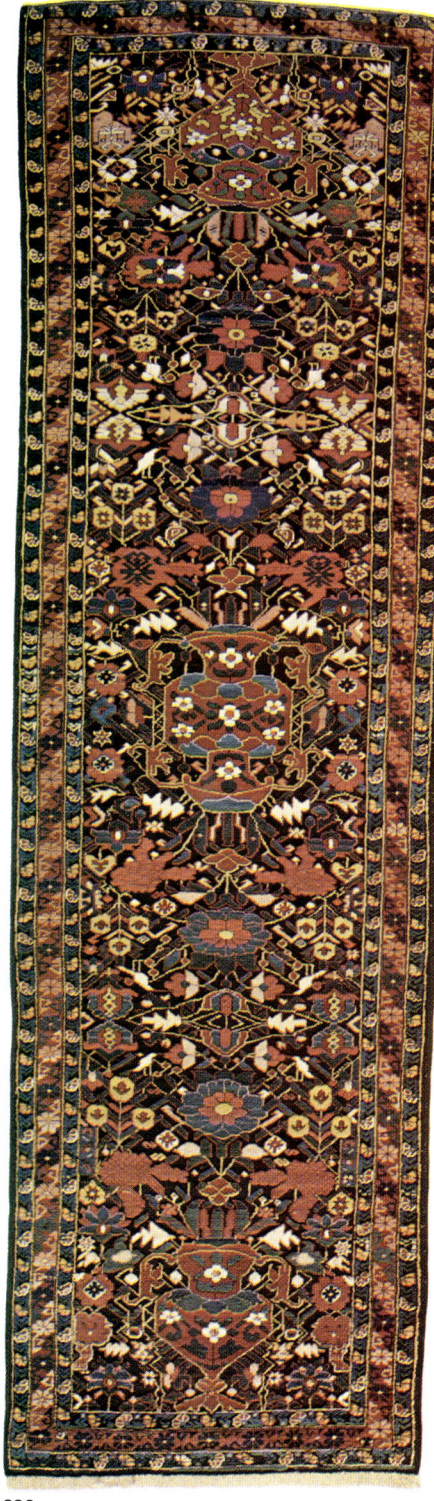

302 KUBA   ALPAN-KUBA

399

400

Alpan-Kuba continued
linked closely not only with other groups of 19th century Caucasian rugs, particularly the 'star' Kazaks (cf. no. 1) and the 'Kasim Ushag' Karabaghs, but also with Iranian tribal weavings, especially those of the Afshar and Baluch, and with earlier Caucasian carpets. It seems probable that the composition as it appears on the Alpan-Kuba rugs is a highly stylised and degenerate version of the large floral palmettes with flanking lanceolate leaves seen on Caucasian floral carpets of the late 17th and 18th centuries. It is interesting to note that Spuhler *et al.*, in their discussion of the old piece mentioned previously, suggested that the design derived initially not only from Persian carpets but also from ceramic tiles. It is also found on 18th century Caucasian embroideries from the Shirvan area.

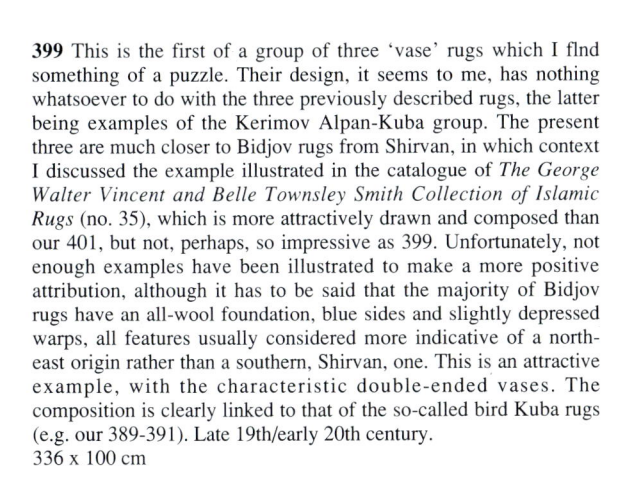

399 This is the first of a group of three 'vase' rugs which I find something of a puzzle. Their design, it seems to me, has nothing whatsoever to do with the three previously described rugs, the latter being examples of the Kerimov Alpan-Kuba group. The present three are much closer to Bidjov rugs from Shirvan, in which context I discussed the example illustrated in the catalogue of *The George Walter Vincent and Belle Townsley Smith Collection of Islamic Rugs* (no. 35), which is more attractively drawn and composed than our 401, but not, perhaps, so impressive as 399. Unfortunately, not enough examples have been illustrated to make a more positive attribution, although it has to be said that the majority of Bidjov rugs have an all-wool foundation, blue sides and slightly depressed warps, all features usually considered more indicative of a north-east origin rather than a southern, Shirvan, one. This is an attractive example, with the characteristic double-ended vases. The composition is clearly linked to that of the so-called bird Kuba rugs (e.g. our 389-391). Late 19th/early 20th century.
336 x 100 cm

400 This rug, with its distinctly more stylised design, is dated 1312 A.H. (A.D. 1894/S). All the rugs of this type have a very Kurdish flavour, this example, with its tri-floral white sprays, particularly so. We should remember that this arcading design is probably a village rendering of what was once a major Safavid workshop production of 'vase' carpets of the 17th and early 18th centuries. Like 'tree' rugs and 'garden' rugs the Kurdish lack of stylisation is clearly visible. It is worth noting that 'vase' carpets with arcading design were also woven by the Afshari of south-west Persia.
345 x 138 cm

401

401 An attractive array of light colours on this piece which none the less has somewhat crude and clumsy drawing, especially obvious when it is compared to 399. In appearance, the rug is strongly reminiscent of Karabagh weaving. Circa 1900.
340 x 140 cm

402

403

402 Zejwa long rugs are uncommon. This example has attractive colours, including a quite vivid green. A high proportion of these rugs have the interlock border composition seen on this example. It should never be assumed, of course, that Caucasian rugs of very similar compositions come from the same area or the same province. Nos. 402 and 403, for instance, do not seem to be of the same group as no. 404. The first two, for instance (and very significantly), have, within the centre of each medallion, the same red diamond *gül* with an octofoil flower head at each point, associated with 'eagle' Chelaberds. Late 19th/early 20th century.
235 x 94 cm

403 Although apparently late and not very attractive, this example is typical of a group of Zejwa rugs which have extra large medallions containing a particularly elaborate latch-hook motif. This, interestingly, seems to combine the Yomut Turkoman *gül* called 'Ogurjali' with a minor motif cut by the edge of the field which resembles the Yomut 'Kepse' *gül*. Probably late 19th century.
183 x 114 cm

Zejwa

These rugs are presumed to have emanated originally from Zejwa, a village a few kilometres to the south of Kuba. The characteristic design consists of a series of large serrate-edged palmettes with ray-like interiors, reminiscent obviously of both Chelaberd rugs from the Karabagh region and also of a certain group of Shirvan rugs (cf. 256-261). The large palmette has also been likened to the so-called 'Ogurjali' *gül* found on certain Yomut Turkoman carpets, with which motif it does, indeed, have much in common.

In general, Zejwa rugs have an all-wool foundation, sides overcast in blue and a knot count of around 1,200 per sq. dm (77 per sq. in.); the ground colour is usually mid to dark blue although a few examples, usually late in appearance, have red fields (e.g. the rug illustrated in Peter Bausback's 1972 catalogue, p. 45).

404 An attractive example with a somewhat misunderstood rendering of the Seichur border. The field contains a wide polychromy, including green, three shades of blue, red, red-brown, dark pink, pink, orange, light yellow and white. Few other Caucasian rugs can match the visual splendour, the almost Byzantine magnificence of the best Kazaks. This piece, however, which, unlike most Kazaks, has a composition of an endless repeat, is one of the few that can. The greatest example of its type I have seen. Second half of the 19th century.
185 x 125 cm

306 KUBA

405

406

405 An interesting rug, with an archaic-looking design of four large *gül*-like medallions forming a reciprocal arrow-head pattern reminiscent of Seljuk Turkish weaving. There are also six clearly recognisable dragon forms, three on each side of the field. Late 19th century.
215 x 109 cm

406 Another rug with an unusual and archaic tribal field composition. The latter is made up of three vertical *gül*-like forms bearing some resemblance to what the Russian scholar Valentina Moskova, in *Die Teppiche der Völker Mittelasiens im späten 19. und 20. Jh.* described as the Kasa-Kalkan emblem. It is also found on old Turkish rugs and on more modern ones—for instance from Melas — and on many Iranian tribal pieces, especially those of the Kurds and Qashqa'i. The border composition is unusual, although the stylised flower motif is found in this form on many tribal carpets. It is interesting to note how the Kotchak medallion of the border, apart from being a most unusual composition to find being used in this part of the rug, relates this piece to a great mass of south-west Caucasian weavings on which it appears in one place or another and in one form or another. Its best known representation is probably on Kazak rugs of the Fachralo and Sewan varieties. It does have the look of an ancient totemic emblem and may once have represented pairs of opposing birds. Late 19th century.
144 x 90 cm

407 A piece closely related in design to the previous example. This particular rendering of the medallion, however, and also the overall vivid polychromy and the octagonal motifs in the main border, are all strongly reminiscent of Kurdish weaving from north-west Persia. A most colourful and attractive rug, with an all-wool foundation. Late 19th century.
140 x 85 cm

407

Daghestan

The name 'Daghestan', used in rug books for some time, was popularised by Schürmann, although to distinguish between Daghestan, Kuba and Shirvan rugs, especially prayer rugs is, as we have noted previously, a task so subjective as to be almost meaningless, and most authors' efforts to define these families in terms of their technical features have not proved very successful.

The fact is that the majority of east Caucasian rugs of any particular design or type can have wool or cotton wefts at random, blue or white sides, a greater or lesser degree of warp displacement and a wide variation in handle. Some can be placed into convenient groups according to design, which does, at least, have the advantage of a useful communicative shorthand; in the case of Daghestan, however, even this is often difficult, and many prayer rugs for instance, are attributed to Daghestan and to Shirvan by different authors.

For the rugs attributed to Daghestan, there would appear to be a wide variety of dates (apart from the interesting phenomenon that so many of them are dated). Five examples in this book are dated between 1884 and 1908 and one 1805/6. This last piece is intriguing and will be discussed at length later. The majority of examples published in recent literature have dates between about 1880 and 1910, with a few in the 1860s. Kurt Erdmann, in *700 Years of Oriental Carpets*, recorded that he had dates for white-ground Daghestan prayer rugs as follows: "1807, 1809, 1811, 1818, 1862, 1865, 1867", etc., going up to 1932. It would be interesting to know how many of the pieces dated in the first three decades of the 19th century had silk, either in the foundation or the pile — the case with the very few examples with such early dates that I have seen, and on which I found the dates believable. There are, however, many examples with early dates which one finds either difficult or impossible to believe (this problem will be more fully discussed in our description of 428). One good example of this is the rug illustrated as no. 31 in the Anglo-Persian Carpet Company's catalogue *Fine and Rare Oriental Rugs and Weavings*, which is dated 1124 A.H. (A.D. 1707)! It should also be noted that the presence of silk, either in the foundation or the pile of a white-ground Daghestan prayer rug, or any other Caucasian rug for that matter, is certainly not an infallible sign of great age.

408

408 This piece has an all-wool foundation and sides consisting of three bundles of two warps overcast in blue wool. It has an attractive border system with two main borders, the outer one of which, with its white ground, creates a strong visual impact; the floral meander contained in the white ground border is, in fact, an unusual feature on rugs of this type. Probably Shirvan or Kuba. Second half of the 19th century.
150 x 105 cm

409 An interesting rug, the long narrow field of which has a composition closely related to some so-called Chichi rugs. The bold and handsome border is characteristic of a group of long rugs usually attributed by recent authors to Daghestan. Perhaps the most beautiful example in recent literature is a rug with an open blue field surrounded by a bold red serration illustrated by Eberhart Herrmann in *Von Lotto bis Tekke* (no. 31), a piece which could possibly be late 18th century in date. However, a very similar border is also found on later Shirvan long rugs — compare, for instance our 255. Probably second half of the 19th century.
271 x 87 cm

DAGHESTAN 309

409

410

410 Again, something of a peculiar mixture, although a very attractive rug notwithstanding. The field composition consists of a somewhat simplified 'Chichi' pattern on an ivory ground and the main border contains the 'Seichur' pattern but rendered in yellow, pale blue and orange, a most unusual colour combination. I see no reason why this piece should not be designated Kuba (compare it with our 358, for instance). Second half of the 19th century.
140 x 89 cm

310 DAGHESTAN

411 This and the following two rugs all have diagonal rows of free-standing angular palmettes (or, in this case, shrubs). It is the type of pattern which all old rug books refer to as Shirvan (or even Kabistan) and there is no reason why they should not continue to be called such (cf. our 243-245). The present piece is a particularly attractive example of this type; an almost identical rug, but with no yellow or orange in it, is in the Metropolitan Museum (*Oriental Rugs in the Metropolitan Museum*, no. 173), catalogued as Shirvan. Second half of the 19th century.
165 x 106 cm

DAGHESTAN 311

412 This attractive white-ground piece has the bat-like palmette encountered on 243 in the Shirvan section; it also has four small animals, two each side of the field about half-way down. Schürmann, in *Caucasian Rugs* (pl. 126) illustrates a far more beautiful example, which also has the unusual feature of a bird and rosette border of the type normally encountered on rugs attributed to Baku (cf. our 288-290 and 305). In this context, it is interesting to note that Jacobsen, in *Oriental Rugs, a Complete Guide*, illustrates (pl. 158) a rug with so-called Lesghi stars which has the 'Khila' bird and rosette border. Schürmann was undecided whether his rug was Daghestan or Kuba. Second half of the 19th century.
167 x 93 cm

413 A more attractive version of the same design with a variant of the border seen on no. 409. A rug with an almost identical composition is illustrated in Peter Bausback's 1977 *Antike Orientteppiche* (p. 267), which has a cotton weft. Bausback shows the rug opposite an illustration of our 358 and catalogues both as Kuba. This attribution, or one even further to the south, might well prove correct. A fine example, second half of the 19th century.
198 x 115 cm

414 A somewhat archaic-looking rug, but not as old as it would appear. The highly stylised ornaments, which are arranged diagonally on the yellow field and which have strong zoomorphic, totemic affinities, should be compared with those on the three Baku rugs nos. 302, 303 and 305. They also appear on a small mat illustrated in a Russian book, Rasim Efendi's *Decorative and Applied Arts of Azerbaijan* (no. 103), which is catalogued as Kuba. It seems likely that, once again, we are dealing with a highly stylised floral palmette, which, in turn, may itself have been derived from a totemic animal group. Certainly, the even more archaic-looking version of the motif seen on the superb 18th century rug illustrated by Schürmann in *Caucasian Rugs* (pl. 128, catalogued, presumably, because of its bright yellows and greens, as Lesghi), lends some credence to this developmental hypothesis. Probably late 19th century.
165 x 105 cm

415 Another strange rug, the attribution of which to Daghestan seems controversial. The star motifs seem to relate to both Kuba rugs and to various soumaks (cf. our discussion of the Kuba rug no. 308), and there is a strong suggestion of an endless repeat in the use of the fractional motifs at the four sides of the field. The white-ground 'crab' border and the diagonal stripes of the minor borders can be compared with the border system of no. 363. As we noted in our discussion of that piece, there are a few rugs with white-ground crab borders, all of which are usually catalogued as Baku or Kuba. Probably late 19th century.
153 x 99 cm

416 This rug is possibly from Derbend, the principal town of the Daghestan region, which is associated with coarsely woven pieces in a variety of styles. Cotton is almost always present in the foundation, the wool is usually hard and the handle is rough and loose. This piece has a Karabagh design and palette. However, a Derbend attribution is not absolutely certain. One cannot help noticing the similarity of its palette to the Lenkoran we illustrate as 189 for instance. Late 19th/early 20th century.
350 x 120 cm

314 DAGHESTAN

417 This somehwat uninspired rug is dated 1317 A.H. (A.D. 1899/1900); the colours are very similar to no. 419 which, coincidentally, bears the same date and which, like the present rug and no. 418, has a design based on a series of hooked diamonds.
265 x 141 cm

418 This rug has certainly the most attractive version of the hooked diamond composition of the three variations we illustrate. The ivory ground, clear spacing and small animals combine to form a pleasant design. A glance back to illustrations 256-261 indicates the relationship to rugs attributed to Shirvan. Probably late 19th century.
198 x 101 cm

419 This rug is also dated 1317 A.H. (A.D. 1899/1900). It is more pleasantly composed than 417 but looks to be of poorer quality. It appears to have a synthetic orange dye, which has run in the main ivory-ground border. Rugs of this type are very common.
126 x 91 cm

DAGHESTAN

420 Dated 1325 A.H. (A.D. 1907/08), this is an interesting rug for a number of reasons. Firstly the floral lattice is drawn in the opposite direction to the date in the top left-hand corner. This means, almost certainly, that the weaver was illiterate and simply wove the date upside down. More fascinating, however, is the presence of the two particular shrubs which are associated with a group of Kuba prayer rugs and which are discussed in our note to 329. Despite its coarseness, a good-looking rug.
137 x 97 cm

421 Another coarse floral-lattice rug, probably of the same vintage as the previous piece.
138 x 95 cm

420

421

422 All the coarse, floral lattice rugs illustrated in this section may have been woven in Derbend. The present piece has surprisingly well-drawn Kufic borders and an attractive red ground. Probably early 20th century. 173 x 106 cm

423 This has a design close to the type of floral lattice associated with Daghestan white-ground prayer rugs. Possibly late 19th century. 147 x 110cm

424 An attractive rug, although somewhat spoiled by the insignificant white-ground main border with its dull geometric flower composition. This border is often encountered on Karadja rugs of the Persian-Caucasian border region. Late 19th/early 20th century.
172 x 134 cm

425 This is the first of the white-ground prayer rugs we illustrate, which different authors have attributed to Daghestan or Shirvan. There is a considerable number of dated examples known, including the following: Kurt Erdmann, *700 Years of Oriental Carpets*, (fig. 219) 1284 A.H. (A.D. 1867/8); A.F. Kendrick, *Victoria and Albert Museum – Guide to the Collection of Carpets*, 1915 (pl. XXVI), and again in Kendrick and Tattersall, *Handwoven Carpets*, (pl. 116) 1287 A.H. (A.D. 1870/1); Jerome A. Straka and Louise Mackie, *The Oriental Rug Collection of Jerome and Mary Jane Straka* (no. 106) 1292 A.H. (A.D. 1875/6); Charles W. Jacobsen, *Oriental Rugs, A Complete Guide* (pl. 150) 1310 A.H. (A.D. 1892/3); *Prayer Rugs,* Textile Museum, Washington (no. XXXI) 1311 A.H. (A.D. 1893/4); Luciano Coen and Louise Duncan, *The Oriental Rug* (pl. 34) 1311 A.H. (A.D. 1893/4); Ian Bennett, *The Book of Oriental Carpets and Rugs*, (p. 102) 1331 A.H. (A.D. 1912/3). The majority of examples have an all-wool foundation and knot counts of between 1,900 and 3,100 per sq. dm (123 to 200 per sq. in.). Although it seems fairly obvious that the great majority of the small, finely woven white ground prayer rugs which are not dated were made late in the 19th or early in the 20th century, they are persistently called mid- to early 19th, or even 18th century, by many writers. The present piece has an unusual cone-like motif which I have seen on some north-west Persian examples. Late 19th century.
132 x 108 cm

425

426 A typical example of a north-eastern Caucasian prayer rug. The outer floral minor border suggest that this particular piece may be from further south, possibly even Shirvan. Late 19th century.
126 x 105 cm

426

427 This rug is dated 1309 A.H. (A.D. 1891/2). It is unusually long and narrow for a prayer rug of this group and would seem to be coarser than most. Its bright colours (the pinks may be synthetic) resemble those on another late rug illustrated in Ian Bennett's *The Book of Oriental Carpets and Rugs* (p. 102), which is dated 1331 A.H. (A.D. 1912/3); the latter, however, is better drawn and is also of interest in that it has within the arch the odd motif seen in the same position on our Kuba prayer rug no. 326. In drawing, colour and in the handling of minor borders our piece can be related to a number of Kuba rugs. 145 x 65 cm

322 DAGHESTAN — PRAYER RUGS

429 This piece is dated 1301 A.H. (A.D. 1883/4), just what we would expect. The use of only one floral shape in the lattice is a little unusual.
149 x 100cm

430 Another late piece, the field composition being in the slightly flattened style of 325. The guard stripe inside the *medachyl* border is an unusual feature. Late 19th century.
122 x 98 cm

428 This rug constitutes something of a puzzle. It is dated 1220 A.H. (A.D. 1805/6), although at first glance, this would seem to be impossibly early. The overall appearance of the rug is static and stiff, qualities not normally associated with early pieces. Technically, it is of very fine quality and our colour reproduction does not do it justice; it will be found more accurately reproduced in Peter Bausback's *Antike Orientteppiche* (p.236). According to Bausback, the piece has a wool warp and weft and is partly piled in silk. Although these are structural characteristics associated in particular with older pieces, I think the date is probably 'wrong'; the rug itself does not appear to have the same age as the superb, if wrecked, example on a silk foundation dated 1232 A. H. (A.D. 1817/8) sold at Lefevre's in London on 5 October, 1979. It should be noted, in addition, that the use of silk, either in the foundation or the pile, is not necessarily an indication of old age. It is arguable that we might be dealing with a copy of an old rug made perhaps in the early 20th century, but incorporating the date which appeared on the model.
136 x 103 cm

430

431 A rare red-ground piece with unusual drawing and polychromy in the lattice itself. A not particularly attractive rug. Probably late 19th century.
128 x 92 cm

432 This piece has cotton wefts and the floral lattice on its yellow field resembles that found on Marasali rugs. I would certainly posit a Shirvan origin for the piece. Second half of the 19th century.
136 x 102cm

431

PRAYER RUGS

DAGHESTAN 325

432

Lesghistan

With this name, we encounter another of the mysteries of east Caucasian weaving which scholarship has still to resolve satisfactorily. The Lesghi are one of many tribes who once inhabited the north eastern area of the Caucasus. There would seem to be little evidence for attributing to them the rugs which are currently described in the West by many dealers and writers as 'Lesghi' — in most cases, this means pieces which have on them large serrate-edged square-section stars, the so-called 'Lesghi' stars. It would not take a beginner long to realise that out of the many examples he can see illustrated and described by this name, there is not one, but many entirely different groups.

Murray Eiland has commented that only one recent Russian book, D. Chirkov's *Daghestan Decorative Art*, illustrated rugs attributed to the Lesghi: "Schürmann identifies a number of rugs as having been woven by the Lesghi, but they are entirely different from the five Lesghi rugs illustrated by Chirkov." These five pieces are not much help since they are probably fairly recent products and their weaving area is not clear.

Another author and rug dealer, Richard Purdon, in *Shirvan and Related Weavings from the North Caucasus,* comments on a rug with Lesghi stars in his exhibition: "This design . . . is found on multitudes of different rugs from all parts of the the Caucasus." Certainly the variation to be found in such compositional details as the main border is considerable. For instance, we illustrate nine Lesghi star rugs which have no less than seven distinct border designs; these include Kufic (433-434), 'running diamond' (435), 'interlock' (436), 'stencil S' (437), narrow *medachyl* (438), 'octagon with stars' (439, 441) and 'Chichi' (440). To these we could add examples with the 'leaf-and-calyx' main border. Charles W. Jacobsen in *Oriental Rugs, A Complete Guide* (pl. 158) illustrates a rug with a white-ground Baku-Khila 'bird and rosette' border (cf. our 288-290) and in the Jerome Straka catalogue (p. 116), there is an example with a white-ground hexagon and brackets composition, very similar to our long rug 409 but closer in feel and colour to the splendid old Daghestan illustrated in Eberhart Herrmann's *Von Lotto bis Tekke* (no. 31). Two examples with 'Seichur' borders can be found in recent literature, one in Murray Eiland's *Oriental Rugs* (pl. 158) and the other in Inge Lise Jensen's *Kaukasiske Taepper en Dansk privatsamling* (pl. S); the latter has a double 'Seichur' border, the inner in yellow and blue and the outer in blue and white. A very fine rug, sold by Lefevre (London on 22nd June 1979), had a white-ground border containing a stencil-like pattern resembling trees resting on square brackets (for examples of the 'stencil S' border, see 29, 145, 224, 277, 299, 419, 470). Another rug sold by Lefevre, and illustrated in *Caucasian Carpets* (pl. 47), had a very narrow red field framed by a wide dark blue ground border containing a continuous series of Lesghi stars of the same proportions as those in the field. The example illustrated in *Shirvan and Related Weavings from the North Caucasus* (no. 13) (and by Herrmann in *Von Lotto bis Tekke*, no. 39) has a white-ground border containing cruciform motifs with zig-zag outlines of the type frequently encountered on Anatolian and Caucasian kilim. Another unusual border is encountered on a fine rug illustrated in *Alte Orientteppiche* (no. 64); this has a somewhat crude and naïve rendering of a Turkoman border. The long rug catalogued as Kazak by Raymond Benardout in *Caucasian Rugs*, catalogued as Kazak, has a white-ground border with continuous 'spindly' eight-pointed stars (cf. our 242 for identical motifs). An obviously Kazak example, with the same 'arrow head' border pattern as seen on our Karachov no. 33, was included in Rippon Boswell's London sale (29th November 1980, lot 72). Finally we should mention the extraordinary example illustrated by Rasim Efendi in *Decorative and Applied Arts of Azerbaijan* (pl. 113), which has a white-ground Marasali border and Marasali-type *boteh* used as ornaments in the field; this is described by the Russian author as Shirvan.

continued on p.328

433 A handsome long rug with a pleasing use of green. This particular shade seems to appear in a particular group of east Caucasian rugs, although its attribution to a particular region or tribe remains unproven. Probably late 19th century.
352 x 125 cm

434 A more crowded version of the previous piece, with nine stars instead of eight. Probably from the same group as the previous piece, attributable to Kuba. Late 19th/early 20th century.
258 x 103 cm

434

435 For a piece of this design, this rug is unusually long and narrow. The polychromy of the top half, with particularly pleasing shades of red, emerald green, dark aubergine brown and sky blue, is more pleasing than that of the bottom half. In colour, shape and compositional lay-out, it resembles closely certain rugs from Baku, e.g. our 299 and 305. Second half of the 19th century.
331 x 95 cm

435

Lesghistan continued

Although this list of Lesghi star rug border ornaments is not exhaustive, we have here an apparently homogeneous group of rugs with closely comparable field designs but no less than eighteen distinct border designs. This argues against a small, centralised area of production. In field design, there is a wide, but less obvious variation in the drawing of the stars; most examples have three or more stars on the vertical axis, although some have two rows; there are also prayer rugs with Lesghi stars in the *mihrab*. The degree of stepping to the sides of the stars varies considerably, some examples being almost straight-sided.

In colour, the famed Lesghi green and yellow hues do appear on several examples, but in just as many they do not. There are also those who believe that the principal distinguishing colour of Lesghi rugs is, in fact, a particularly vivid shade of red. In construction, there is a certain degree of consistency among pieces of reasonable age, although I think that this is largely coincidental; with one exception, all the rugs I have examined, or for which I have seen structure analyses, have all-wool foundations (Heinrich Jacoby, writing in 1951, remarked that one characteristic of Lesghi weaving was the fine brown wool used for the foundation). The one exception is the strange piece illustrated by Peter Bausback in *Antike Orientteppiche* (p. 253), which has, apparently, an all-silk foundation dyed with cochineal and has a deep blue field, three huge stars — two red and one white — and a white-ground leaf-and-calyx border.

436 This piece has beautiful, mellow colours and unusually shaped stars, giving it a very archaic quality. Some experts have voiced the opinion that this is, indeed, a very fine and genuine old Lesghi rug. It is easily noted, however, that the style of composition is not typical of those rugs usually ascribed to the Lesghi, and the stars are not actually Lesghi stars. Both chromatically and stylistically, the nearest comparison that can be made is with the 'star' Kazaks, such as our 1 (the interlock border is also not found very often on north-east Caucasian rugs). Note also the Memlinc *güls* between the large stars, changing to a mini version of the large stars between the bottom two. A very rare and interesting piece. Probably mid-19th century.
245 x 121 cm

437 This example seems totally atypical of east Caucasian weaving; it hails almost certainly from further west, possibly from Moghan or Gendje. An almost identical example in the Victoria and Albert Museum has been attributed to the Kazak-Gendje region (cf. *Hali*, vol. 7, no. 2, p.100, fig. 12). Second half 19th century.
168 x 118 cm

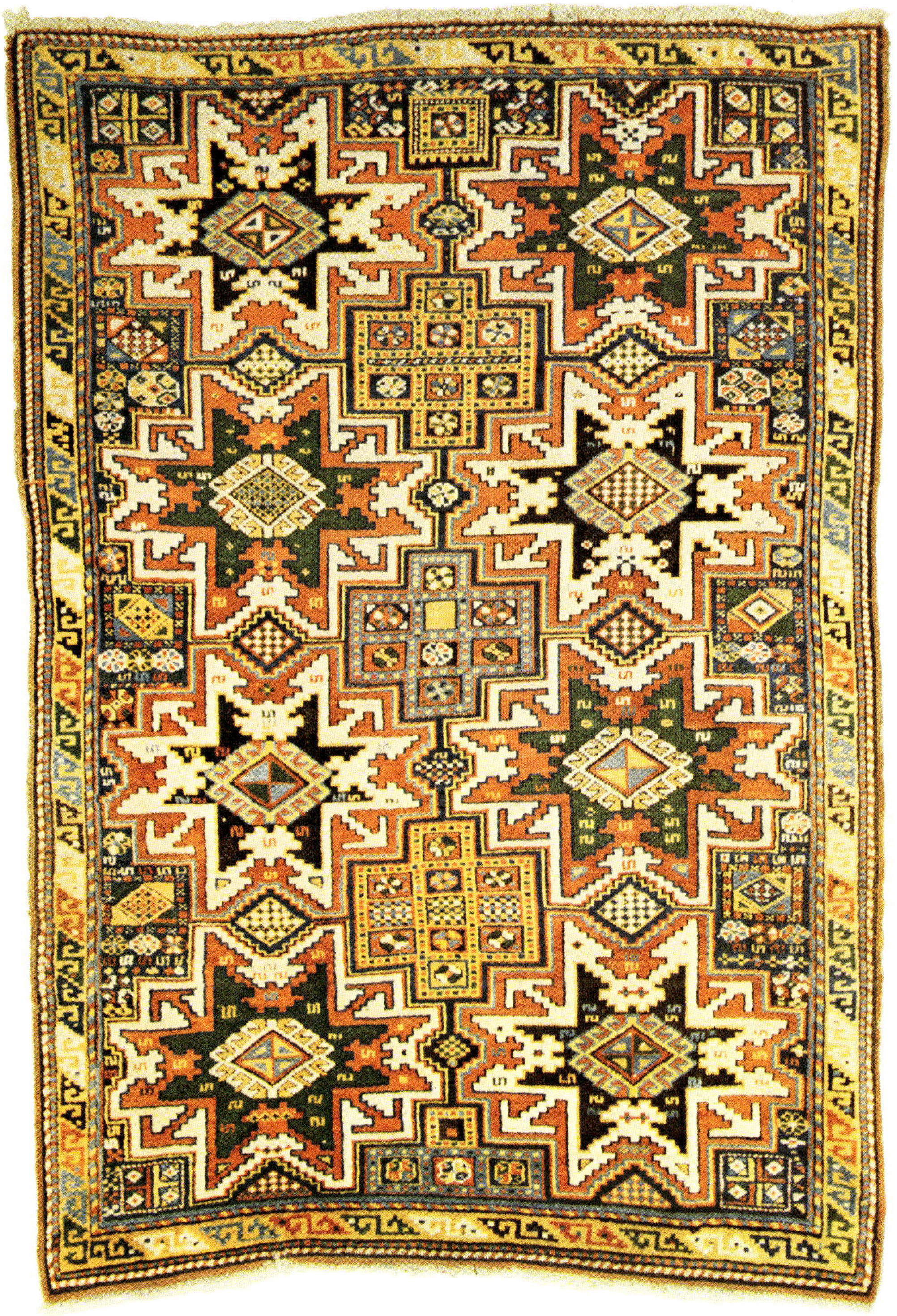

437

330 LESGHISTAN

438

439

438 This rug has diagonal rows of stars, a most unusual feature, and only a very narrow guard border with a *medachyl* design. The tight overall effect, seen at its strongest in this piece, reminds one strongly, both in design and colour, of 15th and early 16th century 'Small Pattern Holbein' rugs from Anatolia. Perhaps, like the Konagkend rugs with their resemblance to the Anatolian Lotto pattern, what we are looking at is a late provincial rendering of a once fluid classical style of court carpet design. On a dark blue ground, this piece probably dates from the late 19th century.
281 x 140 cm

439 This exceptionally large rug has a dark blue ground but a less crowded composition than the previous example (although it lacks that rug's archaic quality). Probably late 19th century.
370 x 200 cm

440 This is a typical example of a late rendering of this composition, although it has the unusual feature of a Chichi pattern border. The colour range is unadventurous and the field composition stiffly regular. It is difficult to know exactly where or when such rugs were made, but one example seen at auction (Messrs. Loudmer et Poulain, Paris, 29-30 September, 1979) was dated in western numerals 1943! Early 20th century.

440

332 LESGHISTAN

441

442

441 A number of rugs with Lesghi stars woven in the soumak technique are known. There are also many of the small, jewel-like, soumak bag-faces so prized by today's collectors. Perhaps one of the most beautiful examples of the latter is illustrated in Joseph V. McMullan's *Islamic Rugs* (pl. 57), and is now in the Metropolitan Museum; another example, a complete pair of bags (*khordjin*), is illustrated in this book (no. 490). The McMullan collection also contained a full-size Lesghi star soumak rug (*ibid*, pl. 56) which is, again, in the Metropolitan Museum. A particularly beautiful example, with four large stars on a pale red field, is illustrated as plate 47 in the catalogue of *The George Walter Vincent and Belle Townsley Smith Collection of Islamic Rugs* (this has an interesting stencilled double S main border composition). Our example, although approximately half the size, is fairly close to the McMullan rug in style. The border on both contains a continuous series of octagons, although on the McMullan rug these have more interesting central ornaments. Probably late 19th century.
151 x 89 cm

442 We now come to the first of four rugs attributed to Lesghistan which do not have the characteristic Lesghi star. The present rug, which is dated 1330 A.H. (A.D. 1911/2) is so close in the composition of both its field and border to 409, and both are so closely related to certain Kuba rugs, especially of the Konagkend and Chichi types, that an attribution to Kuba makes more logical sense. The attribution to the Lesghi is probably based on certain compositional similarities to the beautiful prayer rug illustrated by Schürmann in *Caucasian Rugs* (pl. 129), although Schürmann's attribution of that piece to the Lesghi seems to rest solely on its colour. The Schürmann rug is dated 1279 A.H. (A.D. 1862/3)
296 x 116 cm

443 This rug has an all-wool foundation and sides overcast in blue cotton. In his 1973 catalogue, Peter Bausback attributed it to Daghestan, which is a plausible alternative. This is an attractive piece; note the swastikas within the octagons along the bottom border. Probably second half of the 19th century.
160 x 99 cm

443

444 (*overleaf*) This and the following rug present another problem. They are both striking, handsome pieces with exceptionally beautiful colouring — especially the particular green-yellow tonality which Schürmann says is indicative of a Lesghi origin. However, the use of several vivid shades of green and yellow was also favoured by west Caucasian weavers, especially those of the Kazak and Karabagh regions. Neither can the use of the bold, angular motifs seen on both these pieces be taken as an indication of a Lesghi origin. Similar motifs appear on many rugs attributed to Shirvan — note especially our nos. 224-226, the last of these also having a very similar palette. The present rug has particularly attractive dark blue-green and black *medachyl* minor borders and a Chichi pattern main border. Its closest relative in recent literature is the distinctly more beautiful rug illustrated by Schürmann in *Caucasian Rugs* which he catalogues as a particular type of Daghestan called *Mahatschkala*. I prefer an attribution to Shirvan or possibly Kuba. Second half of the 19th century.
125 x 93 cm

445 (*overleaf*) The attribution of this prayer rug, the date of which has been interpreted as 1306 A.H. (A.D. 1888/89), is strengthened for believers in the Lesghi label not only by its colours but also by its admittedly superficial resemblance to a famous prayer rug first published by Roy Macey in *Oriental Prayer Rugs* (pl. 32) and subsequently by Schürmann in *Caucasian Rugs* (pl. 130), and attributed by both authors to the Lesghi. Both this and the previous piece are of considerable beauty and both represent the type of Caucasian rug coveted by today's collectors.
141 x 105 cm

334 LESGHISTAN

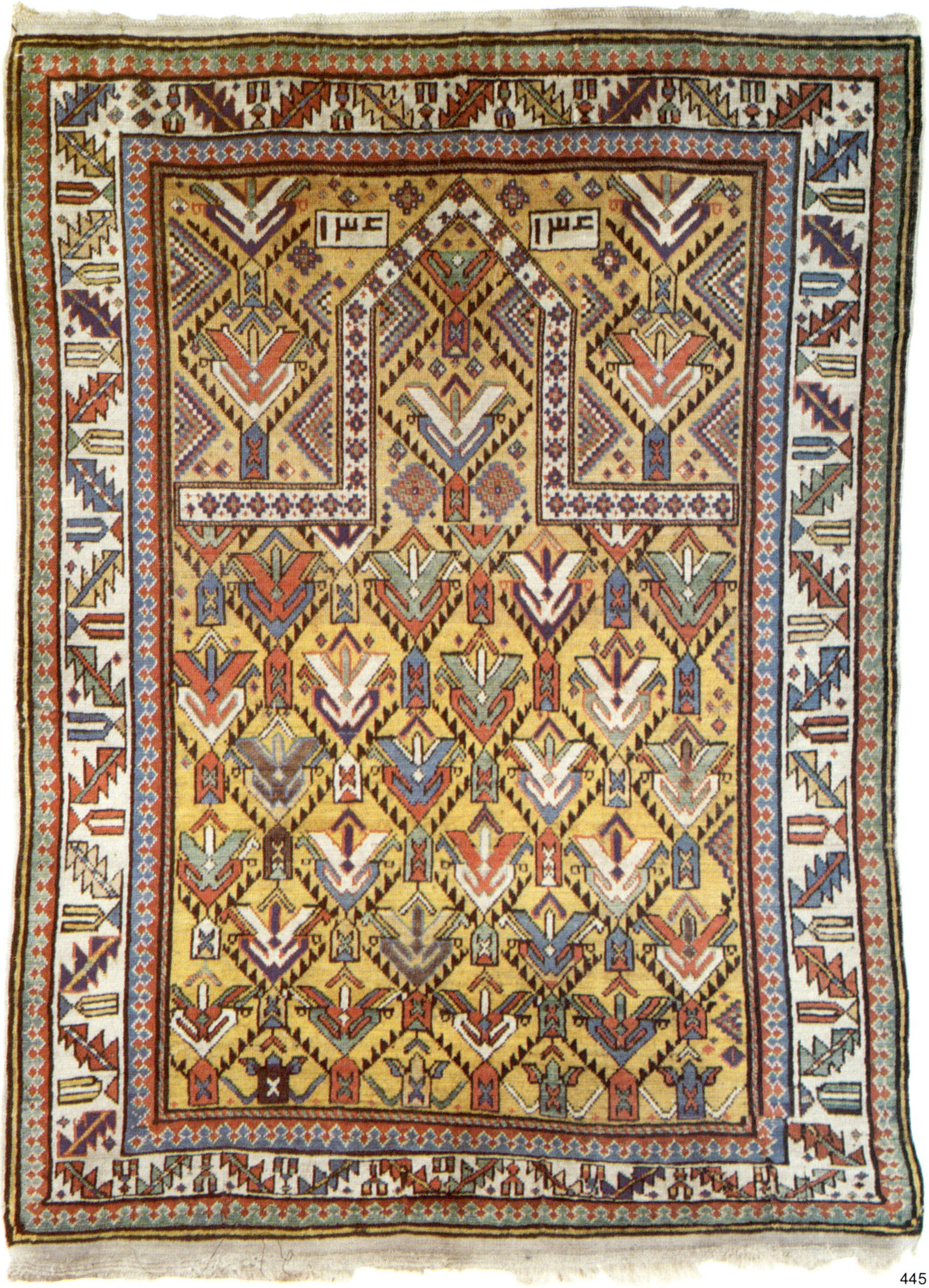

445

Flat Weaves

Although we have encountered a few examples before, the next section is devoted to a wide variety of Caucasian flat-woven rugs, saddle-bags and other artifacts (although the Caucasian attribution is, as we shall discuss, open to question in some instances).

The principal difference, of course, between these pieces and the majority of those that have been illustrated, is that they are not pile-knotted but woven in a variety of tapestry and embroidery techniques; this has the effect of somewhat limiting the fluidity of line, especially on pieces in the slit-tapestry technique, and of making the resultant design flatter, more two dimensional. One compensation is, however, that Caucasian flat-weaves, like their Anatolian and Persian counterparts, have a boldness of design and vividness of colour which, many people would argue, are virtues more consistently present in such pieces than in pile-knotted rugs.

In the East, all flat-weaves, regardless of the technique used, are described as Kilim, or Gilim (or a variety of different spellings); although this is partly true of Western usage, there is a tendency today to use 'kilim' specifically to denote pieces woven in the slit-tapestry technique, certainly the most widespread and simple type of flat-weave; terms such as 'soumak', 'weft-float brocade', 'reverse soumak', *et al.*, are used to denote other specific techniques, as well as, in the case predominantly of Caucasian flat-weaves, terms such as 'sileh' and 'verneh' which have stylistic and geographic connotations as well as technical ones. There are also those who prefer to use the word 'palas' to denote specifically Caucasian slit-tapestry woven rugs, as opposed to pieces woven in the same technique from other countries. It should be noted also that there are many pieces which combine two or more techniques and which are usually referred to as 'mixed technique' or 'mixed method' weavings. To my knowledge, however, the use of flat-weaving and pile-knotting on one piece (excluding the end and side finishes, of course) is not found on Caucasian rugs, as it is on the products of some tribes, such as Lori, Bakhtiari and the Baluch.

Slit-tapestry rugs

These are the rugs which Western writers and dealers now tend to call kilim, using that word in a strictly technical sense to distinguish slit-tapestry rugs from those in other flat-woven techniques.

In basic terms, the slit-tapestry technique can be described as a system whereby the wefts are interlaced over and under the warps, hiding the latter and creating the pattern (hence some writers refer to slit-tapestry rugs as being weft-faced). The wefts in each colour area are discontinuous, each weft turning back on the last warp in each colour area; this causes the appearance of 'slits' between each area of colour, which is how the technique gained its popular name. This system of weaving imposes certain structural limitations, one of which is the virtual impossibility of weaving straight vertical lines and circular lines; thus most slit-tapestry motifs have diagonal or stepped outlines.

The kilim of the Caucasus (where, apparently, the correct word to describe rugs woven in this technique is 'palas') are usually divided into two main groups, the 'Kuba' or north Caucasian variety and the 'Shirvan' or south Caucasian type being the most famous. Kuba kilim design is represented by 452-453 and the best-known Shirvan design by 447-451 (often referred to as banded kilim).

There are other varieties of Kuba kilim not represented in our selection. These include those which have compositions of large starred squares (decahedrons) and those with diamonds or stepped octagons arranged chromatically in diagonal rows; the reader is referred to Yanni Petsopoulos' monograph *Kilims* for the different types and also for further variations on the type of Kuba kilim we illustrate.

446 Among recently published examples of this type, the closest to the present piece is that which appears as no. 25 in the catalogue of *The George Walter Vincent and Belle Townsley Smith Collection of Islamic Rugs*, where it is almost certainly described incorrectly as Turkish. This latter piece has the same stepped octagons containing diamonds with *kotchak* appendages and the same hour-glass main border motifs (which can also be seen on three of the palmette Kuba kilim illustrated by Yanni Petsopoulos in *Kilims*, nos. 279, 283 and 290). It also has small octagonal motifs between the large octagons similar to those found on Shirvan banded kilim, e.g. 449. Most significantly, however, the Smith kilim has a motif at one end identical to those found on a group of Shirvan pile-knotted rugs, 256-261; indeed, the strong similarity between the composition of the Smith kilim, and by extension, this example and the group of Shirvan piles rugs is a strong pointer to the flat-woven examples having been produced in the same area. Probably late 19th century; similar examples could even date from the early 20th century.
333 x 170 cm

447 A typical Shirvan banded kilim, one of the characteristics of which is that the composition has no border. The filler ornament within the hexagons, consisting of a diamond with *kotchak* appendages, is typical. Kilim of this type do not have an overall field colour, the colour of each band contrasting with the next — in this case, blue-green, red, blue, ivory, blue-green, red, ivory and blue-green. The ribbon motifs in the minor guard bands are attractive alternatives to the usual small diamonds; the same motifs can be seen in a Shirvan kilim illustrated by David Black and Clive Loveless in *The Undiscovered Kilim* (pl. 38). Ours is an attractive example, with good colour and spacing. Probably late 19th century.
187 x 116 cm

447

448 This and the following piece are examples of a distinctive type of Shirvan banded kilim which has dark blue main bands, red secondary bands and white minor guards. On the dark blue bands sit massive hexagons with tiny stepping to their outlines (necessitated by the slit-tapestry technique, which does not allow for straight vertical or diagonal lines); each hexagon contains a large hooked motif with *kotchak* forms. 448 has the same ribbon motifs in the guards as the previous example and that illustrated in the Black/Loveless catalogue, the latter being of the same type as this kilim but with the slightly squashed and elongated hexagons seen on the next piece. Probably late 19th century.
249 x 101 cm

449 This is perhaps the finest of the examples of this type we have mentioned. Here, the minor band, which on 448 was given almost equal weight as the main band, is a distinctly secondary element which has been combined with the guards to form a fast-moving counterpoint to the massive sonority of the main bands. A most beautiful piece which typifies the qualities of boldness and archaicism most admired by collectors of kilim. Probably late 19th century.
276 x 168 cm

450 Although of typical Shirvan banded format, the motifs between the bands, heavily stepped octagons flanked by two small crosses one on top of the other, are arranged to form an unusual composition. Probably late 19th century.
316 x 174cm

SLIT-TAPESTRY RUGS

FLAT WEAVES 339

451 Another typical, but very fine, Shirvan banded kilim of similar design to 447 but with a more vivid palette, exciting design and with the addition of zig-zag motifs down each of the long sides, motifs which terminate the composition of the kilim horizontally, a feature not encountered on the other examples of the group illustrated here. Probably late 19th century.
287 x 158 cm

'Kuba' kilim

Nos. 452 and 453 represent two variations on one of the most powerful kilim compositions; diagonally arranged rows of highly stylised palmettes containing diamonds with arrow bars pointing north and south. Some subtly different outlines to these palmettes are known, several of which are illustrated in Petsopoulos' *Kilims* (nos. 279-291). There is also variation in the central diamond and arrow bars motif; an example illustrated in *From the Bosporus to Samarkand* (pl.1) has the diamond with the usual upward pointing arrow bar but the downward bar ends in a pair of *kotchak*. This latter motif is sometimes found replaced by small diamonds or even a pair of lines, as on Petsopoulos, no. 280. A kilim illustrated by Patricia Fiske in her 1974 Textile Museum show, *Caucasian Rugs from Private Collections* (pl. 31), has the palmette itself drawn in the form of an elongated bar-like medallion with protrusions and two pairs of wheel-like forms at top and bottom (it resembles nothing so much as an oldfashioned racing car seen from above!); another example is illustrated in Petsopoulos, no. 288.

Unusual variants include an example sold by Nagel (Stuttgart, on 6 May 1978) which had rows of rectangular medallions placed very close together so as to form an almost solid block, each medallion containing a diamond with small diamond appendages at either end. A rug in the Victoria and Albert Museum, illustrated by Kendrick and Tattersall in *Hand-woven Carpets* (pl. 118b), has medallions almost identical to those on our 452 but also has curious rectangular panels of different sizes at irregular intervals down each side of the field. A third variant is that illustrated by Housego in *Tribal Rugs* (pl. 20); this has slightly elongated versions of the medallions which appear on the kilim illustrated in *From the Bosporus to Samarkand*, but is notable because there are two palmettes to a row, between the medallions are small ornaments (including

continued on p.340

451

'Kuba' Kilim continued
animal and human figures), and some of the motifs are brocaded.

The main border of this group usually contains the zig-zag and bars seen on 452 and 453. Other variants include an hour-glass composition in the main border with an outer minor zig-zag and bars border, as illustrated in Raymond Benardout's *Caucasian Rugs* (p. 55) (this piece is also illustrated in Petsopoulos' *Kilims*, no. 283). Several variants on the hour-glass motif will be found illustrated in *Kilims*, including a reduction to a pair of opposing Greek 'e' motifs. The book also contains two examples with Memlinc *gül* main borders, one with a running dog and the other with a carnation outer border, and one example (no. 289) with a finely drawn *medachyl* border. An example on the New York market (cf. *Hali*, vol. 1, no. 1, p. 88) had a narrow border containing small diamonds; it also had the unusual design feature of four small versions of the main diamond and arrow bars motif flanking the principal rendering of the motif itself. Finally, an example sold by Christie's (London, 15th November 1979, lot 7) had a narrow reciprocal border with simplified half hour-glass motifs; this rug was also noteworthy for its size — at 471 cm the longest example I have encountered (and probably a very late one).

Although popularly called Kuba or north Caucasian kilim, several authors prefer to call them Shirvan and Mrs. Housego, discussing the example illustrated in her book, remarked: "the rich riot of human figures, some with typical Azarbayjani hats, animals, birds, pitchers and angular ornamentation indicate the work of the Persian weaver." She prefers an attribution to north-west Persia, as does John Siudmak in his cataloguing of the unusual Christie example mentioned above.

A few pile-knotted rugs, usually attributed to Shirvan, have the same field composition; Roger Gardiner, in *Oriental Rugs from Canadian Collections*, illustrates one (no. 22) which seems to have a structure characteristic of north Caucasian weaving but an older, greatly superior piece sold by Lefevre (London, 14th April 1978, lot 17) seems certainly Shirvan, as does our 248. Most of

452 The so-called Kuba kilim have either red or dark blue fields, the former usually with a dark brown border and the latter with an ivory-ground one. The present piece has a somewhat gloomy palette and one thinks in terms of it being late.
290 x 158 cm

'Kuba' Kilim continued

these piled versions are smaller than the flat-woven examples; however, a full-sized pile-knotted rug with exceptional colouring, was sold by Lefevre (London, on 30th November 1979, lot 38). This has an almost identical border system to our 213, including the linked S guards, and is clearly from the same area. It is important to recall that these palmettes also occur on our Akstafa no. 244, yet another indication of a southerly origin.

The medallion itself has been linked with the shield-like lotus palmettes of that group of 18th century Caucasian rugs called the 'Shield' group, a design which is thought to have derived from old Persian and Anatolian textiles; the Shield group carpets are generally thought to have been woven in the Shirvan area, and the 'Kuba' kilim may represent a decadent continuance of this tradition, the zig-zag and bar border being a degenerate rendering of the curled leaf border found on the Shield group.

However, there is an equal chance that these kilim were produced over a wide area of the Caucasus and north-west Persia, the view taken by Petsopoulos in *Kilims*, to judge by his map. He reproduces a photograph of a dealer's shop in the Caucasus taken in the late l9th century, also used in E. Markov's *Aspects of the Caucasus*, (published in Moscow in 1904) and more recently in Marvin Lyon's *Russia in Original Photographs,* 1860-1920. The early Russian book also has a picture of a Shirvan banded kilim covering an open ox-cart in Georgia.

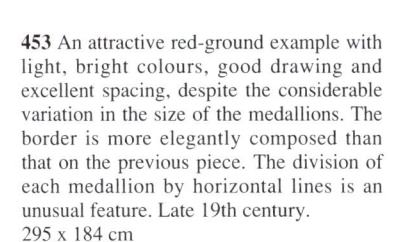

453 An attractive red-ground example with light, bright colours, good drawing and excellent spacing, despite the considerable variation in the size of the medallions. The border is more elegantly composed than that on the previous piece. The division of each medallion by horizontal lines is an unusual feature. Late 19th century.
295 x 184 cm

Brocaded Rugs

The rugs and bags contained in this group represent one of the muddier areas of modern carpet scholarship. Writers could probably be neatly divided between those who ascribe them to north-west Persia/south Caucasus and those who consider them to be Anatolian. The best-known group of brocaded rugs is represented here by 454, 456 and 459. These pieces are in weft-float brocading on a plain-weave ground. The wefts which form the pattern are supplementary to the ground which is in plain weave; the pattern wefts are discontinuous, being confined to their own areas of pattern; there is, in other words, more than one set of wefts.

The three rugs we have mentioned are often described as *verneh* by those who consider them to be Caucasian, although they are not in the same technique as the other group of flat-weaves called by the same name (cf. 479-480), which are either in all-over soumak brocading or in soumak brocading on a slit-tapestry ground.

I take the view that the rugs illustrated in this section are east Anatolian. Landreau and Pickering, in *From the Bosporus to Samarkand,* were undecided but seemed to favour a Turkish origin; Michael Franses, in his *World of Rugs* catalogue, illustrated an example (no. 13) of which he said: "The design of this piece points to the Kurdish weaving of eastern Anatolia. We believe that most of these pieces were marketed in Erivan in Armenia."

The composition of these rugs consists, basically, of a series of large squares which seem to float on a checkerboard or diamond-lattice ground. There is a group of such rugs, however, woven in the same technique, which differs in colour and which does have compositional elements which suggest a north-west Persian/south Caucasian origin. A good example is illustrated by Jenny Housego in *Tribal Rugs* (plate 1); another (plate 2 in the same book) has a diamond lattice arranged chromatically to form a large multi-layered diamond and a third, a long rug, is illustrated in the catalogue of the Jerome and Mary Straka collection (no. 123). A fourth will be found illustrated in this book, no. 77.

These latter rugs are united into a group by their use of a double 'T' bracket motif either in the squares or in the borders (usually both), and can be closely relaited to certain south-west Caucasian pile-knotted rugs – for instance 28, 34, and 35 (Karachov Kazak) and 67, 76 and 78 (Kazaks). A comparison of 77 with 454, 456 and 459 will surely demonstrate, even to a novice, that we are dealing here with two different groups of brocaded rugs, albeit ones which are related. It is, perhaps, the confusion of these two groups which has caused the Anatolian examples to be lumped together with the Persian/Caucasian rugs.

It is possible, of course, that both groups were woven by the same people living in different areas. An attribution to the Kurds is possible for both groups, or even to Armenians. J. Iten-Maritz, in his study of predominantly modern Anatolian weaving, *Turkish Carpets*, unfortunately gives only cursory attention to east Anatolian rugs, although he does reproduce a pile-knotted piece (p.338) which he describes as a 'Kagizman' carpet "produced in the villages between Erzurum and Kars"; this has rows of squares containing geometric motifs and seems obviously related to the

454 A large and typical example. These rugs are often woven in two pieces. An example with similar colouring but with a composition of large squares enclosing diamonds-within-squares motifs, and woven in two pieces, is illustrated by Spuhler, König and Volkmann in *Alte Orientteppiche* (no. 34); an attribution to either Anatolia or the Caucasus is posited. Another closely related piece is illustrated in *From the Bosporus to Samarkand* (no. 69), which is tentatively ascribed to Anatolia. Peter Bausback, who reproduced our 454 in his 1975 catalogue, prefers a central Caucasian attribution. Probably late 19th century.
183 x 86 cm

brocaded rugs under discussion.

More interesting, however, is Iten-Maritz's attribution of closely related brocaded rugs to western Anatolia – 'Bergama Verneh' and 'Yuntdag kilim' (pp. 130 and 134). Of these, the author remarks, "The town of Stepanakart, formerly called Shusha, in the Karabagh region of southern Caucasus, is the home of *verneh kilims*. Nowadays, this town lies within the Soviet state of Azerbaijan. It is from here that the kilim weavers now living in the Bergama region originally came..." Although Iten-Maritz gives no evidence for these statements, it is possible that some of the brocaded rugs we illustrate may come from west, and not east, Anatolia.

455 This piece is woven in two sections and, despite its tight diamo lattice, has a border which relates it closely to the previous piece. Unlike 454, 456 and 459, it is red-warped, as are other published examples of its type and is probably late 19th or even early 20th century.
178 x 145 cm

456 Another standard composition, with a lighter, more checkerboard-like appearance, than 454 and 459. An almost identical example is illustrated by Jean Lefevre in his *Caucasian Carpets* (no. 60), although he describes it as a 'Verneh' from the east Caucasus, an attribution with which I cannot agree. A rug illustrated in *From the Bosporus to Samarkand* (plate 70) has a related composition but has only three rows of five squares, each of which lacks the central square ornament of the present piece. The latter rug is, in turn, related to the example illustrated in *Alte Orientteppiche* (no. 34), which has four rows of six squares, each with a central diamond-within-square motif, and to the example illustrated by Michael Franses in *The World of Rugs* (pl. 13), which has only six large squares, each with a large central diamond on a field of small interlocking triangles, the squares themselves floating on a diamond lattice ground. Our example is probably late 19th century.
281 x 102 cm

457 This bag seems unrelated to the other bags and rugs illustrated in this group and may be Persian tribal work. There are several groups of white-ground rugs with soumak brocading which resemble the type and style of decoration seen on this piece. Among these, the closest parallel stylistically is the rug illustrated in the *Yörük* catalogue (no. 42), which has three motifs—trees, shrubs and horned deer—arranged in alternate rows and brocaded in various colours on a pale ivory ground; the piece is made of five narrow strips sewn together and attributed to north-west Persia. A very similar piece, woven in six strips, was once in the McMullan collection (*Islamic Rugs,* pl. 60), although the latter has the double T border which, as we have discussed, does seem to be a characteristic motif of north-west Persian/south Caucasian brocaded rugs. Both these examples are much more delicately drawn than the five-strip example reproduced (upside down) as plate 15 in Jenny Housego's *Tribal Rugs* and attributed to the Shahsavan. A complete *khordjin* illustrated in *The Warp and Weft of Islam* catalogue (no. 65) is attributed to the Bakhtiari tribe of south Persia; the field has an intricately worked composition of geometric motifs and small birds principally in red and blue soumak brocading on an ivory ground, the corners of the bag being pile-knotted. This type of decoration was particularly favoured by the Lori and Bakhtiari tribes of south Persia. Another piece which closely resembles the present bag in style is the white-ground (cotton) panel with soumak brocading inset into the re-
continued

BROCADED RUGS

FLAT WEAVES

457 continued
verse side of a soumak and pile-knotted bag in the Straka collection (cat. no. 95), which is attributed to the Lori or Bakhtiari. We should also mention the stylistically not dissimilar horse-cover illustrated by Jenny Housego in *Tribal Rugs* (pl. 95), although this differs technically, the motifs being pile-knotted on a plain-weave ground; this piece is attributed to south Persia. Probably late 19th century.
78 x 68 cm

458 As we mention in connection with the bedding bags reproduced later, there is considerable controversy as to the origin of this particular group of objects, although it seems fairly certain that they were produced by many different groups in Anatolia, the Caucasus and Persia. This particular weft-float brocaded example is probably of Anatolian manufacture, possibly from the region of Lake Van. A piece of very similar type is illustrated in *From the Bosporus to Samarkand* (no. 81), where it is tentatively attributed to Anatolia. Probably late 19th century.
106 x 51 x 54 cm

459 Almost identical in composition to 454 and of similar date, with only some minor differences in design. This example has the light, bright palette frequently encountered on Anatolian rugs. Probably late 19th century.
196 x 106cm

Embroidered and Slit-tapestry Rugs

These narrow banded kilim in mixed technique form a specific group, which are thought to have been made specifically for use as covers at weddings. Again, their place of manufacture is controversial but an attribution to Azerbaijan, in the Persian/Causasian border area, seems reasonable. 460 and 462 are in mixed technique, with bands of weft-float brocading on a plain-weave ground, and red-ground bands, with geometric motifs of X shape, in slit-tapestry. 461, however, has no slit tapestry. Published examples of this type are difficult to find; a fragment in weft-float brocading only, is illustrated in *From the Bosporus to Samarkand* (pl. 80), where it is attributed to either Turkey or the Caucasus; it has virtually the same composition as our 461, which, in turn, is in the same technique as 458.

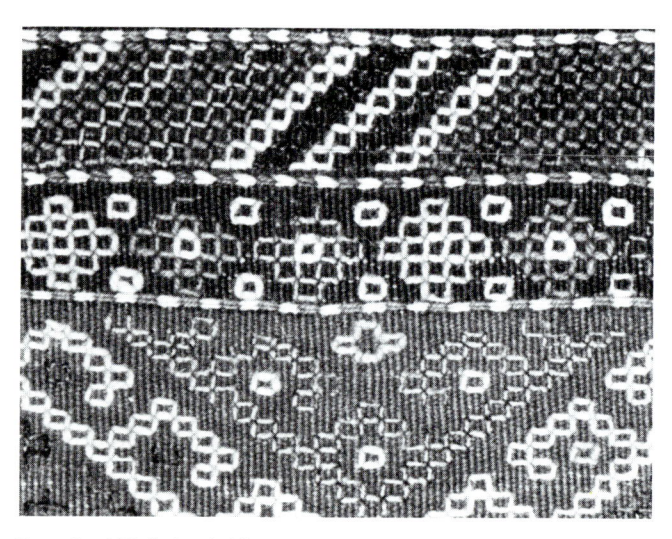

Example of 'Holbein stitch'

460 An attractive example with typical colour range. Some writers, particularly in Germany, refer to weft-float brocading of this type as 'Holbein stitch', since it is encountered in medieval European textile art. It has been suggested that they may have been made in Baku, in the north-east Caucasus. Probably late 19th century.
255 x 165 cm

461 An interesting piece with the minor slanting guards of the previous example, as well as the broad brocaded bands; it lacks the slit-tapestry bands, however. Late 19th century.
213 x 165 cm

EMBROIDERED SLIT-TAPESTRY RUGS — FLAT WEAVES

462 An almost identical piece to 460 but with a more attractive and complex link chain composition in the narrow guards between the slant stripe guards. Probably late 19th century.
266 x 170 cm

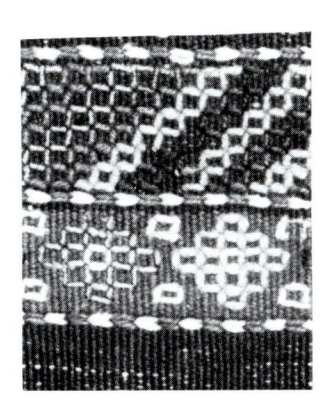

462 front

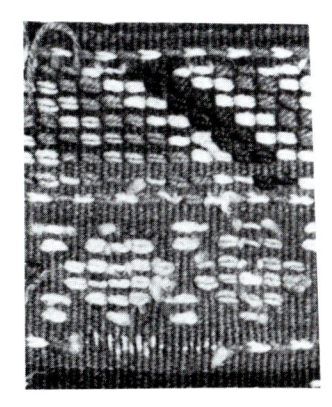

462 back

The Soumaks

The large Caucasian soumak rugs are amongst the most grand and distinguished of all eastern flat-weaves. Many of them have designs which are not found on pile-knotted rugs, while others, such as the so-called 'dragon' and 'blossom' soumaks, have compositions which hark back to the earliest known groups of pile rugs; these archaic designs seem to have lived on in flat-woven form. The earliest dated examples can be placed within the first two decades of the 19th century, while well-drawn and finely composed examples, despite the inevitable use of harsh, synthetic colours, are still being made today (although it is difficult to pinpoint when an indigenous village craft gave way to an export industry—probably around the second decade of the present century).

The term soumak is used to refer to a specific type of brocading which is defined in *From the Bosporus to Samarkand* as a technique in which "the sequence of the progressive wrapping of warp by weft is consistently forward over and back under, with a span ratio, usually, of 2:1." Various differences in this basic technique will be found, including 'soumak wrapping' in which there is no ground weave between the wrapping wefts and, the most often encountered type, 'soumak brocading' in which there are discontinuous wrapping wefts supplementary to the ground weave. In the majority of cases, all the wrapping wefts lie in the same direction ('plain soumak') although, when the direction changes from row to row, this is sometimes called 'countered soumak'. Again, on most examples, the weft threads are left hanging at the back; rare examples which have a finished pattern on both sides are called 'reverse soumak', a technique most often encountered on small pieces such as bag-faces.

463 Of the several variant compositions of the so-called 'dragon' soumak, this is the one least often encountered. Despite its boldness of design and intricacy of drawing, and despite such other noteworthy features as the brilliant blue of the main border and the superbly drawn 'running dog' outer guards, this piece may be a late example. It is of the type which some writers—e.g. Jean Lefevre in *Caucasian Carpets* (no. 56) prefer to call 'blossom' soumak, since the admittedly highly stylised animals which can be discerned on some examples —e.g. our 465 —have completely disappeared, to be replaced either by equally highly stylised floral or geometric motifs. Nevertheless, the present piece, despite probably being younger than the example illustrated by Lefevre, has some intriguing compositional details not encountered on the latter rug, not least of which are several anthropomorphic motifs, seen most clearly in the top and bottom borders and in the top and bottom halves of the field itself. These motifs form an intriguing link with some earlier Caucasian rugs which have winged enthroned figures, including the 'tree' carpet reproduced by Kurt Erdmann in *Seven Hundred Years of Oriental Carpets* (fig. 131) (and again by Serare Yetkin in *Early Caucasian Carpets In Turkey,* vol. 1, pl. 103) and the Afshan carpet reproduced by Charles Grant Ellis in *Early Caucasian Rugs* (pl. 27). A late 18th/early 19th century date for these two rugs, the former in the Turk ve Islam Museum, Istanbul, and the latter in the St. Louis Art Museum, seems probable and I know of no other late 19th/early 20th century examples with similar motifs, motifs which are assumed to have derived from Persian Safavid embroideries. The large stylised ewers each side of the bottom of the field, which are echoed in the main border design, are also unusual features on such rugs. Late 19th/early 20th century.
314 x 256cm

464 *(overleaf)* Although closer in colour and design to the more usual dragon soumaks, this example, nevertheless, has several unusual features. The positioning of the highly stylised dragons themselves is uncharacteristic; three pairs of white-ground rectangles with triangular heads, serrate-edged feet and containing red and blue comb-like motifs, are positioned at equal distances down each side of the field, sitting on the broad blue or green leaves; these are the dragons which, as in the next example, are found more normally on the red field between each leaf system, spaces occupied in this example by yellow and blue (or white and blue in the case of the topmost pair) geometric configurations which have only the slightest hint of zoomorphism. This is a beautiful rug, with a very attractive border system (the outer red-ground running dog guard, seen at top and bottom, having been removed from the sides). Its age is difficult to determine—cf. the discussion of the age of dragon soumaks in relation to the next rug. Probably second half 19th century.
317 x 171 cm

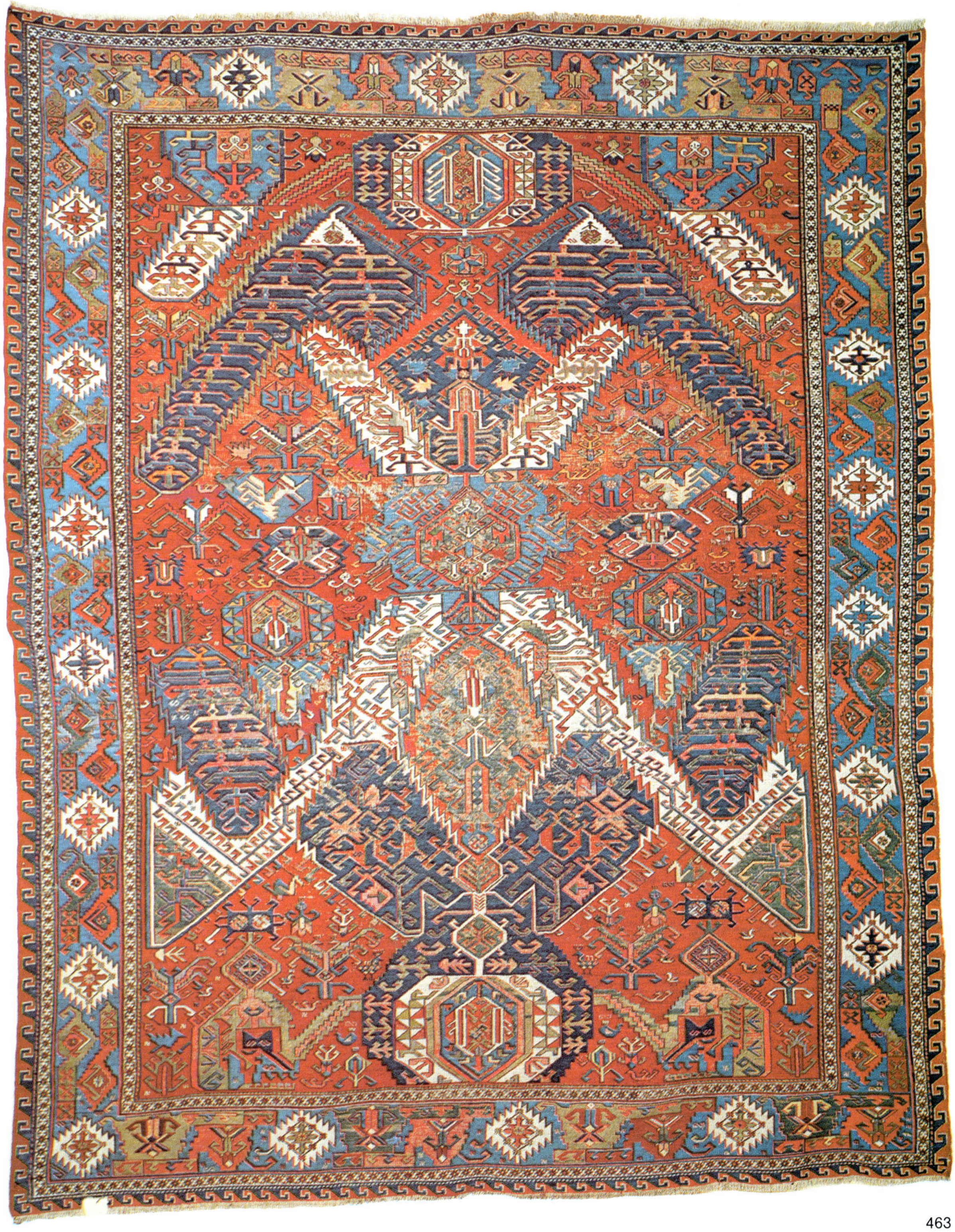

463

465 This is the classic dragon soumak composition. The earliest recorded example, in the Wher collection, is dated 1223 A.H. (A.D. 1808/9) and other examples are known with dates only slightly later in the 19th century. Despite the usual warnings against placing too much faith in the dates found on Caucasian village weavings, the Wher collection piece is certainly of sufficient quality to give us some confidence in the authenticity of its date. It has a particularly beautiful range of colours—a light red ground, ivory, pale blue and very pale green (leaves), and a frequent use of an unusual shade of light aquamarine blue. Its composition is much more open and freely drawn than that found on our 464, and it has the usual outer red-ground running dog guard. An interesting point, however, is that the dragons on the Wher carpet have already reached a very exaggerated degree of stylisation, perhaps even more so than those on the undated, but obviously early, example in the Metropolitan Museum (Dimand, *Oriental Rugs in the Metropolitan Museum of Art,* fig. 242), the latter having a main border composition related to those seen on our 463 and 467, and which is found on soumaks with a wide variety of field compositions. The Metropolitan Museum example is very close both in field and border compositions to the rug illustrated by Schürmann in *Caucasian Rugs* (pl. 119), another example with exceptionally beautiful colour. A third example closely related to the Metropolitan Museum rug was sold at auction by Lefevre in London on 26 November, 1976 (lot 17); this had harsher colours and more spikey drawing than the Schürmann piece. Another rug sold by the same auctioneers on 9 February, 1979, had the same wide spacing as the Wher example, as well as a very similar colour range (although its main border was of the same type, but slightly more ornate, as the Metropolitan Museum rug). The present soumak has dragons no more stylised than those seen on the Wher and Metropolitan Museum examples; indeed, the bottom pair, with yellow bodies, dark blue heads and light blue legs, which flanks the eagle medallions between the two complete series of interlocking leaves, is, if anything, slightly less stylised. Note also the pair of two opposing small blue and red motifs seen clearly a quarter of the way down each side of the bottom large white-ground leaf, motifs which have been interpreted as mini-renderings of the dragon and phoenix combat. The place of manufacture of this group of Soumak rugs probably does not differ from rugs of other designs in the same technique, many of which, as can be seen from the following examples, have similar borders, minor details of composition and a closely allied colour range. John Mumford, in one of the most influential early 20th century carpet books, *Oriental Rugs,* remarked in the preface to the fourth edition of 1915, that in the Shirvan region there had been an independent Khanate of Soumaki, which had existed until the Russian military conquests in the first half of the 19th century. In the map found in an early 19th century travel book by the Hon. George Keppel, *Personal Narrative of Travels in Babylonia, Assyria, Media and Scythia in the Year 1824,* extensively quoted by Jean Lefevre in the introduction to his book *Caucasian Carpets,* we find marked in the Shirvan area the name Schamachin, which in Schürmann's map in *Caucasian Rugs,* has become Soumak. In the

465 continued

text of his book, Keppel describes 'Nova Shumakia' — "Its present possessors, the Russians, are repairing the ravages inflicted by Aga Mohumud, who wrested it from the Tartars in the latter end of the last century." The town was built near the ruins of another, much older, town of the same name, "once the seat of government of a Tartar prince . . . ". We recall that some current authorities incline to the view that the dragon pile-knotted rugs of the 16th and 17th centuries were probably not made in the town of Kuba, to which they were attributed by an older generation of writers, but in royal workshops established by the Khans further south. The town of Shusha in the Karabagh has been mentioned in this context but Soumak, not so far to the north, seems to offer itself as just as likely a candidate. Not a few Soumak rugs have many details of composition in common with pile-knotted rugs attributed to the eastern Caucasus. Indeed, the unusual dragon soumak illustrated by Roger Gardiner in *Oriental Rugs from Canadian Collections* (no. 80), which would seem to be a very late example with an uncharacteristic floral ground, has an outer Seichur border, a composition not normally encountered on rugs made outside the eastern regions; it is also found on many soumaks of differing designs. The minor blue-ground guards of the present piece, with their rows of tiny flower-heads, are also characteristic features of Shirvan weaving, being found on many pile-knotted rugs from this region. Probably second half 19th century.
264 x 205 cm

465

466 *(overleaf)* The most frequently encountered composition on Caucasian soumak rugs consists of a series of large medallions, usually three, on a red ground; 468 represents the best-known type, but the eight-pointed squared stars seen on this rug are not unusual. In overall composition, these pieces resemble certain pile-knotted Shirvan rugs, in particular those from Akstafa (although they lack the the large fan-tailed birds); it is interesting that our Akstafa rug 214 not only has clear compositional affinities with this and similar soumak rugs, but also has palmettes which link it to the distinctive group of kilim (cf. 452-453) which I am inclined to think hail from Shirvan rather than Kuba. 466 has Seichur borders usually attributed to Kuba but clearly not confined to that region. The piece is dated 1309 A.H. (A.D. 1891/2). Had it not been so dated, many people would probably have considered it to be a few decades older.
159 x 127 cm

467 *(overleaf)* Although bold and powerful in composition, it is not to my taste. The huge, latch-hook sided octagons have some points in common with those found on the 'garden' Surahani rugs but there the resemblance ends. The only pile-knotted rug I know which has a closely related field composition is illustrated by Schürmann in *Caucasian Rugs* (pl. 133) and it is attributed to the Lesghi. The three hooked octagons on that rug contain almost the same motifs as seen on the present piece, motifs clearly derived from animal, possibly dragon forms. The unusually wide main border contains an interesting composition linked to that found on the dragon soumak in the Metropolitan Museum (see text to 465); it is a design difficult to interpret, although the complex figures seen between the red and white saw-edged diamonds seem clearly zoomorphic. Probably late 19th century.
167 x 134cm

352 FLAT WEAVES SOUMAKS

467

468

468 This rug has one of the best-known and beautiful of the Caucasian soumak compositions, and one which, in its basic elements, consists of large, flattened, irregular octagons in blue (and sometimes green), flanked by yellow ground octagons of regular form and inward-pointing bell-like motifs in dark blue and black. The best, and possibly earliest, examples have only three very large medallions, the centre one of which is often green; one of the most beautiful rugs of this type, which, however, lacks the flanking octagons and has an unusually wide main border with a conjoined octagon composition, will be found illustrated in *From the Bosporus to Samarkand* (no. 19). The zig-zag main border of the present piece is typical, although on some examples of this type and of other related types, the Y shaped motif is larger and more complex. Probably late 19th century. 268 x 218 cm

469 A smaller rug with an unusual variation of the composition seen on the previous piece. The octagons have been replaced by serrate-edged diamonds and the bell-like forms by floral palmettes. Like all such soumaks of this and related types, it has a red ground. Probably late 19th century. 160 x 143 cm

SOUMAKS
FLAT WEAVES 355

469

470 A number of soumak rugs are known with designs which can be associated with pile-knotted rugs from various parts of the Caucasus. This might suggest that the soumak rugs themselves cannot be confined to a particular area, since the earlier examples were probably not woven for export; thus there would have been no need for the weaver to copy designs popular among western buyers. The present rug is of the Chelaberd design attributed to the Karabagh and stylistically very close to some examples—compare, for instance, our 94, which is dated 1346 A.H. (A.D. 1927/8); an attribution of the previous piece to the same region is not impossible. Late 19th/early 20th century.
320 x 165 cm

471 Woven with a dark blue ground, this is an unusual and attractive piece. In design, it can be related to the smaller rug illustrated by Kendrick and Tattersall in *Hand-woven Carpets* (pl. 146). It would seem to have some affinities with Kuba weaving and may be from the Seichur area. Late 19th/early 20th century.
353 x 161 cm

Detail of 472

472 This is a particularly attractive and pleasing soumak with beautiful colour. It represents one of those designs which, in terms of ground to field relationships, is ambiguous. On one level, the composition can be read as a vertical series of octagon-square-diamond-within-diamond medallions on a red ground flanked on either side by a series of irregular brown zig-zags and quartered red and yellow diamonds, each quarter containing a stylised animal. In fact, we are dealing with an endless design cut on all sides by the borders; the central part is a continuous diamond section with a red ground on which sit the red medallions; the actual ground colour is the dark brown which appears as a zig-zag on either side; this means that the composition reads as a series of vertical red diamond-sided blocks alternating with vertical rows of quartered diamonds on a dark brown ground. Probably second half of the 19th century.
348 x 179 cm

Details of 473

473

473 The reciprocity between the field and design which we saw on the last piece is present here also, although to a less marked extent. The dark blue half diamonds cut off by the side borders are, in fact, the field of a composition which, by implication, extends endlessly from side to side with multiple rows of large blue stars on a red zig-zag ground. Note the presence of duck-like motifs in these blue half diamonds, motifs which suggest that this may be a highly stylised garden design. Late 19th/early 20th century.
330 x 219 cm

474 This is one of the best-known soumak designs and can be related to some rare stem-stitch embroideries, an old and particularly beautiful example of which is illustrated in *From the Bosporus to Samarkand* (pl. 82). The same catalogue also reproduces an exceptionally fine example of the present composition (no. 18), the rug being almost of square format; the three star medallions sit in a vertical row on a wide field, and are not slightly cramped, as in the present piece. Surrounding each medallion are pairs of small octagons which echo the shape of the space left between the medallions, and down each side of the field are large palmettes of ornate form which link the design to earlier Caucasian floral carpets. Covering the ground is a broken lattice of spiky branches ending in small tri-pronged motifs; these are almost identical to the motifs found on the grounds of 16th and 17th century Anatolian Ushak carpets of the medallion and star varieties and which are found growing from the *gül* of Tekke main carpets. Another link with Turkoman weaving is found in the main border composition, which is a slightly better drawn version of that seen on the present piece; the zig-zag meander with tuning fork motifs in the spaces is probably a simplified version of the so-called Turkoman line border associated principally with the Yomud (many eastern dealers suggest that the rendering of the motif seen between the meander, as it appears on Baluch rugs, is a highly stylised Kufic inscription denoting the name of Allah). The present rug is a later version of the Washington rug and has conjoined stars in the field; it is notable for its plethora of bird figures, as well as other animals and two humans, who flank the top-most star. The Turkish influence is not so apparent here as it is on the Washington rug, although there would appear to be a fairly clear relationship with certain Kazak rugs, specifically those of the Fachralo group. However, many of the same features as appear on the Washington piece, including the broken lattice ground, appear also on our 466, which has the same spacing and very similar side medallions. Late 19th/early 20th century.
262 x 151 cm

474

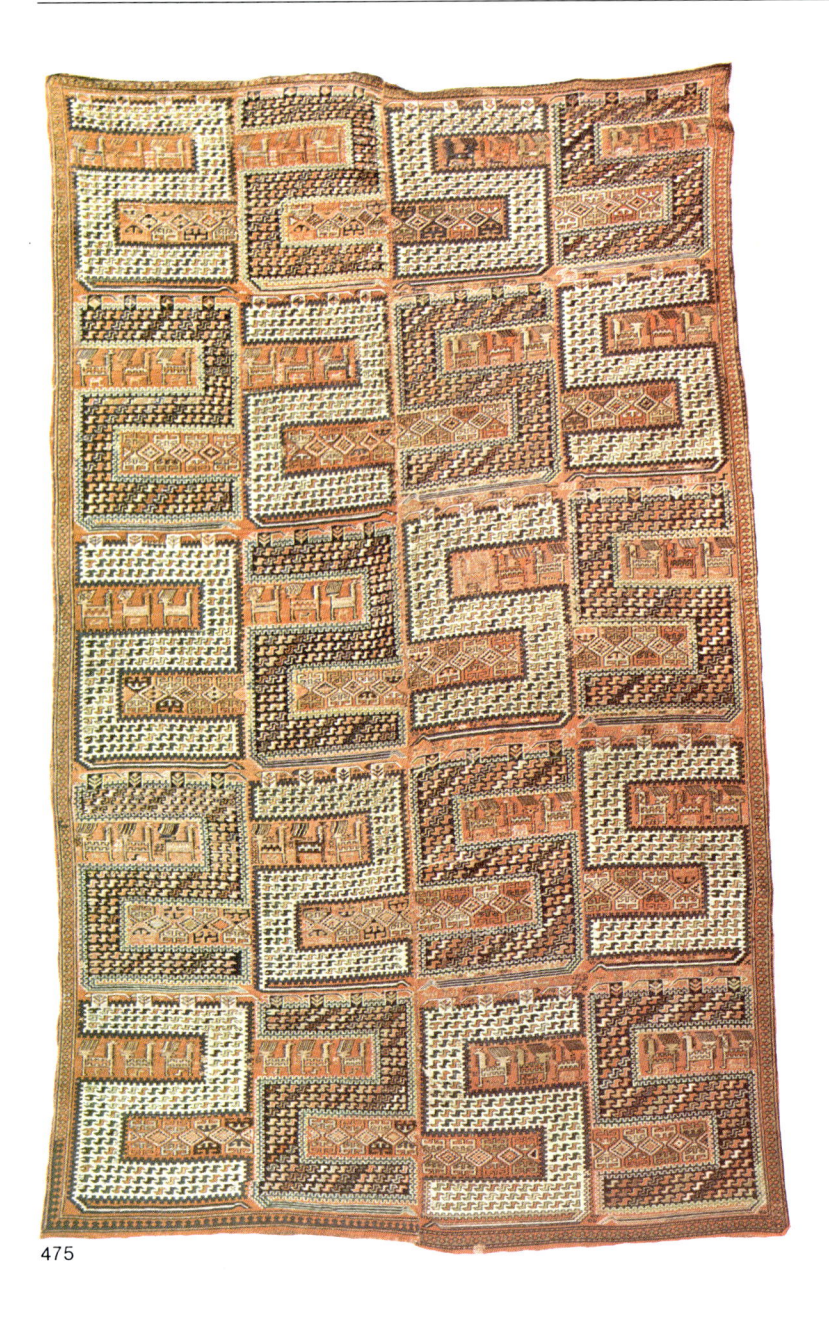

'Dragon' Sileh

Nos. 475-478 are representatives of a well-known group of Caucasian flat-weaves called generally 'dragon' sileh (or silé). They are, in fact, extremely common, although there is a considerable variance in both colour and quality. In design, there are two principal types, both of which are represented here. The difference between these two types is determined by the presence of a small zoomorphic motif in the jaws of the dragon, i.e. in the top half of the S; it is present in our 478 and absent in the other examples we illustrate.

In technique, these rugs are in all-over soumak brocading—in other words the same technique as the majority of the preceding soumak rugs; almost all examples are made in two halves sewn together vertically along the selvedges. Considerable controversy exists about the chronology and place of manufacture. Many experts incline to the view that the pieces with the zoomorphic motifs are the oldest, or if not the oldest, the ones with the 'purest' rendering of what is, in any case, a highly stylised design. As I will show, there is little evidence for such a view, and, indeed, slightly stronger evidence that the opposite is the case.

Only two dated dragon soumaks are known to me, one being the example illustrated by Schürmann in *Caucasian Rugs* pl. 121). Although difficult to read, the date on this rug would appear to be 1261 A.H. (A.D. 1845). The unusual features of this piece, apart from the date itself, are (l) it is woven in one piece and (2) its exceptionally rich colouring, including a wide range of blues and greens. In composition, it is one of the minority group which have the dragons all facing in one direction; usually they face in opposite directions on each side of the two halves (although we should note such variations as our 478, which has all the dragons facing in one direction except in the bottom row, a most unusual feature).

The Schürmann rug also lacks the zoomorphic motifs, a fact which, in view of the rug's early date, suggests that the theory concerning the dating of rugs *with* the motif is incorrect. This is enforced by another dated non-zoomorphic example, apparently bearing the date 1258 A.H. (A.D. 1842/3), illustrated in my *Rugs and Carpets of the World* (p. 253); this has all the dragons in one direction but is woven in two halves. We should also mention the obviously early, although undated, example sold by Lefevre in London and illustrated in Eberhart Herrmann's *Von Lotto bis Tekke* (no. 29); this again is a non-zoomorphic design of a most unusual format — four rows of only three huge dragons on a particularly long, narrow rug woven in one piece.

475

475 This rug has the fairly muted colour range of (probably) late examples. It lacks the zoomorphic motif. In most respects, a typical piece, woven in two halves, although it has one feature which I have not encountered on any other dragon sileh: instead of the usual two ears, this rug has four atop each dragon. It is difficult to say why this should be, unless we accept the somewhat banal explanation that the weaver considered the ears as mere decorative appendages with four having a more harmonious compositional effect than two. One other point is worth reiterating: it is often said of the dragon sileh with the zoomorphic motif that not only are they the older and purer of the two groups but that they also tend to have animals within the dragon shapes, whereas the non-zoomorphic examples have the usual hour-glass motifs. In fact, the latter observation, in percentage terms, does seem to be true, although we illustrate this non-zoomorphic piece *with* animals and a zoomorphic piece (478) with hour-glass motifs; as usual, nothing is certain! Probably late 19th century.
353 x 170cm

The colour, although not as rich as that of the Schürmann piece, is mellow and most attractive and even if Herrmann's suggested 18th century dating cannot be followed, it must, nevertheless, be one of the oldest published examples.

It might be asked how the rugs came to be called dragon sileh. One could argue, of course, that a motif so bold and simple could not be a mere abstraction but must represent an extreme stylisation of some floral or animal original. Certain features strongly suggest that it is, in fact, a very formalised rendering of a dragon, that most ubiquitous of creatures in eastern weaving. Fortunately, however, one does not have to rely on intuition alone. There exists one extraordinary and unique rug in which the form has not deteriorated into a mere S with 'ears' and a 'tail' but is still, by comparison, almost a lifelike creature. This is the famous McMullan rug now in the Metropolitan Museum, New York, and well-known from its illustration on the dust jacket of McMullan's own catalogue of his collection.

Woven in two pieces and joined down the centre, the McMullan rug, being unique, is a little difficult to use as a yard-stick. In technique, it is markedly different from the type of dragon sileh we illustrate; its composition, however, is typical. It has rows of basically S shaped animals all facing in the same direction; it has an assortment of small filler ornaments and tiny animals as well as a version of the zoomorphic motif. By reference to the McMullan rug, we can interpret the comma-like appendages which appear at the top of the S as ears and the single line which runs parallel to the base of the S as an abbreviated rendering of a pair of hind legs. McMullan himself presumed his piece to be at least 18th century. An early to mid-19th century date seems more likely, especially as we know that an apparently archaic rendering of a composition can often co-exist chronologically with an apparently late and decadent rendering. Perhaps the greatest mystery about the McMullan rug, however, is why only one example should have survived, when so many hundreds of the normal version are known.

Where these rugs were woven and why they are called sileh are further questions not to have received satisfactory answers. The majority of current writers refer to them as sileh and ascribe them to the eastern Caucasus. Schürmann attributed his dated example to Daghestan, although he also remarks in his introduction that both sileh and verneh probably originated from the Karabagh.

The rugs we illustrate as nos. 479-480 are usually called verneh; the stylistic relationship

476 This is, perhaps, the standard form of the non-zoomorphic dragon sileh. It is of a more pleasing format than the previous piece, being squarer, and it would appear also to have a darker, richer palette, with attractive blues and greens used in the minor ornaments. It should be noted that regardless of the direction in which the dragons face, the ears and feet all point in the same direction; this is in contrast to the previous piece but is a fairly normal feature and one which would suggest, once again, that regardless of what interpretation is placed on this design in the West, it was lost on many Caucasian weavers. Again woven in two pieces, it has a multi-coloured selvedge and is probably somewhat older than 475. Probably second half of the 19th century.
340 x 224 cm

362 FLAT WEAVES — SILEH

477 This comparatively small and square rug is, again, typical in design, although it differs from the previous two in having all the dragon motifs facing in one direction. One unusual minor decorative feature, however, is the outer meander border in place of the *medachyl* border which appears on almost all rugs of this type. The colours are bright and pleasing and it seems that this sileh was woven in one piece. Late 19th century.
231 x 188 cm

'Dragon' Sileh continued

between them and the various groups of north-west Persian/ south Caucasian animal covers is obvious (cf. for example our 481-483). The latter are usually attributed to the Shahsavan, who inhabit large areas of Persia below Tabriz, as well as being found in the Caucasus, most predominantly in the Moghan region.

However, there are writers who refer to sileh as verneh and *vice-versa*. Among these is the Soviet author Rasim Efendi who in his *Decorative and Applied Arts of Azerbauan*, calls a dragon sileh (pl. 120) a 'Verni' and attributes it to the Karabagh, and what most western writers would call a verneh he describes as a 'Zili', and attributes it to Baku. He also illustrates one of the closely related animal covers (pl. 122) which again he calls a Zili but which he attributes to 'Kazakh'. For our purposes, however, we will follow the now generally accepted terminology, with the warning that there is no guarantee of its accuracy.

478 The only zoomorphic dragon sileh we illustrate (such rugs are considerably rarer than the non-zoomorphic type); it is also the smallest and most beautiful. It is difficult to interpret what the motif seen in the upper half of the dragon might have been intended to represent in its original form, but in its present state, it has a hint of the ancient totemic animal and tree symbol. Although there are tiny animals between the hour-glass and zoomorphic motifs in the bends of the dragons, the hour-glass motifs are abandoned in the upper halves of the two dragons at bottom right in favour of large fan-tailed birds (peacocks ?); another interesting and unusual minor detail is the fact that the dragons have, alternately, double or single tails. The dragons themselves have alternate ground colours of blue and yellow; this is considerably rarer, and to collectors, more desirable than the usual blue and white alternation. The design and spacing of this piece are outstanding, as can be seen by comparing it to the previously illustrated, and considerably more mundane, examples. Woven in two pieces. Second half of the l9th century.
220 x 158 cm

'Verneh' Rugs

The majority of these rugs are produced in soumak brocading on a slit-tapestry ground (480), although there is also a rarer group in allover soumak brocading (479). We have discussed the possible attribution to Azerbaijan-south Caucasus in the introduction to 'dragon' sileh. There are several varieties of so called bird verneh rugs, and even a superficial comparison of our two examples reveals that they are of different types. 480 is the most frequently encountered variety, and examples are still made today. The composition of this Foup varies very little, and the outer red, inner blue and central red are typical. Many almost identical examples can be found in carpet literature, including From the Bosporus to Samarkand (no. 95) and Rasim Efendi's Decorative and Applied Arts of Azerbaijan (described as a l9th century Zili from Baku). An example in the Victoria and Albert Museum, illustrated in Kendrick and Tattersall's Hand-Woven Carpets, has the usual lay-out and colour but in the majority of segments there are large double-headed animals with tiny birds on their backs, in place of the normal large peacock accompanied by a smaller bird, as on our 480; two other examples were illustrated in Hali (vol. 1, no. 3, pp. 25 and 220). Another variant on 480 will be found illustrated in From the Bosporus to Samarkand (pl. 97). This has two borders divided into segments containing animals, birds, or other motifs, framing a large open field.

479 continued
unbalanced look. This example seems closer in design to the Persian animal covers and may be by the Shahsavan. However, a closely related rug illustrated in *From the Bosporus to Samarkand* (pl. 20), has three bands of motifs in the central panel identical to the stylised serrate-edged dragon motifs which appear on a group of rugs attributed to Kuba, motifs which are a late rendering of the Afshan pattern (cf. our 312). It may be, therefore, that Rasim Efendi's attribution of rugs of this type (actually of the type represented by our 480) to Baku should be given closer scrutiny. Second half of the 19th century.
213 x 119 cm

480 This piece falls into a wider group of flat woven rugs and animal covers using large fan-tailed birds as their principal decorative motif (sometimes replaced by animals) and, through this motif, they can be linked with the so-called Akstafa rugs (cf. 210-218) thought to have been woven in the region where the Karabagh, Moghan and Shirvan areas converge. 480 appears to be in mint condition and is in every way typical. A late date is possible.
199 x 145 cm

479

479 This rug, considerably rarer and finer than 480, has all-over soumak brocading. Although the basic lay-out is the same, and on dark blue and red grounds, the wealth of ornamentation and the use of a vivid shade of green give the piece a richer appearance. Unfortunately, the border has been removed from the sides, giving the rug a somewhat

'VERNEH' FLAT WEAVES 365

480

481

Animal Covers

No one has catalogued definitively the many groups of north-west Persian and Caucasian animal covers with the distinctive shape of our 481-483. The majority have animal and bird motifs arranged in three or more rows in the bottom half, with a contrasting design in the upper part and are woven in two or more pieces.

Because so many similar groups of these covers are woven over so wide an area, attributing specific provenances to them has proved very difficult. Sometimes a small but consistent variation has led to a particular sub-group being assigned to one tribe or place. For instance, some examples do not have straight sides but have indentations at the end of each of the narrow 'flaps' and many experts consider these to be from Shiraz in south-west Persia. There is also the very beautiful group which is woven in six vertical strips alternately blue (or black) and white, the bottom half woven with animals and/or birds, the top half with rows of tri-floral sprays. The best known example of this group, which is comparatively rare, is illustrated in *From the Bosporus to Samarkand* (p. 30). Some examples may have only two of the vertical strips in blue and there are some with all-white strips; covers such as these are illustrated in *Tribal Animal Covers from Iran* (pls. 4 and 5). This group is firmly attributed to the Shahsavan. The pieces we illustrate are in soumak brocading on a plain-weave ground, like the majority of such covers.

482

481 An attractive and typical piece. whose colour, minor border elements and tri-floral motifs in the upper half all suggest a Persian origin, probably Shahsavan, but even an attribution to the Afshar of south-west Persia is possible. Jenny Housego in *Tribal Rugs* (pl. 5) attributes a somewhat similar example to the Shahsavan. The long knotted fringes on this piece are typical of south-west Persian tribal weavings. Late 19th century.
170 x 158 cm

482 This piece has motifs which relate it more closely to the bird verneh rugs, especially the three rows of fan-tailed motifs in the upper half. Once again, however, the minor border elements and the colour indicate a Persian origin and an attribution to the Shahsavan. One very unusual and attractive compositional feature is the placing of human figures with water-ewers between each of the huge birds in the central row in the bottom half of the piece. Late 19th century.
157 x 125 cm

483 A cover apparently of the same group as 481 but possibly older. The animals and birds are particularly well drawn, with a splendidly heraldic appearance. The lattice in the top half contains bell-like boteh, with the occasional substitution of a shrub for variety. Second half of the l9th century.
167 x 149 cm

484 There are various different artifacts made by the Caucasian and Persian tribes which combine a large area of netting with small flat-woven bands and/or bags. According to Jenny Housego, who illustrates a very similar example in *Tribal Rugs* (pl. 27), "the netting is purely decorative, and used to adorn the sides of a tent, while the bag stores small domestic valuables." She adds that such weavings were also used as animal trappings. Mrs. Housego attributes her piece to the Shahsavan of Hashtrud in north-west Persia. The style of ornamentation on our piece certainly suggests a Persian origin; this is especially true of the ivory-ground brocaded band, the design of which should be compared with that on the bag-face of our 457 (and to the related weavings mentioned in connection with that piece). The design of the small and delicately woven soumak bag, with its two medallions and rows of bird and tree motifs similar to those found on Yomud Turkoman *asmalyk*, should be compared to the composition of a complete *khordjin* illustrated by Jenny Housego (pl.7); this latter piece was found by the author in a Shahsavan tent of the Seyyitler clan near Mount Savalan in north-west Persia; she was told by its present owners that it was the work of another Shahsavan clan, the Mughanlu. Our piece is a rare and particularly beautiful example with fine colours and, apparently, in almost perfect condition. Late 19th century.
225 x 74 cm

485 The attribution of this large bag, which has been opened along the sides, to the Caucasus is, again, not certain. Its origins are discussed in greater detail in the note to bags 491-494, which are very similar. Probably late 19th/early 20th century.
143 x 105 cm

485

486 This is a complete soumak double bag, probably for a donkey, and is called a *khordjin*; examples were made by the majority of tribes in the Caucasus, Anatolia and Persia. The present piece has a design and palette which links it with the dragon sileh rugs and was probably made in the same area. Jenny Housego, in *Tribal Rugs* (pl. 18), illustrates one half of an almost identical bag and comments: "(It) has a common Shahsavan design. It features on the large weft-wrapped rugs they still make today." She goes on to suggest that the dragon sileh themselves may have also been woven by the Shahsavan, a view not far removed from that of some current Soviet authors but not one generally held in the West. Probably early 20th century.
47 x 128 cm

487 This appears to be one half of a soumak *khordjin* which has been made into a cushion. It is brightly coloured and well-drawn; I consider it to be north-west Persian Kurdish or even east Anatolian in origin. Late 19th century.
43 x 40 cm

489 *(opposite page)* This is, perhaps, one of the most famous soumak bag designs, seen here on a complete *khordjin*. The design itself, multi-coloured diagonal bands on which sit small S-like shapes, is also found on pile-knotted rugs usually attributed to Gendje (cf. our 163, 171 and 172). Fine soumak bags with the same field composition are illustrated in *From the Bosporus to Samarkand* (pl. 49) and Jenny Housego's *Tribal Rugs* (pl. 16). A particularly fine example was sold at auction by Sotheby's in London on 12 October, 1978; this was dated 1271 A.H. (A.D. 1854/5). There is a surprising unanimity of opinion about the origin of these pieces, the south Caucasus being widely accepted; this would presuppose that they were woven further south than Gendje, despite the similarity in design between the pile-knotted and flat-woven pieces. Second half of the 19th century.
128 x 53 cm

486

487

488 This is an attractive soumak on a plain-weave ground, the distinctive shape of which shows it to be a salt-bag. The greatest number of these artifacts is attributed to tribes from the Fars region of south-west Persia, and also to the Bakhtiari, Afshar and Kurds; a smaller number were woven in east Persia by the Kurds and Baluch. The present piece would seem to me to be by north-west Persian Kurds. Late 19th/early 20th century.
61 x 68cm

488

489

490

490 A pair of soumak bags (*khordjin*) which have been separated in the centre. The design, fairly common on such pieces, is of 'Lesghi' stars, surrounded by a beautifully composed ivory ground border with bird and pole design, surrounded, in turn, by another principal border with large florettes. As noted in the section on Lesghi rugs, the finest published soumak bag-face with Lesghi stars appears in Joseph V. McMullan's *Islamic Carpets* (pl. 57). It seems that McMullan interpreted the composition as being of blue-outlined red stars with "a secondary motif (of) a continuous pattern created by the spaces left by the star medallions". The composition can also be read as red stars diagonally arranged within a red trellis, the whole composition being placed on a dark blue ground. The McMullan piece has a narrow, heavily slanting S guard and a main white-ground border of the stencil type with H motifs between inward pointing V-shaped brackets—one of the most frequently encountered soumak bag border compositions. The field has that element of beautifully constructed reciprocity which is often taken as a hall-mark of good early weaving and it is interesting to note how three factors of the McMullan bag-face—the colour, the combination of stars and octagons and the kaleidoscopic nature of the design—put one in mind of Mamluk carpet design. Another Lesghi star bag-face with inner white-ground bird and pole borders and an outer border of octagons containing stars, is illustrated by Richard Purdon in *Shirvan and Related Weaving from the North Caucasus* (no. 18). A more standard example in *From the Bosporus to Samarkand* (no. 52 has one and three quarter stars in the field, the compositional treatment of which is closer to our example; the main border, however, is of the same type as the McMullan bag-face. Another bag-face in the same catalogue (no. 54) has a field composition of rows of bird and tree motifs similar in colour and drawing to those which appear in the main border of our piece. Another good example, with one large central star in the field flanked on two sides by rows of smaller stars and with a wide reciprocal border of crude X-like forms, is illustrated in *The Warp and Weft of Islam* (pl. 34). A fine complete khordjin is illustrated in *Yoruk* (no. 53); this has one large star framed by a wide border containing large octagons, with an outer border
continued on p.372

491

492

490 continued
containing the typical spiky leaf forms of the type often encountered on kilim. The description of soumak bags of this design as Caucasian seems to be followed by most authors (although the compilers of the *Yoruk* catalogue refer to their *khordjin* as the work of the Shahsavan of north-west Persia). Both the colour and design of our piece suggest an origin in the north east Caucasus but, like the pile-knotted rugs which employ this design, it is possible that examples were woven by different groups over a wide area. Late 19th century.
51 x 56 cm

491-494 These four bedding bags are very similar in type to 485. The first three are in soumak brocading and the fourth in slit-tapestry, with the narrow white-ground bands in soumak. The attribution of these bags is controversial; the first three are of the type which can be found attributed to north-west Persia, east Anatolia or the southern Caucasus, although the relationship of the fourth piece to so-called Shirvan kilim would leave its origin in less doubt. The Caucasian provenance for bags such as this, in all-over soumak brocading with the central area in plain-weave, was adhered to by Landreau and Pickering in *From the Bosporus to Samarkand*. In the *Yoruk* catalogue, however, published in 1978, no. 52, a very similar bedding bag to our 485, was attributed to the Shahsavan (although this does not necessarily obviate a Caucasian provenance); in the same catalogue, a bag (no. 21) very similar to our 491 was attributed to the Yoruk of south-west Turkey. In the catalogue *The Warp and Weft of Islam*, two examples (nos. 88 and 89), the former close to our 493 and the latter to our 494, were both attributed to the Bakhtiari tribe of Persia, the editors pointing out that bedding bags of this type were called *rakhtekhab-pich*. Several examples illustrated by Jenny Housego in *Tribal Rugs* (plates 9, 17, 28, 30, 31 and 33) are attributed to the Shahsavan; one example (no. 9) can be compared to our 485 and is attributed to the Shahsavan of Hashtrud. Late 19th/early 20th century.
491   322 x 50 cm
492   332 x 51 cm
493   345 x 43 cm
494   286 x 45 cm

SOUMAK BAGS FLAT WEAVES 373

493

494

Bibliography

CAUCASIAN RUGS

Aga-Oglu, M.: *Dragon Rugs: A Loan Exhibition* (exhib. cat.). Textile Museum, Washington, 1948.

Anon.: "The Eskenazi Dragon Carpet". In *Hali*, vol. II, no. 1, p.65.

Benardout, Raymond: *Caucasian Rugs*. Raymond Benardout, London, 1978.

Buchanan, Glenn: *Antique Rugs from the Caucasus* (exhib. cat.). The Australian Society for Antique Rugs, Melbourne.1974.

Dall'Oglio, Marino: "A White Ground Dragon Carpet: a study of the Design and Relevant Comparisons". In *Hali*, vol. II, no. 1, pp. 16-18.

Dimand, M.S.: "A Loan of a Caucasian Rug". *In Bull, Metropolitan Museum*, New York, 1941, pp. 185 ff.

Dournovo, Lydia A. with Sirarpie Der Nersessian: *Armenian Miniatures*, London, 1961.

Eder, Doris: *Orientteppiche Band 1: Kaukasische Teppiche*. München, 1978.

Efendi, Rasim: *Decorative and Applied Arts of Azerbaijan (Middle Aged)*. Baku, 1976.

Ellis, Charles Grant: "A Soumak-woven Rug in a 15th century International Style". *In The Textile Journal*, 1/2, 1963, pp. 3-21.

Ellis, Charles Grant: "Caucasian Carpets in the Textile Museum, Washington". In *Forschungen zur Künst Asiens. In Memoriam Kurt Erdmann*, Istanbul, 1970.

Ellis, Charles Grant: *Early Caucasian Rugs* (exhib. cat.). The Textile Museum, Washington, 1975.

Ellis, Charles Grant: "Review of Serare Yetkin's *Early Caucasian Carpets in Turkey*". In *Hali*, vol. I, no. 4, pp. 377-382.

Farensadeh, Schamil: *Kaukasische Teppiche. Braunschweig*, 1971.

Fiske, Patricia: *Caucasian Rugs from Private Collections* (exhib. cat.). The Textile Museum, Washington, 1975.

Gombos, A.: "Les Tapis Anciens Arméniens". In *Ars Decorativa*, vol. 3, pp. 41-59, Museum of Decorative Arts and Hopp Museum of Far Eastern Art, Budapest, 1975.

Gombos, A.: "Old Caucasian Rugs". In *Hali*, vol. I, no. 4, pp. 368-370.

Gombos, Karoly: *Régi Kaukazsni Azerbajdzsán Szönyegek* (exhib. cat.). Museum of Applied Arts, Castle Museum, Nagytétény, 1977.

Hofrichter, Z.: *Armenische Teppiche*. Vienna, 1937.

Jensen, Inge-Lise: *Kaukasiske Taepper en dansk privatsamling*. Køge, 1974.

Kerimov, Lyatif: *Azerbaidzhanskii Kovyor*. Akademiya Nauk Azerbaidzhanskoi SSR, Baku, 1961.

Kerimov, Lyatif: *Folk Designs from the Caucasus*. New York, 1974.

Lang, David Marshall: *Armenia, Cradle of Civilization*. 2nd corr. ed. London, 1978 (1st ed. 1970).

Ledaks, K.A.: "Armenische Teppiche". In *Heimtex*, Oct. 1968 – Mar. 1969.

Lefèvre, Jean with Thompson, Jon, and Blikslager, Bert: *Caucasian Carpets*. London, 1977.

Lynch, H.F.B.: *Armenia, Travels and Studies*. New ed. Beirut, 1965 (1st ed. London, 1901).

Pinner, Robert with Franses, Michael: "Caucasian Shield Carpets". In *Hali*, vol. I, no. 1, pp. 4-22.

Pinner, Robert with Franses, Michael: "The Cambalios Carpet". In *Hali*, vol. I, no. 2, pp. 200-201.

Pope, A.U.: "The Myth of the Armenian Dragon Carpets". In *Jahrbuch der Kunst*, 11, 1925, pp. 147 ff.

Pope, A.U.: "Les Tapis à Dragons". In *Syria*, 1929, pp. 181 ff.

Purdon, Richard: *Shirvan and Related Weavings from the North Caucasus* (exhib. cat.). Thornborough Galleries, Cirencester, 1978.

Raphaelian, H.M.: *Rugs of Armenia*. New York, 1960.

Sakisian, A.: *"Les tapis arméniens"*. In *Révue des Etudes arméniens*, 1, 1920, pp. 121 ff.

Sakisian, A.: "Les tapis à dragons et leur origins arméniennes". In *Syria*, IX, 1928, pp. 238 ff.

Sakisian, A.: "Les tapis armeniens du XVe a XIX siecles". In Revue de l'art Ancien et Moderne, LXIV, 1933, pp. 21 ff.

Sakisian, A.: "Nouveaux documents sur les tapis arméniens". In *Syria*, XVII, 1936, pp. 177 ff.

Sakisian, A.: *Pages d'Art Arménien*. Paris, 1940.

Schürmann, Ulrich: *Kaukasische Teppiche*. Braunschweig, 1961.

Schürmann, Ulrich: *Caucasian Rugs*. Repr. 3rd imp. Ramsdell, 1974 (1st German ed. *Teppiche aus dem Kaukasus*. Braunschweig, 1964).

Spuhler, F.: *Kaukasische Teppiche* (exhib. cat.). Museum für Kunsthandwerk, Frankfurt, 1962.

Tschebull, Raoul: *Kazak, Carpets of the Caucasus*. New York, 1971.

Tschebull, Raoul: "The Development of four Kazak Designs". In *Hali*, vol. I, no. 3, pp. 257-261.

Yetkin, Serare: *Early Caucasian Carpets in Turkey*, 2 vols. London, 1978.

GENERAL

I have, in the main, confined myself to books, catalogues and articles containing significant material —either text or illustrations or both—concerning Caucasian rugs, or which have been mentioned in the text.

Achdjian, Albert: *Le Tapis—The Carpet*. Paris, 1949.

American Art Association: *The V. & L. Benguiat Private Collection of Rare Old Rugs* (auction cat.). New York, 4-5 Dec., 1925.

Anglo-Persian Carpet Company: *Fine and Rare Oriental Rugs and Weavings* (exhib. cat.). London, 1976.

Bacharach, Jere L. with, Bierman, Irene A.: *The Warp and Weft of Islam* (exhib. cat.). The Henry Art Gallery, University of Washington, 1978.

Bausback, Peter: *Alte und Antike Meisterstücke orientalische Teppichknüpfunst* (exhib. cat.). Mannheim, 1972.

Bausback, Peter: *Alte und Antike Meisterstücke orientalische Teppichknüpfunst* (exhib. cat.). Mannheim, 1973.

Bausback, Peter: *Antike Meisterstücke orientalischer Knüpfkunst* (exhib. cat.). Mannheim, 1975.

Bausback, Peter: *Antike orientalische Knüpfkunst* (exhib. cat.). Mannheim, 1976.

Bausback, Peter: *Alte orientalische Flachgewerbe* (exhib. cat.). Mannheim, 1977.

Bausback, Peter: *Alte orientalische Knüpfkunst* (exhib. cat.). Mannheim, 1977.

Bausback, Peter: *Antike Orientteppiche*. Braunschweig, 1978.

Beattie, May H.: *The Thyssen-Bornemisza Collection of Oriental*

Rugs. Castagnola, 1972.

Bennett, Ian: *The Book of Oriental Carpets and Rugs.* Feltham, 1971.

Bennett, Ian: *The Country Life Book of Rugs and Carpets of the World.* Feltham, 1978.

Black, David with Loveless, Clive, Petsopoulos, Yanni, et al.: *The Undiscovered Kelim* (exhib. cat.). London, 1977.

Bode, W. von and Kühnel, Ernst: *Antique Rugs from the Near East* (trans. Charles Grant Ellis). London, 1970.

Cammann, Schuyler V.A.: "Symbolic Meaning in Oriental Rug Patterns". In *The Textile Museum Journal*, vol. III. Washington, 1973.

Cloudman, Ruth H.: *A Rich Inheritance* (exhib. cat.). Joslyn Art Museum, Omaha, 1974.

Coen, Luciano with Duncan, Louise: *The Oriental Rug.* London, 1978.

Cselenyi, Ladislav: *Oriental Rugs from the Collection of Mr. John Schorscher.* (exhib. cat.). Royal Ontario Museum, Ontario, 1972.

Dimand, M.S.: *Peasant and Nomad Rugs of Asia.* New York, 1961.

Dimand, M.S. with Mailey, Jean: *Oriental Rugs in the Metropolitan Museum of Art.* New York, 1973.

Dilley, A.H.: *Oriental Rugs and Carpets* (rev. M.S. Dimand). New York, 1959.

Diyarbekirli, Nejat: "New Light on the Pazyryk Carpet". In *Hali*, vol. I, no. 3, pp. 217-221.

Dodds, Dennis R.: "Heritage of the Middle East". In *Hali*, vol. I, no. 1, pp. 48-51.

Dodds, Dennis R.: "Fisher Collection of Oriental Rugs, the Virginia Museum of Fine Arts, Richmond, Virginia". In *Hali*, vol. I, no. 2, pp. 149-155.

Dodds, Dennis R.: "Allen Art Museum Rug Exhibition". In *Hali*, vol. I, no. 4.

Eiland, Murray: *Oriental Rugs.* Rev. ed. Boston, 1976, pp. 365-367.

Eiland, Emmett and Murray: *Oriental Rugs from Western Collections* (exhib. cat.). University of California Museum, 1973.

Ellis, Charles Grant: "The Rugs from the Great Mosque at Divrigi". In *Hali*, vol. I, no. 3, pp. 269-274.

Erdmann, Kurt: *Seven Hundred Years of Oriental Carpets* (trans. May H. Beattie and Hildegard Herzog). London, 1970.

Erdmann, Kurt: *Oriental Carpets* (trans. C.G. Ellis). Fishguard, 1976.

Ettinghausen, Richard: *Ancient Carpets from the L.A. Mayer Memorial Institute for Islamic Art* (exhib. cat.). Jerusalem, 1977.

Formenton, Fabio: *Oriental Rugs and Carpets.* Feltham, 1972.

Franchis, Amedeo de with Housego, Jenny: *Tribal Animal Covers from Iran* (exhib. cat.). Tehran, 1975.

Franchis, Amedeo de with Wertime, John: *Lori and Bakhtiyari Flatweaves* (exhib. cat.). Tehran, 1976.

Franses, Jack: *European and Oriental Rugs.* London, 1973.

Franses, Michael: *The World of Rugs* (exhib. cat.). London, 1973.

Gardiner, Roger: *Oriental Rugs from Canadian Collections* (exhib. cat.). Toronto, 1975.

Gombos, Karoly: *Régi keleti Szónyegek (Old Oriental Rugs)* (exhib. cat.). Keresztény Museum, Esztergom, 1977.

Grote-Hasenbalg, Werner: *Der Orientteppich, Seine Geschichte u. seine Kultur.* 3 vols. Berlin, 1922.

Grote-Hasenbalg, Werner: *Masterpieces of Oriental Rugs.* London, 1925.

Gregorian, Arthur T.: *Oriental Rugs and the Stories they Tell.* Rev. ed. London 1978 (1st ed. 1967).

Hali: International Journal of Oriental Carpets and Textiles, published quarterly, 193a Shirland Rd., London W9 2E.

Hempel, Rose with Gräfin Preysing, Maritheres: *Alte Orientteppiche.* Museum für Kunst und Gewerbe, Hamburg, 1970.

Herrmann, Eberhart: *Von Lotto bis Tekke* (exhib. cat.). München, 1978.

Housego, Jenny: *Tribal Rugs.* London, 1978.

Hubel, Reinhard G.: *The Book of Carpets.* London, 1969.

Hubel, R.G.: *Orientteppiche und Nomadenknüpfarbeiten vergangener Jahrhunderte, Sammlung R.G. Hubel* (exhib. cat.). Städtischer Museum, Wiesbaden, 1969.

Jacobsen, Charles W.: *Oriental Rugs, A Complete Guide.* 11th printing, New York, 1971.

Jacoby, H.: *How to Know Old Oriental Carpets and Rugs.* London, 1967.

Jajczay, J.: *Symbology of the Oriental Carpet.* Budapest, 1975.

Jensen, Inge-Lise: *Orientalsk Taeppekunst i dansk privateje* (exhib. cat.). Valby Kunstforening, 1964.

Kendrick, A.F.: *Guide to the Collection of Carpets.* Victoria and Albert Museum, London, 1915.

Kendrick, A.F. and Tattersall, C.E.C.: *Hand-Woven Carpets, Oriental and European.* Reprint of 1st ed. of 1922, New York, 1973.

Landreau, A.N. and Pickering, W.R.: From the *Bosporus to Samarkand, Flatwoven Rugs* (exhib. cat.). The Textile Museum, Washington, 1969.

Landreau, Anthony N. (ed.): *Yoruk, the Nomadic Weaving Tradition of the Middle East* (exhib. cat.). Museum of Art, Carnegie Institute, Pittsburgh, 1978.

Lanier, Mildred B.: *English and Oriental Carpets at Williamsburg.* Colonial Williamsburg, 1975.

Lettenmair, J.G.: *Das Grosse Orient-teppiche-buch.* New ed. München, 1977 (lst ed. 1962).

Macey, R.E.G.: *Oriental Prayer Rugs.* Leigh-on-Sea, 1971 (1st ed. 1961).

Mackie, Louise W.: *Prayer Rugs* (exhib. cat.). The Textile Museum, Washington, 1974.

Mackie, Louise W. with Ettinghausen, Richard and Dimand, M.W: *The Mayer Collection of Rugs* (exhib. cat.). The Textile Museum, Washington, 1974.

Martin, F.R.: *A History of Oriental Carpets before 1800.* Vienna, 1908.

McMullan, Joseph V.: *Islamic Carpets,* New York, 1965.

McMullan, Joseph V. with Reichart, Donald O.: *The George Walter Vincent and Belle Townsley Smith Collection of Islamic Rugs* (exhib. cat.). Springfield, N.D.

Mumford, J.K.: *Oriental Rugs.* New York, 1900.

Neff, Ivan C. and Maggs, Carol V.: *Dictionary of Oriental Rugs.* London, 1977.

O'Bannon, George: *Oriental Rugs from Western Pennsylvania Collections* (exhib. cat.). The Westmoreland County Museum of Art, Greenburgh, 1975.

Petsopoulos, Yanni: *Kilims.* London, 1979.

Robert, Ernest H.: *Islamic Carpets from the Museum Collection.* Special issue of *The Bulletin of the Allen Memorial Art Museum,* Oberlin, Ohio, XXXVI, 1978-80.

Sarre, F. and Trenkwald, H.: *Ancient Oriental Carpets* (trans. A.F. Kendrick). Vienna, 1929.

Spuhler, Friedrich, König, Hans and Volkmann, Martin: *Alte Orientteppiche: Meisterstucke aus deutschen Privatsammlungen*

(exhib. cat.). München, 1978.
Spuhler, Friedrich: *Islamic Carpets and Textiles in the Keir Collection*. London, 1978.
Straka, Jerome A. with Mackie, Louise W.: *The Oriental Rug Collection of Jerome and Mary Jane Straka*. New York, 1978.
Thornborough Galleries: Exhibition Catalogue. Cirencester, 1976.
Walker, Daniel S.: *Oriental Rugs in Cincinnati Collection* (exhib. cat.). Cincinnati Art Museum, 1977.

THE ANTIQUE COLLECTORS' CLUB

The Antique Collectors's Club was formed in 1966 and now has a five figure membership spread throughout the world. It publishes the only independently run monthly antiques magazine *Antique Collecting* which caters for those collectors who are interested in widening their knowledge of antiques, both by greater awareness of quality and by discussion of the factors which influence the price that is likely to be asked. The Antique Collectors's Club pioneered the provision of information on prices for collectors and the magazine still leads in the provision of detailed articles on a variety of subjects.

It was in response to the enormous demand for information on 'what to pay' that the price guide series was introduced in 1968 with the first edition of *The Price Guide to Antique Furniture* (completely revised, 1978 and 1989), a book which broke new ground by illustrating the more common types of antique furniture, the sort that collectors could buy in shops and at auctions rather than the rare museum pieces which had previously been used (and still to a large extent are used) to make up the limited amount of illustrations in books published by commercial publishers. Many other price guides have followed, all copiously illustrated, and greatly appreciated by collectors for the valuable information they contain, quite apart from prices. The Antique Collectors' Club also publishes other books on antiques, including horology and art reference works, and a full book list is available.

Club membership, which is open to all collectors, costs £19.50 per annum. Members receive free of charge *Antique Collecting*, the Club's magazine (published ten times a year), which contains well-illustrated articles dealing with the practical aspects of collecting not normally dealt with by magazines. Prices, features of value, investment potential, fakes and forgeries are all given prominence in the magazine.

Among other facilities available to members are private buying and selling facilities, the longest list of 'For Sales' of any antiques magazine, an annual ceramics conference and the opportunity to meet other collectors at their local antique collectors' clubs. There are over eighty in Britain and more than a dozen overseas. Members may also buy the Club's publications at special pre-publication prices.

As its motto implies, the Club is an organisation designed to help collectors get the most out of their hobby: it is informal and friendly and gives enormous enjoyment to all concerned.

For Collectors — By Collectors — About Collecting

5 Church Street, Woodbridge, Suffolk, IP12 1DS
Tel: 0394 385501. Fax: 0394 384434

Market Street Industrial Park, Wappingers' Falls, NY 12590
Tel: 914 297 0003. Fax: 914 297 0068.

Books on Textiles from the
ANTIQUE COLLECTORS' CLUB

Oriental Rugs Vol. 2 Persian
by Erich Aschenbrenner

10 x 8½in., 268pp., 141 col. illus., 15 line drawings

ISBN 0 907462 12 X

Gives the collector the information he requires, in a clear and concise manner, to assess not just museum quality pieces, but the wide variety that pass through shops and auctions. Each area of carpet manufacture is divided into the various towns and villages whose carpets display individual characteristics and these are categorised under the headings: sizes, colours, patterns, foundation, knots, pile and quality. If you glance through the illustrations in this book you will see why the Persian carpet is held in such high regard by people throughout the world. **Persian Rugs** is an important volume in an expanding series which, by virtue of the practical help it gives to the collector, is being accepted as the standard literature on the subject.

Oriental Rugs Vol. 3 The Carpets of Afghanistan
by R.D. Parsons

10 x 8½in., 196pp., 90 b. & w. illus., 154 col.

ISBN 1 85149 144 9

This revised edition of the most detailed analysis of the Afghanstan rug production ever published is a consequence of the recent civil war and the resultant changes within that country's carpet industry. A new introduction, two additional chapters and forty supplementary colour plates combined with the original text and illustrations, guide the keen collector and the first-time buyer through a labyrinth of fascinating choices. The author treats the reader to not only a veritable feast of carpets and rugs, all with their attendant tribal origins and motifs vividly explained, but also to a fascinating journey through the history of a diverse, colourful, multiracial country. Afghan rugs open up a whole new vista for the collector, from sumptuous piled purdahs to flat woven prayer rugs.

Oriental Rugs Vol. 4 Turkish
by Fritzsche and K. Zipper

10 x 8½in. 212pp., 15 b. & w. illus., 210 col.

ISBN 1 85149 091 4

Turkey lies in a geographical position of some importance, separating as it does the Eastern and Western cultures. Despite the proximity of the Persian influence, Turkish rug makers largely retained their own traditional motifs and the language of their designs and ornaments is fully explained in this comprehensive book. The main text leads into a full colour pictorial catalogue which illustrates rugs from the numerous towns and villages throughout Anatolia. Comprehensive and detailed captions describe some 225 examples, ranging from antique and very rare museum exhibits right through the good quality modern pieces which are readily available today. This is an essential volume for all lovers of fine carpets and will appeal equally to the acknowledged expert and the fascinated but inexperienced beginner.

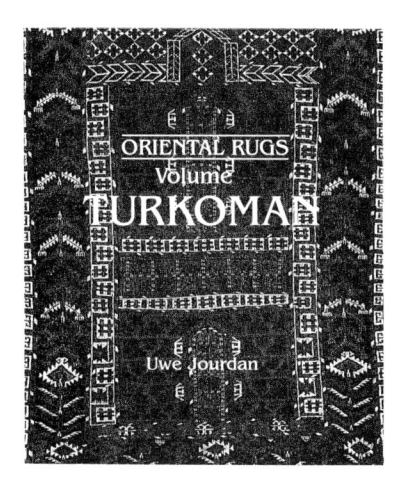

Oriental Rugs Vol. 5 Turkoman
by Uwe Jourdan

11 x 8½in. Approx. 328 pages, 300 col. illus
ISBN 1 85149 136 8

This is the first major book to have appeared on Turkoman rugs for nearly a decade and it is perhaps unrivalled in its comprehensiveness. The author both entertains the specialist and enlightens the novice through the scope and depth of his pictorial survey. Thus the book, the fifth in the Antique Collectors' Club Oriental Rugs series, is both an invaluable record of Turkoman weaving and, at the same time, a lesson in connoisseurship. Turkoman weaving, that marvellous functional product of the nomadic tribes of Central Asia, has attracted specialist collectors for over a century. This book will assure itself an important and continuing place in any carpet library and is the best general guide to the splendours of Turkoman weaving anyone could hope to find in the foreseeable future.

European and American Carpets and Rugs
by Cornelia Bateman Faraday

11 x 8½in. 484 pp., 326 b. & w. illus., 112 col.
ISBN 1 85149 092 2

Until recently European and American production of carpets and rugs has been largely ignored in spite of the huge range of material which is available. This book is packed with information and, as it was written at the very height of interest in Art Deco, it includes important designer rugs by names hitherto unknown or unconnected with rugs and carpets as well as a wealth of unique information about technique and styles. Some 70 new colour plates have been added to this important reprint and the distinguished expert Ian Bennett has contributed an introduction which incorporates the findings of more recent scholarship into this important new area of interest. The result is a standard work of reference.

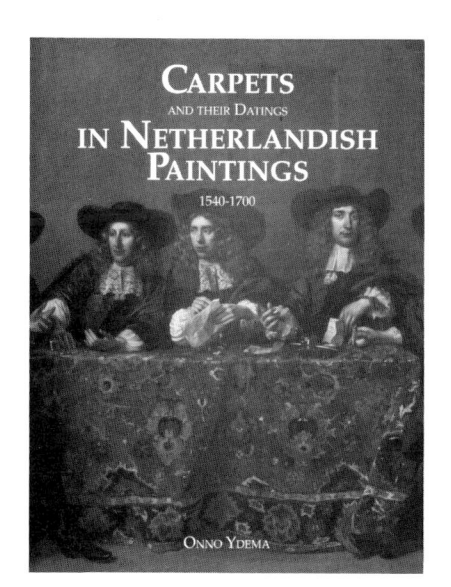

Carpets and their Datings in Netherlandish Paintings 1540-1700
by Onno Ydema

11½ x 9in. 208 pp., 290 b. & w. illus., 44 col.
ISBN 1 85149 151 1

In the sixteenth and seventeenth century Oriental carpets were rare commodities in Western Europe and were, therefore, considered as extreme luxuries. As a consequence, they were often proudly used as props in paintings: in portraits for instance the value of a depicted carpet emphasised the portrayed's (or patron's) social status, whereas in genre paintings they suggested a general atmosphere of wealth. Understanding the early history of carpets and carpet making would be impossible without the legacy of European paintings of the sixteenth and seventeenth century, upon which the process of dating most early carpet types crucially depends. The examples included in this book (nearly a thousand), provide an impressive survey of information to be found in Dutch and Flemish paintings of this period.

Other publications from the
ANTIQUE COLLECTORS' CLUB

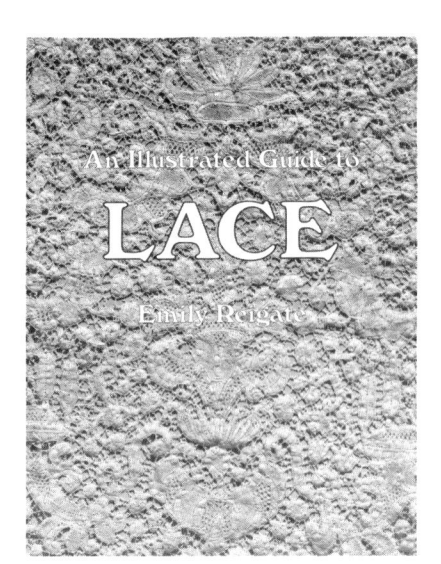

An Illustrated Guide to Lace
by Emily Reigate

11 x 8½in. 264 pp., 700 b. & w. illus., 12 col.

ISBN 1 85149 003 5

Emily Reigate's book is copiously illustrated with lace from all manufacturing centres and all ages. With 700 black and white photographs, it is believed to be the best illustrated book on the subject ever published. The text has been limited to facts. The combination of a visually interesting book with fine photographs of examples, most of which have never been published before, with the sensible comments of an experienced collector and needlewoman, makes this a key book on the subject. The author was Chairman of the Royal School of Needlework for ten years and for five years was a member of the Advisory Council of the Victoria and Albert Museum.

The Decorative Arts of the China Trade
by Carl L. Crossman

11 x 8½in., 464 pp., 325 b. & w. illus., 136 col.

ISBN 1 85149 096 5.

From the late 1700s an increasing number of sailing vessels brought back loads of exotic objects from China. An insatiable interest in things oriental resulted in an enormous range of exquisite objects created specifically for the western market, and a veritable flood of goods made their way to the West throughout the 19th century. The technicalities of trading with the Chinese are followed in detail while fascinating particulars of life and objects brought in China are depicted throughout the book. This is the definitive source book and essential reference on the decorative arts of the China trade.

Gardens of Central Europe
Text by Patrick Bowe

12½ x 9½in. 216pp., 200 col. illus.

ISBN 1 85149 152 X

As political changes focus world attention on the cultures of Central Europe, this book presents a unique opportunity to explore the exotic gardens of this region. The gardens and gardening traditions, with sources both in Europe and in the Orient, have never before been published as a group in an English language text. The author takes the reader on a tour of the great royal and significant gardens of the past as well as the smaller monastic gardens up to, and including a more recent tradition of urban gardens. The book is divided into chapters according to countries and regions: Eastern Germany, Poland, Czechoslovakia, Hungary, Yugoslavia, Western Romania and includes such gardens as Sans Souci, Prague Castle gardens, Esterháza, Brancusi sculpture garden, Trsteno Park. Each chapter contains an introduction describing the cultural history of that country's garden design, detailing climatic conditions, flora and plants imported to complement local characteristics. This is then followed by a detailed description of selected gardens with specially commissioned photographs. **Gardens of Central Europe** is an appealing and beautiful book.

George Chinnery 1774-1852
Artist of India and the China Coast
by Patrick Conner

11 x 8½in., 320 pp., 189 b. & w. illus., 113 col.

ISBN 1 85149 160 0

Among British artists George Chinnery is a special case. After a promising early career in England and Ireland, he spent the rest of his long life in the Far East – twenty-three years in India, and twenty-seven on the China coast, where he lies buried. Untouched by the changing fashions of nineteenth century England, Chinnery's art retained the spirit of the 1790s, when the rising star was Sir Thomas Lawrence and the young J.M.W. Turner was his close contemporary at the Royal Academy Schools.

This book represents the first thorough study of Chinnery's life and work; it also presents a vivid picture of life in the remote outposts of European empires.

A Dictionary of Russian and Soviet Artists
by John Milner

11 x 8½in. Over 5,000 entries. Approx. 550 pp., 293 b. & w. illus., 90 col.

ISBN 1 85149 182 1

In recent years there have been many exhibitions of Russian art, particularly the art of the last hundred years, and these have created a good deal of interest. It is likely that much more Russian art will appear in exhibitions and in the saleroom as communications with the West grow again after the long period of the Cold War. **A Dictionary of Russian and Soviet Artists** is designed to make relevant information available in English so that scholars and collectors can gain access to what was once written about mostly in Russian. The **Dictionary** also lists further reading and details of collections holding works by Russian painters, sculptors and printmakers. The subject is highly rewarding and this **Dictionary** aims to make it more so by providing the basic background to the work of Russian and Soviet artists from about 1420 to the 1970s.

Roy Lancaster Travels in China:
A Plantsman's Paradise
by Roy Lancaster

11 x 8½in., 520 pp., 253 b. & w. illus., 413 col.

ISBN 1 85149 175 9

This book successfully combines a most enjoyable and detailed account of the well-known author's many journeys through China. First and foremost, **Travels in China** provides a practical assessment of the plants that are either of ornamental merit or botanical interest to gardeners in the West, and on his extensive travels Roy Lancaster follows in the footsteps of the great Victorian plant hunters. He describes, in this, his *magnum opus*, some 1,000 different plants in their natural habitat. Over 400 of the author's own attractive and colourful photographs are reproduced in this book, interspersed with fascinating descriptions and anecdotes from his travels. Most of all this is a book about plants from a country so rich in variety that there are 50% more species on one mountain in China than in the whole of the British Isles. The wide range of climatic conditions in a country as vast as China makes this book relevant to all gardeners, be they from Norway or Spain, the United Kingdom or Canada.

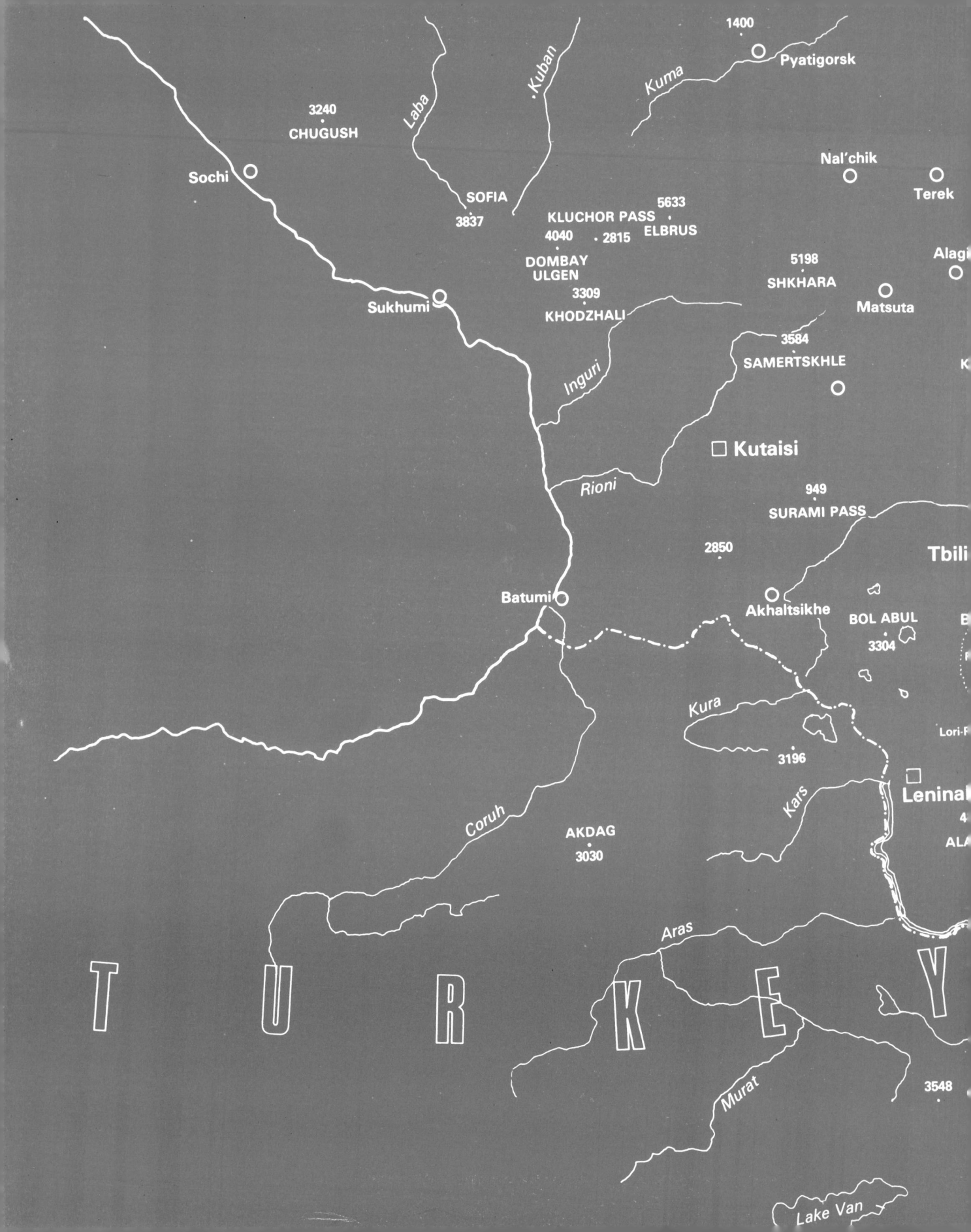

Location	Elevation
CHUGUSH	3240
Pyatigorsk	1400
Sochi	
Nal'chik	
Terek	
SOFIA	3837
KLUCHOR PASS	4040
ELBRUS	5633
	2815
DOMBAY ULGEN	
SHKHARA	5198
Alagi	
Matsuta	
KHODZHALI	3309
Sukhumi	
SAMERTSKHLE	3584
Inguri	
Kutaisi	
Rioni	
SURAMI PASS	949
	2850
Tbili	
Batumi	
Akhaltsikhe	
BOL ABUL	3304
Kura	
	3196
Lori-	
Kars	
Leninak	
Coruh	
AKDAG	3030
ALA	
Aras	
TURKEY	
Murat	
	3548
Lake Van	